AMERICA'S NEEDY
Care and Cutbacks

Timely Reports to Keep
Journalists, Scholars and the Public
Abreast of Developing Issues, Events and Trends

Editorial Research Reports
Published by Congressional Quarterly Inc.
1414 22nd Street, N.W.
Washington, D.C. 20037

About the Cover

The cover was designed by Staff Artist Robert Redding

PRINTED IN THE UNITED STATES OF AMERICA

Editor, Hoyt Gimlin
Associate Editor, Martha V. Gottron
Editorial Assistants, Laurie De Maris, Elizabeth Furbush
Production Manager, I. D. Fuller
Assistant Production Manager, Maceo Mayo

Library of Congress Cataloging in Publication Data

Main entry under title:

America's needy.

Bibliography: p.
Includes index.
1. Public welfare — United States. 2. United States — Social policy. 3. Poor — Government policy — United States.
I. Congressional Quarterly, inc.
HV95.A74 1984   362´.973   84-4359
ISBN 0-87187-322-2

Contents

Foreword

Few problems have lain so long and uneasily on the American political landscape as those of caring for the nation's needy — the poor, ill, infirm and elderly. Conscience has been pitted against pocketbook in the sometimes strident debates that erupt periodically. The public-policy question of how, and how much, to care for the needy may lie dormant for years and then blossom full-blown, demanding attention on the political agenda. This occurred in the Depression Thirties and again 30 years later during Lyndon Johnson's "war on poverty." It has returned once more, since President Reagan came into office determined to stop the "welfare state" dead in its tracks.

He has been cheered by people troubled by the huge costs of federal domestic spending and what they perceive as an erosion of self-reliance fostered by public welfare. Others have decried his spending cutbacks as the handiwork of an uncaring government bent on recreating some of the social ills Charles Dickens described so graphically in 19th century England. In this election year, especially, the president is trying to deflect charges from the political opposition that his programs and policies are unfair to the needy and overly generous to the well-to-do.

This is the "unfairness issue," which is examined in the first report and elaborated in some aspects in other of the nine reports that make up this book. They deal with hunger, the homeless, medical care, aid for the disabled, treatment of minorities and the elderly. There is also discussion of a renewed emphasis on volunteerism — on private charity doing more to fill the gap between the need and what is provided by the government.

All of these reports were initially published on the dates they bear, going back to mid-year 1982. While new information is offered, when pertinent, in editors' notes at the beginning of several of these reports, their basic thrust remains unchanged from the time they were written. We offer them here in the hope the reader will gain a better understanding of this topic of national importance and, often, of intense personal interest.

Hoyt Gimlin
Editor

April 1984
Washington, D.C.

SOCIAL WELFARE UNDER REAGAN

by

Robert Benenson

Mar. 9
1 9 8 4

SOCIAL WELFARE
UNDER REAGAN

A T ISSUE in this presidential election year is the three-year-old question of whether President Reagan's social welfare programs are fair to the nation's poor. Reagan's critics claim that his economic recovery program has been built on the backs of the poor, that federal programs to help low-income individuals and families have been cut to finance an unnecessarily large defense program and to compensate for massive income tax cuts of benefit primarily to the wealthy. Reagan and his supporters counter that the welfare program reductions were needed to curb the excessive federal spending that was fueling double-digit inflation and creating a dependency on the federal government.

The growth of social welfare programs has been a central issue of American domestic policy since the mid-1960s. Conservatives condemned the steady expansion of these programs, claiming they had placed an unacceptable burden on the American taxpayer while doing little to alleviate the long-term problems of the poor. Dissatisfaction with welfare programs helped propel Reagan into the presidency in 1980, and he moved quickly to slow the rate of growth in domestic spending.

From the beginning, Reagan has said that his budget-cutting efforts have been aimed only at those low-income individuals who had been able to obtain substantial incomes by combining their earnings from work with federal cash assistance and "in-kind" benefits.[1] The poorest individuals — the "truly needy" — would be spared from the budget ax. "Those who through no fault of their own must rely on the rest of us, the poverty-stricken, the disabled, the elderly, all those with true need, can rest assured that the social safety net of programs they depend on are exempt from any cuts," said Reagan in February 1981.

But advocates of social welfare programs claim that Reagan's policies have been unfair to the poor. The destitute have maintained their eligibility for means-tested entitlement programs, such as Aid to Families with Dependent Children, food stamps,

---

[1] Cash assistance programs — commonly referred to as "welfare" — provide cash grants to families and individuals who meet income requirements. In-kind benefit programs provide services such as housing, medical care and job training, or vouchers for discount purchases, such as food stamps.

housing assistance and Medicaid; but critics contend that many of the poor have had their benefits reduced by direct cutbacks, deferred increases and hikes in rents and other fees. Opponents also say that the "working poor" whose benefits were eliminated have been thrust back into dire poverty.

Reagan administration officials have consistently denied that their programs are unfair to the poor. But the "fairness issue" is apparently going to be central to the Democrats' efforts to unseat Reagan in this year's presidential election. "The Reagan record reflects an insensitivity to the needs of poor Americans that is unique in the post-Depression era," Democratic contender Gary Hart said in a recent interview.[2]

The major budget cuts of Reagan's presidency occurred early in his first year. Within seven months of Reagan's inauguration, Congress had enacted the largest spending and tax cuts in its history, slashing fiscal 1982 spending $35 billion below projected levels and reducing personal and corporate income taxes by $37.7 billion. About $25 billion in cuts — some 70 percent of the budget savings — were made in programs affecting the poor.[3] Congress was not as receptive to Reagan's budget-cutting requests in the following years, although some cuts in poverty programs were enacted.

Perhaps the biggest change was to reduce benefits for the working poor and focus federal welfare assistance primarily on the non-working poor. Congress, for example, amended the major cash benefit program, Aid to Families with Dependent Children (AFDC), to eliminate most payments to working parents.[4] According to the Congressional Budget Office (CBO), "Of the 450,000 to 500,000 families with earnings estimated to be receiving AFDC at the time of the [1981 program] changes, about one-half are estimated to have lost eligibility because of [those changes]. Another 40 percent are estimated to have had their AFDC benefits reduced, and the remaining 10 percent to have received unchanged or higher benefits. The other ... changes, which affect primarily non-earners, are estimated to have made at least another 100,000 families ineligible and reduced benefits significantly for another 100,000."[5]

---

[2] Published in *Public Welfare,* winter 1984, p. 9.
[3] Congressional Quarterly Inc., *Budgeting for America,* 1982, p. 99.
[4] The payments to AFDC recipients in each state are provided on approximately a 50-50 basis by the federal and state government (overall, the federal government pays about 54 percent of all AFDC costs). Benefits are based on a "standard of need," a subsistence level of income set by the states. Standards of need vary widely between states, with monthly benefits for families of three ranging from lows of $96 in Mississippi and $118 in Alabama, to highs of $674 in Alaska and $526 in California.
[5] Unless otherwise noted, quotes and figures attributed to the Congressional Budget Office were taken from the August 1983 CBO report entitled "Major Legislative Changes in Human Resources Programs Since January 1981."

Changes in Major Welfare Programs

The following table lists the major federal welfare programs and those changes made during the first three years of the Reagan administration that resulted in significant spending cuts. Hundreds of other program changes were made that also affected the poor and near-poor.

Aid to Families with Dependent Children (AFDC)	**Purpose:** Federal-state program providing cash support to low-income families with children **Major Changes:** Reduced eligibility for families with earned income by limiting "work incentive" benefits; eliminated or reduced benefits for students beyond high school; limited benefits for pregnant women with no children to last trimester of their pregnancy.
Medicaid	**Purpose:** State-federal program to pay for medical care for the poor **Major Changes:** Reduced federal Medicaid grants to states 3 percent in 1982, 4 percent in 1983 and 4.5 percent in 1984 (states could avoid reduction by reducing error rates and benefit growth); states could require recipients to pay part of costs.
Food Stamps	**Purpose:** Coupons, good for food purchase, issued to low-income households **Major Changes:** Eliminated inflation adjustment in 1982 and postponed later adjustments; revoked eligibility of households with monthly incomes over 130 percent of the poverty line, unless they have elderly or disabled members; penalized states for excessive error rates in food stamp distribution.
Housing aid	**Purpose:** Rent subsidies for low-income families; aid to public-housing projects to help cover construction and operating expenses **Major Changes:** Gradually increased the tenant share of rent from 25 percent to 30 percent (the federal government pays the remainder); eliminated most federal housing construction subsidies.
Title XX Social Services	**Purpose:** Grants to states for providing services such as day care, foster care and family planning **Major Changes:** Congressional Budget Office (CBO) estimated funding cut of 22 percent.
Community Services Block Grant	**Purpose:** Grants to local community action agencies for social services to low-income persons **Major Changes:** Community Services Administration abolished and its programs made into a block grant. CBO estimated 39 percent funding cutback.

Congress in 1981 and 1982 made changes in the food stamp program that, according to CBO, eliminated about 4 percent or one million people from the rolls. Deferrals in adjustments for inflation affected most people still receiving benefits. Although Congress refused Reagan's request to put a cap on the federal contribution on Medicaid, the state-run health care program for the poor, it did reduce federal Medicaid grants to the states and allowed the states to require Medicaid recipients to pay for part of the cost of their care.[6] In addition, since AFDC recipients are automatically eligible for Medicaid, many of those eliminated from the AFDC rolls lost their medical benefits as well.

Congress abolished altogether the public service employment (PSE) program, which provided jobs for the unemployed in state and local governments and in non-profit agencies. PSE was one of the most controversial of the low-income-targeted programs. Its advocates said PSE provided many poor individuals with work experience that eventually helped them move completely into the unsubsidized job market. However, opponents said the program provided dead-end, make-work jobs; news reports on mismanagement and provision of jobs to non-needy individuals further tarnished the program's image.

The administration also targeted the Work Incentive Program (WIN) for cutbacks. The program, which provides job search and training assistance, has been mandatory for AFDC recipients without children under age 6 since its inception in 1967. However, Reagan's budgeters claimed the program was neither successful nor cost-effective in reducing welfare dependency. Although Congress rejected requests to eliminate the program, the number of registrants dropped from 1.6 million in 1981 to one million in 1982. Other major spending cuts affecting the poor were made in federal housing assistance programs, social services, and community services, school lunch programs, compensatory education and emergency energy assistance.

Savings Resulting From Welfare Changes

The Reagan administration takes pride in slowing the growth of federal programs for low-income individuals. "Between 1954 and 1981 the constant dollar cost of federal means-tested benefit programs increased *eleven-fold* — from $6 billion to $68 billion," said the authors of the fiscal year 1985 budget document.[7] "Although Congress has not adopted all of the reforms proposed by the administration, estimated 1984 current law real

---

[6] The Reagan administration and many economists say that overuse of medical services by participants in private insurance plans and recipients of public medical benefits has contributed to the rapid rise in health care costs. See "Rising Cost of Health Care," *E.R.R.*, 1983 Vol. I, pp. 253-272.

[7] Figures used are based on 1985 constant dollars.

costs will be lower than 1981, as will the means-tested budget share of the GNP [1.8 percent compared with 1.9 percent in 1981]."

The CBO reported in August 1983 that the impact of the changes is even greater if the current spending figures are compared with the spending that would have occurred under the laws in effect at the beginning of 1981.[8] CBO found that, compared with pre-1981 law, AFDC and food stamps for fiscal years 1982-1985 had been cut by almost 13 percent; child nutrition programs had dropped about 28 percent; housing assistance fell 4.4 percent; Medicaid was cut by 5 percent.

Some non-entitlement programs were slashed even deeper: general employment and training funds (not including public service employment) were cut 35 percent; the Work Incentive program was cut 33 percent. Funding for the Community Services Block Grant was 39 percent below that of the Community Services Administration programs it replaced. The only programs to be increased compared with 1981 projections were Supplemental Security Income for the elderly, blind or disabled and the supplemental feeding program for women, infants and children (WIC); both programs went up about 4 percent.

CBO's calculations cast some doubt on the administration's claim that the spending cuts would not affect the truly needy. CBO assessed the impact of budget actions on all "human resource" programs, including those not targeted to low-income Americans, such as Social Security, Medicare, and Civil Service and veterans' pensions, and found that "... the means-tested benefit programs, which primarily benefit low-income households, were cut by about 8 percent overall, while the non-means-tested programs, whose beneficiaries are likely to have higher incomes on the average, were reduced about 4 percent. Further, much of the savings in non-means-tested programs comes from the Medicare reductions, most of which do not directly affect individuals [because the payments go directly to health care providers and not to the individuals]. . . ."

The CBO report found that households with incomes under $10,000 would lose an average of $470 (in 1982 dollars) in benefits in the 1982-1985 period, and households with incomes between $10,000 and $20,000 would lose $360 in benefits; meanwhile, households with incomes over $80,000 would lose $170 in federal benefits. About 70 percent of the reductions would affect those households with annual incomes below $20,000 — 48 percent of the population. The report also noted that because

---

[8] CBO's calculations were based on its February 1983 budget projections, and did not include subsequent fiscal year 1984 or 1985 budget action.

there are households in those income categories that receive no benefits at all, "...the impacts of benefit reductions or increases on those who are affected will generally be larger than the averages for the entire income group suggest."

Effects on Working Poor, Truly Needy

One of the prime targets of administration budget-cutters was the work incentive portion of the AFDC program. Enacted in 1967, the program made eligible for AFDC payments those parents who worked but did not earn enough to support their families. The idea was to encourage people totally dependent on welfare to seek jobs. "The fact is over that period of 15 years, there was no significant increase in the number of people getting jobs," said Robert B. Carleson, special assistant to President Reagan for policy development, in a recent interview. "But [the program] made millions of people and families eligible for welfare who had not been eligible in the past..." [9]

Carleson, who served as director of the California Department of Social Welfare in the early 1970s under then-Governor Reagan, couched the administration's assault on benefits for the "working poor" in terms of fairness. According to Carleson, by dipping into the limited pool of welfare resources, persons with other earnings were taking money that could have been used to raise basic benefits for people who had to rely entirely on public assistance. Also, he added, welfare benefits for workers were supported in part by tax dollars paid by those not much better off: "You had people side-by-side making the same income, one person paying taxes and not receiving benefits, and the other person at the next desk or the next work station receiving a welfare benefit, and that's not fair."

To advocates of AFDC payments to the working poor, however, the cutbacks have had an impact they find more unfair than the one described by Carleson. According to figures published by the Center for the Study of Social Policy in 1983, in 13 states families with a working parent who lost supplemental AFDC benefits had less income after taxes than AFDC families with no working parent. The difference was only marginally in favor of the working parent in several other states.

Many analysts predicted that the loss of AFDC benefits would force thousands of parents to give up their jobs and return to the welfare rolls. Studies have shown this not to be the case. The Research Triangle Institute of North Carolina reported in April 1983 that in the 40 counties and 27 states it surveyed, only 15 percent of the workers whose AFDC benefits had been cut off in October 1981 had returned to welfare a year later.

---

[9] Unless otherwise noted, quotes in this report come from interviews by the author.

To Carleson, these statistics prove the administration's contention that the working poor could survive without government support. "In effect," Carleson said, "we weaned these people away from dependency on that system and there was no decline in the work effort after those changes were made."

According to Robert Greenstein, executive director of the Center on Budget and Policy Priorities[10] and head of the federal food stamp program during the Carter administration, the work ethic among the poor is so strong that most of the people who lost AFDC payments would stay on their jobs even though it

meant financial loss. "But while it is the case that most of those people did not quit their jobs, it is the undeniable fact that their living standards were reduced ... and that they and their children were poorer than they were before," Greenstein said.

Demonstration, Washington, D.C.

The Reagan administration stands firmly behind its contention that it has protected the truly needy, making only justifiable spending cuts to relieve the burden of transfer payments on the American taxpayer. According to the fiscal 1985 budget document, "Contrary to the claims of some critics, the social safety net is as strong today as it was in 1981 as measured by constant dollars of budget resources: the difference is that unsustainable, unnecessary, and socially counterproductive expansion has been stopped."

The Census Bureau reported last September that, through 1982, the administration had succeeded in stemming the growth of federal benefit programs and had made gains toward its goal of retargeting the programs on the poorest of the poor. The agency found that, despite the deepening recession, the number of households receiving one or more benefits had dropped from 14.7 million in 1981 to 14.6 million in 1982. Of all food stamp recipients, 72.3 percent were below the poverty line in 1982, compared with 67.5 percent in 1981; the number of Medicaid recipients in poverty went up from 54.3 percent to 59.1 percent.

---

[10] The Center on Budget and Policy Priorities in Washington, D.C., was founded in 1981 to analyze the impact of domestic federal spending reductions on low-income families and individuals.

But the administration's opponents insist that while the truly needy have not been removed entirely from the rolls, they have lost benefits. Greenstein noted the increase, to 30 percent from 25 percent, in the share of rent paid by all residents of subsidized public housing. He also observed that delays in food stamp benefit increases affected all recipients. "The bulk of the savings came not from throwing people off the program, but by reducing benefits for people below the poverty line," Greenstein said. "What is *completely* disingenuous is for the administration to claim that it has never tried to go after the people at the bottom."

Congress over the past three years has rejected a number of administration proposals that might have affected the truly poor. One of these would have raised rents for all families and elderly persons living in subsidized housing who also receive food stamps. For every $100 a month received in food stamps, rents would have risen $30. According to Greenstein, because food stamp allotments increase as income decreases, the poorest families would have incurred the largest rent increases.

Growth of Poverty Aid

PROVIDING CHARITY for the poor has been an obligation of virtually all major religions throughout the centuries. Traditionally, aid to the poor was borne by individuals and institutions, such as churches, that would today be described as part of the "private sector." By the 16th century, the idea that the state should play a role in alleviating the effects of poverty was embodied in the English Poor Laws, which formed the basis for the treatment of the poor in the American colonies. As in the mother country, the New England colonies required each locality to support its indigents. Residence requirements were established to discourage itinerant beggars. Indigent persons, including children, were bound as indentured servants; workhouses and "poor farms" followed.

In the early years of the United States, it was thought that state aid to the poor would destroy the incentive to work and create a permanent population of indigents. An 1818 report issued by the Society for the Prevention of Pauperism in New York asked: "Is not the partial temporary good which [relief payments] accomplish, how acute soever the miseries they relieve, ... more than counterbalanced by the evils that flow from the expectations they necessarily excite; by the relaxation of industry, which such a display of benevolence tends to produce...?" The report warned that, if the poor were relieved of the "anxiety to provide for the wants of a distant day," they would fall into a "state of absolute dependence" and become "a burden to the community." [11]

Attitudes toward relief began to shift by the mid-1800s. Massachusetts created a state board of charities in 1863; other states followed by creating homes for poor persons who were mentally or physically impaired. In 1911, Illinois and Missouri passed "mothers' aid" laws that provided assistance to mothers of young children whose fathers had died, deserted or were disabled. By 1926, 42 of the 48 states had similar laws; by 1933, more than half provided old-age assistance.

Federal social welfare programs evolved more slowly than state programs. But as the Industrial Revolution led to urban growth, explosive immigration created teeming slums, and "muckraking" journalists and social workers exposed vile conditions of poverty, pressure grew for federal action. In 1912 Congress created the Children's Bureau, the first federal program for poor mothers and children. In 1921 Congress passed a law to fund state programs that provided health care for pregnant women and infants.

It was the Great Depression, though, that forced a sea change in public attitudes toward federal welfare efforts. With a quarter of the work force unemployed, millions of former wage-earners had no money for food or shelter. The destitute, so long seen as responsible for their own plight, were now viewed as victims of national economic vagaries.

Soon after Franklin D. Roosevelt assumed the presidency in 1933, Congress passed the first federal public assistance law — the Federal Emergency Relief Act. Roosevelt himself actually had a traditional view of cash relief. "The quicker they are taken off the dole the better it is for them for the rest of their lives," he said shortly after taking office, adding that work "is the saving barrier between them and moral disintegration." Many of Roosevelt's New Deal programs — the Civilian Conservation Corps, the Works Progress Administration, the Public Works Administration, the National Youth Administration — were aimed at putting people back to work.[12]

It was the Social Security Act of 1935 that laid the groundwork for the vast expansion of federal payments in the next half-century. The law set up the Social Security and unem-

---

[11] Quoted in Charles A. Murray, "Safety Nets and the Truly Needy," The Heritage Foundation, 1982.
[12] See "Federal Jobs Programs," *E.R.R.*, 1982 Vol. II, pp. 949-972.

ployment insurance systems; both were contributory programs for which all workers were eligible regardless of socioeconomic status. It also created assistance programs for special categories of the poor — Old-Age Assistance, Aid to the Blind, and Aid to Dependent Children (ADC).[13]

Johnson's Great Society; War on Poverty

Initially there was no great surge in participation in the federal welfare programs. This can be attributed, at least in part, to the negative attitude toward the "dole" harbored even by the poor. Although nine million people remained unemployed in 1940, only 372,000 families received relief through the ADC program that year.

The employment boom during World War II and the economic growth and general affluence of the 1950s diminished poverty as a national issue. The dawn of the 1960s renewed concern about poverty. The Census Bureau reported in 1959 that 18.5 percent of all Americans had incomes below the poverty line; 48.1 percent of all blacks lived in poverty. Books such as John Kenneth Galbraith's *The Affluent Society* (1958) and Michael Harrington's *The Other America* (1962) discussed the nation's "forgotten poor"; the civil rights movement cast a spotlight on the problems of black poverty.

In his 1964 State of the Union address, President Lyndon B. Johnson declared "unconditional war on poverty in America." Pursuing his goal of a "Great Society," Johnson convinced Congress to pass a number of programs aimed at eliminating the roots and symptoms of poverty. Manpower Development and Training Administration programs were expanded, and the Job Corps for underprivileged youths was created. Model Cities and other urban development programs were established, as were educational aid programs.

Congress also expanded the means-tested entitlement programs for the poor. The experimental food stamp program begun in 1961 was made permanent in 1964. In 1965, Medicaid was founded to provide medical care to the poor. Enrollment in AFDC was expanded in 1967 to include families with working parents. The efforts of "welfare rights" organizations to inform individuals of their eligibility and to encourage them to take advantage of the programs also added people to the rolls.

Reports such as CBS News' "Hunger in America" and studies such as the one by the Field Foundation in 1967 that found

---

[13] In 1950, the Aid to the Permanently and Totally Disabled program was added. In 1962, the ADC program, which previously had provided payments only for the support of needy children, added support for their parents and was renamed Aid to Families with Dependent Children. In 1974, the programs for the elderly, blind and disabled poor were merged into the Supplementary Security Income (SSI) program.

widespread hunger and malnutrition in America increased pressure for expanded federal nutrition programs. In May 1969, President Nixon called for an expansion of the food stamp program: "That hunger and malnutrition should persist in a land such as ours is embarrassing and intolerable. The moment is at hand to put an end to hunger in America itself for all time." Congress broadened eligibility, and the program grew explosively; federal outlays for food stamps grew from $248 million in 1969 to $577 million in 1970 and $1.6 billion in 1971.

Dissatisfaction With Welfare Programs

"The belief that the government could help build a more decent society flourished during these years," wrote John E. Schwarz in *America's Hidden Success: A Reassessment of Twenty Years of Public Policy* (1983). A Gallup Poll taken in April 1966 showed that 61 percent of all Americans were favorable to anti-poverty programs. But despite his call to expand the food stamp program, Nixon by 1970 was claiming to represent a "silent majority" that opposed continued expansion of low-income benefit programs. Efforts by Presidents Nixon, Ford and Carter to reform the welfare system were unsuccessful, however. And Congress created new welfare programs or vastly expanded others, such as the public service employment program under Ford and Carter.

Between 1960 and 1980, participation in AFDC rose from 803,000 to 3.8 million families and from 3.1 million to 11.1 million individuals; the federal share of AFDC payments rose from $2 billion to $6 billion. Federal outlays for food stamps, at just $30 million in 1964, soared to $9.1 billion in 1980. Spending for other programs targeted on the poor and near-poor totaled in the tens of billions of dollars.

Dissatisfaction with federal benefit programs helped fuel Reagan's successful run for the presidency in 1980. Critics voiced several objections. One was that the welfare programs contributed significantly to the growth of the federal budget which in turn led to the record rise in inflation and interest rates in the late 1970s. Critics also said that the tax dollars used to pay for the programs, if left in the private economy, would have resulted in investment and job creation that would have had a more beneficial long-term impact on the poor than the welfare programs had.

Traditional conservative beliefs about welfare dependency also gained new currency. Conservatives said that AFDC, for example, encouraged marital breakup because the benefits went mainly to families in which the husband/father was absent. Many families, these critics said, determined they would be

13

better off financially if the male left home. They also blamed the rapid increase in the number of out-of-wedlock and teenage births on the AFDC program.[14]

The critics also claimed that the availability of welfare payments, their favorable comparability to income from minimum-wage employment and the loss of the stigma of the "dole" had destroyed the incentive to work and created a self-perpetuating welfare class. In *Wealth and Poverty* (1980), George Gilder wrote, "The most serious fraud is committed not by the welfare culture but by the creators of it, who conceal from the poor, both adults and children, the most fundamental realities of their lives: that to live well and escape poverty they will have to keep their families together at all costs and will have to work harder than the classes above them. In order to succeed, the poor need most of all the spur of their poverty." To provide that spur, Gilder said, "Welfare benefits must be allowed to decline steadily in value as inflation proceeds."

While avoiding such politically unpalatable suggestions as Gilder's, Reagan administration officials have voiced similar sentiments concerning the destructiveness of federal benefit programs. "There is no question that many well-intentioned Great Society-type programs contributed to family breakups, welfare dependency and a large increase in births out of wedlock," said President Reagan in a radio speech to the nation in December 1983. In his remarks to the National Press Club in the same month, presidential counselor Edwin Meese III said, "In a very real sense, the broken families, dependent mothers and fatherless children that were spawned by a decade of aimless spending are the real victims of a well-meaning but misguided system of governmental aid and regulations."

Questions of Fairness

SUPPORTERS of federal welfare programs claim the Reagan administration and other critics are way off base. In a 1983 booklet entitled "Beyond the Myths: The Families Helped by the AFDC Program," the Center on Social Welfare Policy and Law said that program benefits were hardly generous: Combined average AFDC and food stamp benefits were less than 76 percent of the poverty level for families in 38 states and the

---

[14] According to the National Center for Health Statistics, the illegitimate birth rate increased from 5.3 per hundred live births in 1960 to 18.9 per hundred in 1981.

District of Columbia, and less than 60 percent of the poverty level in 14 states. The center also denied that there is a large permanent welfare group. Citing a 1979 Department of Health and Human Services caseload sample, it reported that more than half of all welfare recipients were on the rolls for less than three consecutive years, while only 7.1 percent were recipients for more than 10 consecutive years.

The idea that reliance on welfare is the result of structural flaws in the economy rather than personal flaws in the individual was bolstered, according to advocates, by the events of the recent recession. According to the Rev. Thomas Harvey, executive director of the National Conference of Catholic Charities: "[F]or many years ... blue-collar laborers were told welfare [recipients] were ripoffs. Then all of a sudden, a lot of their brothers, as mills closed, are caught in structural change that put them in the welfare class. Did they become lazier? What happened in the environment that made it possible for them to make a choice that was always unacceptable to them?"

Determining Poverty: Counting Benefits

Advocates also deny that the money spent during the years of program expansion was wasted. Poverty rates dropped to a low of 11.1 percent in 1973, and remained in the 11-12 percent range through most of the 1970s. Using Census Bureau data, Schwarz figured that without the income transferred to individuals through government programs, poverty would have lingered around 20 percent throughout the period. Schwarz also noted that some of the worst symptoms of poverty — lack of health care, infant mortality and substandard housing — were shown statistically to have eased.

Some conservative commentators, on the other hand, say that the declining poverty rates actually indicate that increased welfare spending is unnecessary. Some even suggest that the poverty rate is overstated because it is based only on income and does not include the value of in-kind benefits that, for many families, can add up to several thousand dollars. Office of Management and Budget Director David A. Stockman told Congress last November that if medical care and housing were included, the poverty rate would drop from 34.4 million or 15 percent of the population to 20 million or 9.6 percent.

Administration opponents claim that such figuring is spurious. They say that when increased doctors' fees cause Medicaid payments to go up, it does not result in an increase in income or standard of living for the benefit recipient. They note that the inclusion of medical benefits in a measure of income has an ironic impact: the sicker a person is, the wealthier he or she will appear. And they contend it is unfair to include in-kind benefits

15

in the income of public assistance recipients when similar benefits, such as employer-paid medical insurance and other fringe benefits, are not included in general income statistics. "This makes for a neat comparison of apples and oranges," said Robert Greenstein.[15]

The debate over how to measure poverty has taken on new importance since 1979 when the Census Bureau began to report yearly increases in the poverty rate. From 11.4 percent in 1978, the rate moved up to 11.7 percent in 1979, 13.2 percent in 1980, 14.0 percent in 1981 and 15.0 percent in 1982. Because the increase began before Reagan took office, the bureau attributes the rise to inflation and the recessions of 1980 and 1981-83. Even with in-kind benefits counted, the poverty rate is rising. The bureau reported Feb. 23 that, counting both cash payments and in-kind benefits, the rate had increased from 6.8 percent in 1979 to 10 percent in 1982 using one statistical formula, and from 9 percent to 12.7 percent using another formula.[16]

Social program backers insist that things are getting worse, both for the long-term poor and the "new poor," mainly the families of middle-class blue-collar workers whose jobs in the basic industries, such as automobiles and steel, were lost to recession or automation. For instance, Steven Fustero wrote in February 1984 that increased unemployment had helped swell the ranks of the homeless, estimated at two million people.[17] Many social issue activists say that the standard of living of those in or near poverty has declined. "I would say that people are having to give up their independent living and move in with friends and relatives," said National Urban League President John Jacob. "I would say that people are having to make choices between heating their homes and eating. I would say that people who ordinarily would be able to send their kids to schools are having to keep them home ... because they can't buy warm clothes for them, or give them lunch money...."

Perhaps the widest gulf between the administration and its critics has been on the subject of hunger. In May 1983 the Center on Budget and Policy Priorities released the results of its survey of 181 emergency food programs across the country: 53.3 percent of the programs reported increases of more than 50 percent in the number of meals or food baskets provided between February 1982 and February 1983; 32.2 percent at least

---

[15] Greenstein, "Stockman is Still Cooking the Numbers," *The Washington Post*, June 19, 1983.

[16] The House Ways and Means Committee reported in February that the purchasing power of welfare benefits had dropped by one-third since 1970 because state increases in benefits had not kept pace with inflation.

[17] Steven Fustero, "Home on the Street," *Psychology Today*, February 1984.

doubled in size; 24.3 percent had to turn people away in February 1983; 68.1 percent limited the number of times the same person could get food assistance.[18] In June 1983, after visiting 28 emergency food centers, the federal General Accounting Office reported that "in almost all cases, the emergency food centers were serving more today than in the past."

The Reagan administration has strongly denied that there is a hunger crisis in the United States. In a news conference Dec. 14, the president said, "We're doing more to feed the hungry in this country today than has ever been done by any administration." Reagan, who appointed a task force on food assistance in August 1983, readily accepted its findings released Jan. 9. While hunger persists in America, the panel said, ". . . we have not been able to substantiate allegations of rampant hunger." [19]

Impact of Economic Recovery on Poor

Reagan administration officials have said that limiting the discussion of "fairness" to a statistical examination of the budget cuts does not tell the whole story. They say that the president's economic recovery program has beneficial effects for the entire economy. They take credit for the falling jobless rate and decline in inflation, from 12.4 percent in 1980 to 3.8 percent in 1983. An improving economy benefits all Americans, said Robert Carleson, "especially those in the lower-income brackets."

Soup kitchen, Washington, D.C.

Administration critics say, though, that a broader view confirms that the overall Reagan economic program is unfair to the poor. The Center on Budget and Policy Priorities calculated the effects of the Economic Recovery Tax Act of 1981 on different tax brackets after inflation and Social Security tax increases were factored in: it found that individuals with earnings over $200,000 a year would pay 15 percent less in taxes, while those with in-

---

[18] The center released its findings in a report entitled "Soup Lines and Food Baskets." The survey period covered the height of the recent recession.

[19] The president had no public comment on a report by the Harvard-based Citizens Commission on Hunger in New England, released Feb. 6, which said, "We have found concrete evidence of hunger in every state we have looked. We found hunger and it wasn't hard to find."

comes under $10,000 would pay 22 percent more in taxes.[20]
Comparing tax breaks provided to corporations under that law
with the administration's actions toward the working poor, Edward Weaver, director of the American Public
Welfare Association, said, "We will give business and industry
all sorts of inducements and incentives to recapitalize and
to renew their industries because they need incentives to do
that, but we will remove [incentives for the working poor] from
the welfare system because poverty is the incentive there. If
you're hungry enough, sick enough, ... you'll get up off your
backside."

The critics say that programs for the poor have been victimized to pay for the 38 percent increase in defense spending,
and note that non-means-tested entitlement programs such as
Social Security have been treated lightly compared with the
means-tested programs.

Carleson denied the alleged unfairness of these budget actions. But Reagan's opponents cite numerous statements made
by the president and his advisers as evidence of insensitivity,
even meanness, toward the poor. Among those noted:

> In an interview with *The Wall Street Journal* published Feb.
> 3, Reagan said that "if there are individuals who suffer from our
> economic program, they are people who have been dropped from
> various things like food stamps because they weren't morally
> eligible for them ... in many cases, weren't even technically
> eligible for them."
>
> On ABC-TV's "Good Morning America" program on Jan. 31,
> Reagan said that many of the homeless were "homeless, you
> might say, by choice." (A White House spokesman said afterward
> that the president was referring to people who had refused assis-
> tance from public authorities.)
>
> During an interview with wire service reporters Dec. 8, Edwin
> Meese III said that he had not heard of "any authoritative fig-
> ures that there are hungry children," and then added, "I know
> we've had considerable information that people go to soup kitch-
> ens because the food is free and that that's easier than paying for
> it."

Fairness and the Presidential Campaign

Each side in the debate over fairness accuses the other of
playing politics with the poverty issue. According to Edward
Weaver, "There are times in my more cynical moments that the
responses of the Ed Meeses and David Stockmans and Ronald
Reagans of the world are very calculated statements that are
geared to assuage the politically powerful at this point in time
... that they are cold and calculating, believing that the power-

---

[20] "Inequity and Decline," Center on Budget and Policy Priorities, 1983.

less people don't have enough friends that will pay any attention ... and yet it assuages their coterie of followers." Robert Carleson countered, "If those people really cared about [the poor], they wouldn't be putting out these misperceptions," and blamed the situation on "the politicians or people who have a financial stake in an expanded welfare system ... the people who earn their livings as advocates."

That the "fairness issue" is going to be enmeshed in the partisan politics of 1984 has already become evident. In an article in the winter 1984 issue of *Public Welfare*, a publication of the American Public Welfare Association, all of the Democratic presidential candidates attacked Reagan's social welfare policies and called for reversal of some or all of the program cutbacks. On the campaign trail, the Democrats have been harshly critical of Reagan. Former Vice President Walter F. Mondale's Feb. 4 speech before a regional conference of the AFL-CIO in Boston, is typical: "Roosevelt gave us the New Deal, Truman gave us the Fair Deal, but this president will go down in history giving us the double deal. To children and the poor he offers a raw deal. To defense contractors the sweetheart deal. To the nation's hungry he says, 'Big deal.' To the corporations he says, 'Let's make a deal.' To the polluters he offers a dirty deal. And to those who need job training he says, 'No deal.' I say it's time to restore fairness by bringing an end to the Reagan double deal in 1984."

Recent public opinion polls indicate that the Democrats will get a sympathetic hearing on the fairness issue. A *New York Times*/CBS News Poll, conducted Jan. 14-21, found that 73 percent of the respondents thought that hunger was a real problem in America. In an ABC News poll completed Jan. 17, 54 percent of the respondents said cutbacks in federal spending for social programs have created serious hardship for many people, and 62 percent said the government should not cut spending for social programs to reduce the federal deficit.

In an interview with *Public Opinion* magazine, published in the December-January 1984 issue, pollster Daniel Yankelovich predicted that Reagan's treatment of low-income Americans will be an important, but probably not decisive, issue in the election campaign. "The fairness issue is one of Reagan's vulnerabilities, and it is a big one," said Yankelovich. "[But] the fairness issue by itself will not defeat Reagan. ... Other issues, such as inflation and leadership, and foreign policy, are too important."

Selected Bibliography

Books

Gilder, George, *Wealth and Poverty*, Basic Books, 1980.

Palmer, John L., and Isabel V. Sawhill (eds.), *The Reagan Experiment*, The Urban Institute Press, 1982.

Schwarz, John E., *America's Hidden Success: A Reassessment of Twenty Years of Public Policy*, W. W. Norton and Co., 1983.

Articles

Carleson, Robert B., and Kevin R. Hopkins, "Whose Responsibility is Social Responsibility?: The Reagan Rationale," *Public Welfare* (a publication of the American Public Welfare Association), fall 1981.

"The Democratic Candidates on Social Welfare Policy," *Public Welfare*, winter 1984.

Reports and Studies

"Budget of the United States Government, FY 1985," U.S. Government Printing Office, 1984.

Center on Budget and Policy Priorities, "Soup Lines and Food Baskets," May 1983.

Center on Social Welfare Policy and Law, "Beyond the Myths: The Families Helped by the AFDC Program," 1983.

Children's Defense Fund, "A Children's Defense Budget," February 1984.

Congressional Budget Office, "Major Legislative Changes in Human Resources Programs Since January 1981," August 1983.

Editorial Research Reports: "Hunger in America," 1983 Vol. II, p. 721; "Rising Cost of Health Care," 1983 Vol. I, p. 253; "The Homeless: Growing National Problem," 1982 Vol. II, p. 793; "Reaganomics on Trial," 1982 Vol. I, p. 1; "Future of Welfare," 1975 Vol. II, p. 845; "Future of Social Programs," 1973 Vol. I, p. 249; "Welfare Reforms," 1967 Vol. II, p. 923; "Persistence of Poverty," 1964 Vol. I, p. 81.

Murray, Charles A., "Safety Nets and the Truly Needy: Rethinking the Social Welfare System," The Heritage Foundation, 1982.

National Urban League, "The State of Black America 1984," January 1984.

Graphics: Cover illustration by George Rebh; pp. 9, 17 photos by Martha Tabor.

NEW OPPORTUNITIES FOR THE DISABLED

by

Marc Leepson

Mar. 16
1 9 8 4

Editor's Note. The U.S. House of Representatives voted 410-1 on March 27, 1984, to stop the Reagan administration from cutting off the Social Security benefits of additional thousands of disabled workers. Federal officials said more than 470,000 had been removed from the disability rolls since March 1981, when the administration began to review the eligibility of those receiving the benefits. Before the vote, it was reported, the administration had tentatively decided to stop the process. This was viewed by some of the House members as an attempt to prevent the vote. The bill they passed was sent to the Senate, where its outcome was uncertain.

NEW OPPORTUNITIES
FOR THE DISABLED

I N LOS ANGELES, at the University of California's Neuro-
psychiatric Institute, parents and their preschool deaf children learn to communicate through sign language and lip reading. In Westmont, Pa., a quadriplegic uses a computerized
system activated by his breath to make telephone calls, tune
in a television and turn on the lights in his house. At the
U.S. Department of Justice in Washington, D.C., blind attorneys use specially adapted "talking" computer terminals to
obtain complete access to legal data banks. In Boston, a paralyzed man uses a sip-and-puff air tube to control the movement of his motorized wheelchair.[1] At Pittsburgh's Rehabilitation Institute paralyzed patients "speak" by staring into a
computerized electronic grid hooked to a video camera that
translates eye movements into synthesized speech. In Dayton,
Ohio, a young woman whose spinal cord was severed in an
automobile accident walks several steps with the aid of computerized electrical stimulation devices attached to her nerves and
joints.

These are just some of the technological breakthroughs that
are helping disabled people lead more normal lives today. Aided
by computerized technology, innovative rehabilitation techniques and laws banning discrimination against the disabled,
many handicapped persons have broken down barriers that
once denied them opportunities most able-bodied persons take
for granted. More handicapped persons than ever before are
receiving formal education, gaining employment and leading
more self-reliant lives. "We are on the periphery now of many
wonderful things," said Dr. Margaret J. Giannini, director of the
Veterans Administration's Rehabilitation, Research and Development Service. "The possibilities are so tremendous that we
can do many, many things for the paralyzed, the blind and the
deaf.... The technology is there and I think 10 years from now
it's going to be even better. I'm very excited about the '80s; I
think many things are going to happen."[2]

An important component in the rising opportunities for disabled persons is an attitudinal change among the disabled as
well as the public at large. A decade ago handicapped citizens

---

[1] A combination of inhalations and exhalations activate and guide wheelchair movement.
[2] Unless otherwise noted, those quoted in this report were interviewed by the author.

began to demand equal rights.[3] Today the message that the disabled have the right to become self-sufficient, independent citizens seems to have taken hold. "People are finally recognizing that disabled people are part of this society, that you can't hide them away," said Michael Winter, executive director of the Center for Independent Living in Berkeley, Calif. "People are realizing that there's nothing wrong with being disabled, that it's a state of being like any other state in society and there are some very positive things about that." Added Jim Norgard of the Courage Center, a Minnesota rehabilitation organization: "We're definitely — in both the minds of the able-bodied and the physically disabled people — getting away from this long-worn stereotype of the poor crippled person that's to be pitied and taken care of. A disabled person doesn't want pity and doesn't want to be taken care of. They want to be given the opportunity to pick themselves up by their own bootstraps and function as independently as possible."

Changes Following Second World War

More than 31 million Americans — about 15 percent of the population — have some type of chronic condition that limits their activities. Some eight million Americans are so handicapped that they are unable to work or participate in other major activities.[4] Some are born with disabilities such as cerebral palsy, spina bifida, Down's syndrome, blindness, deafness and epilepsy. But accidents, disease and war account for at least three-fourths of today's disabled Americans. Crippling diseases that primarily affect the elderly, such as arthritis and diabetes, have increased significantly. "As the life span has increased, so has the probability that an individual will acquire a major disability-inducing disease," rehabilitation specialists Gerben DeJong and Raymond Lifchez wrote recently. "And as the population of the elderly has increased, so has the prevalence of disease and disability."[5]

The marked increase in the number of disabled persons in this country began in the early 1940s with the development and widespread use of sulfonamide drugs, penicillin and other antibiotics. These drugs fight off pneumonia and other infections that physically disabled persons are particularly susceptible to.

---

[3] See "Rights of the Handicapped," *E.R.R.*, 1974 Vol. II, pp. 885-904.
[4] According to the latest fully tabulated data compiled by the National Center for Health Statistics, in 1979 an estimated 31.5 million persons had "some degree of chronic activity limitation" and some 7.9 million persons were "unable to carry on major activity" because of "severe chronic activity limitation." See "Health Characteristics of Persons with Chronic Activity Limitation, 1979," National Center for Health Statistics, "National Health Survey," Series 10, No. 137, December 1981.
[5] Writing in *Scientific American*, June 1983, p. 43. DeJong is associate professor of rehabilitation medicine at the Tufts University School of Medicine. Lifchez is associate professor of architecture at the University of California at Berkeley.

'Handicapped' vs. 'Disabled'

In the past the most commonly used term to refer to the mentally and physically impaired was "handicapped." Today, however, the preferred term is "disabled" — especially among disabled persons themselves. "The militance against the word *handicap* has some elements of a healthy pride and self-assertion about it," wrote Robert L. Burgdorf Jr. in *The Legal Rights of Handicapped Persons* (1980). "It is reminiscent of the Negro/black terminological shift in the black civil rights movement in America."

Burgdorf, who heads the Development Disability Law Project at the University of Maryland School of Law in Baltimore, said, however, that the distinction between "handicapped" and "disabled" "is not completely beneficent, nor, possibly, even logical." Preferring to be called "disabled," he said, "too often has a ring of elitism and favoritism about it. It frequently translates as, 'I'm not like those "handicapped" people. We persons with X disability are better than people with handicaps; we're much more like "normal" folks.' "

Semantically, Burgdorf said, "the implications of the two words have been totally reversed. The word *disabled* clearly derives from roots meaning 'not able,' implicitly not able to do something. *Handicap*, on the other hand, in common usage, in legal contexts, and according to the dictionary, refers to a physical or mental impairment."

This report uses the two words interchangeably.

"Prior to the mass production of penicillin in 1943 many disabling conditions were not a problem because people didn't survive," said George A. Conn, commissioner of the U.S. Department of Education's Rehabilitation Services Administration. "Spinal cord injuries, head trauma, poliomyelitis, smallpox and other problems led either to disability or to death. Eventually secondary infectious disorders led to the demise of these people. . . . That's all changed with advancing medical and pharmacological technology."

These medical advances also meant that beginning with World War II and continuing with the Korean and Vietnam wars a large number of veterans returned home with disabling injuries that would have proved fatal in earlier conflicts. The disabled World War II veterans had a great impact on public sensibilities. "We had never suffered massive disabling conditions in this country until World War II," Conn explained. "The attitude toward returning veterans changed things a great deal. . . . There was a natural empathetic reaction to that. The vets really led the way [in helping change attitudes] in the late '40s, all through the '50s and through most of the '60s." Dr. Howard A. Rusk agreed. "There was a feeling [following World

War II] that something had to be done to help those brave young men," said the founder of New York University Medical Center's Institute of Rehabilitation Medicine.[6]

Growth of Rehabilitation Technology

The influx of returning disabled World War II veterans sparked a new interest in rehabilitation medicine. Since 1947 some 75 hospitals specializing in rehabilitation have been set up throughout the country and researchers at other medical centers have started their own sophisticated rehabilitation programs. Private industry also has become involved in designing and marketing prosthetic, orthotic and other technological devices to aid the disabled. And since 1978 the National Institute of Handicapped Research (NIHR) has been funding research and training centers that work on developing technology to aid the disabled.

An NIHR-funded project at the Rehabilitation Engineering Center at the University of Virginia in Charlottesville, for example, is doing basic research on wheelchairs, something that had never been done until this project began eight years ago. "We're attempting to study the fundamentals much more than trying to design new approaches, although that is part of it," said Colin McLaurin, the program's director. "The people who build wheelchairs, as something goes wrong, they make them a little better. But there hasn't been any scientific study done on design," McLaurin said. His team is working on reducing the rolling resistance of wheelchair tires, making frames lighter, adjusting seat positions to help avoid pressure sores and evaluating newly developed lightweight but powerful batteries for mechanized chairs.

A team of rehabilitation engineers at the Palo Alto, Calif., Veterans Administration's Rehabilitative Engineering Research and Development Center is studying ways to give paralyzed persons control of their arms and hands. Engineers have developed a computer simulation of the mechanical action of a normal wrist to help surgeons analyze its complex system of muscles and tendons. In another effort, the Palo Alto VA is collaborating with Stanford University on a sophisticated, remote-control robotic arm equipped with a video camera. The arm, attached to a moving mechanism, would respond to spoken commands and be programmed to remove food from a refrigerator, for example, or take a specific book off a shelf and bring it to the user. Engineers expect the device to be available commercially in several years.

---

[6] Rusk was quoted by Laurence Cherry and Rona Cherry, "New Hope for the Disabled," *The New York Times Magazine,* Feb. 5, 1984, p. 53.

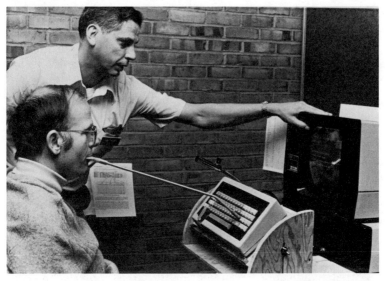

Courage Center staff member advises client on how to operate a computer.

Development of the personal computer has been a boon to the disabled. Engineers have developed ways to modify personal computers to give blind, deaf and paralyzed persons full use of the machines. There are talking computers, computers with Braille keyboards and computers that work with special control levers, mouthsticks or sip-and-puff mechanisms. Personal computers provide many advantages to disabled persons, including new work and educational opportunities. "Putting the right computerized information tools in the hands of the disabled is like giving them an equalizer gun," said Thomas Shworles, who heads the 400-member Committee on Personal Computers for the Handicapped in Chicago. "This technology is like the six-gun in the old West. It puts the weak and the strong, the meek and aggressive on a par." [7]

For the last four years the U.S. Department of Justice has operated a Sensory Assistance Center to give blind lawyers in the federal government access to legal information stored on computers. The center, located in Washington, D.C., uses specially designed computers with Braille keyboards and printouts as well as "talking" terminals that read information aloud. This equipment frees blind lawyers from having to depend on others to help them with research. "It makes things easier because yc can do your own casework on your own time, not to mer producing your own work without" depending on othe͏ the center's manager, Ed Bordley. Most blind lawyer to master the center's equipment after two hours

[7] Quoted in *The Wall Street Journal*, Feb. 7, 1984.

"The most difficult thing is just getting used to synthetic speech," Bordley said. "It's not very hard to use any of the data bases. . . . You can pick up the skills quickly because in law school you really have to learn quickly to keep up."

Landmark Legislation

THE OPPORTUNITIES that have opened up for the disabled in the last 15 years have been spurred in large part by more than two dozen federal laws and scores of state and local statutes to make buildings, education and employment more accessible to the handicapped. "The principle underlying such laws," a U.S. Commission on Civil Rights report noted, is "that handicapped people are entitled, as a matter of social justice, to a fair and equal chance to participate in American society. . . ." [8] These laws, for the most part, do not provide benefits directly to the disabled. Rather, they aim to break down the societal barriers that have denied disabled persons equal opportunities. "Disabled people really want to do things for themselves, and often we find that the environment itself is the handicapping fact of life — not the person's disability," said Conn of the Rehabilitation Services Administration. "When I was first injured [in 1955] there were no curb cuts," said Conn, who uses a wheelchair. "There were no special parking facilities in shopping centers. Public buildings were often inaccessible and you couldn't vote or sign a contract. You couldn't plead a case; you couldn't do a lot of things. It's been changing rather quickly in this country over the last 15 years."

The movement to eliminate physical barriers dates from the mid-1950s. A presidential advisory commission on employing the disabled and the Veterans Administration in 1958 drew up a voluntary plan to make public buildings accessible to the physically handicapped. But without the force of law, the plan was not widely implemented. In 1961, under sponsorship of the President's Committee on Employment of the Handicapped[9] and the National Easter Seal Society, the American National Standards Institute, a private group that sets architectural standards, issued guidelines for making buildings accessible to the handicapped. "The standards specified the minimum require-

---

[8] "Accommodating the Spectrum of Individual Abilities," U.S. Commission on Civil Rights, September 1983, p. 1.

[9] The president's committee was founded in 1947 to promote employment for the handicapped.

Major Federal Disability Laws, 1968-80

Year	Law	Main Requirements
1968	Architectural Barriers Act	Required federally funded public buildings to be made accessible to the physically handicapped.
1970	Urban Mass Transportation Act	Required states receiving federal funds for mass transit to make special efforts to accommodate handicapped persons.
1973	Federal Aid Highway Act	Required federally funded highway projects to be planned, constructed and operated to permit use by handicapped persons.
1973	Rehabilitation Act	Required each federal agency to develop affirmative action programs to hire and advance handicapped persons; employers with federal contracts over $2,500 must take affirmative action to employ and advance handicapped persons; prohibited discrimination on the basis of handicap in any program receiving federal funds.
1975	Developmental Disabilities Assistance and Bill of Rights Act	Required recipients of aid under this law to take affirmative action to employ and advance handicapped persons; established protection and advocacy systems for developmentally disabled.
1975	Education for all Handicapped Children	Assured all handicapped children the right to a free and appropriate public education in the least restrictive setting possible.
1975	National Housing Act Amendments	Required removal of all physical barriers to the handicapped in federally supported housing.
1978	Rehabilitation Comprehensive Developmental Disability Amendments	Established the National Institute for Handicapped Research; provided federal funding for Independent Living centers.

Sources: U.S. Commission on Civil Rights, Congressional Quarterly.

ments and working details for structures such as walkways, parking spaces, ramps, stairs, floor surfaces, mirrors, water fountains, public telephones, control identifications and warning signals," wrote DeJong and Lifchez.[10] But it was not until 1968 that Congress passed the Architectural Barriers Act requiring that all public buildings financed with federal funds be constructed or remodeled to be accessible to the physically handicapped *(see box, p. 29)*.

Far-Reaching Implications of 1973 Law

Five years later, Congress passed the Rehabilitation Act of 1973, frequently referred to as the Civil Rights Act of the Handicapped. The law has two anti-discrimination provisions:

● Section 504 states: "No otherwise qualified handicapped individual in the United States ... shall, solely by reason of his handicap, be excluded from the participation in, be denied the benefits of, or be subjected to discrimination under any program or activity receiving federal financial assistance."

● Section 503 requires that any company or organization with a federal contract worth more than $2,500 take affirmative action to employ and promote the disabled. This provision also provides that any handicapped person who believes he is a victim of job discrimination can file a complaint with the Department of Labor.

Federal legislation, of course, is not always a cure-all. Despite the 1973 law and similar legislation passed by most states, many employers have resisted hiring the disabled, and many qualified disabled persons are unable to find suitable employment. According to the latest Census Bureau data, 22 percent of disabled men and 7 percent of disabled women worked full time for all of 1981, compared with 61 percent of all able-bodied men and 33 percent of able-bodied women.[11]

One reason for this disparity is that many employers believe they need to make expensive accommodations for handicapped persons in the work place. But studies conducted by the U.S. Department of Labor and by E. I. du Pont de Nemours and Co. have found this not to be the case. The overall conclusion of a 20-month study of federal contractors prepared for the Labor Department in 1982 found that "for firms which have made efforts to hire the handicapped, accommodation is 'no big deal.' Rarely did an accommodation involve much cost; 51 percent of

[10] DeJong and Lifchez, *op. cit.*, p. 46. Several state legislatures also adopted laws banning architectural barriers in future construction.

[11] See "Labor Force Status and Other Characteristics of Persons with a Work Disability," 1982, U.S. Bureau of the Census, Series P-23, No. 127. According to the report, more than a fourth of all disabled Americans have incomes below the poverty line.

those reported cost nothing; an additional 30 percent cost less than $500. Only 8 percent cost more than $2,000." [12]

The Du Pont study indicated that disabled workers perform on a par with their able-bodied counterparts. The 1981 survey, which involved more than 2,700 disabled Du Pont employees, found that "the performance of handicapped employees is equivalent to that of their non-impaired co-workers." [13] Larry Volin of the President's Committe on the Employment of the Handicapped said these and other studies "indicate that disabled employees have more than held their own, that their records are as good as, or maybe even slightly better than, so-called non-disabled people in such things as attendance, safety and productivity."

Some experts are optimistic about the future overall employment picture for the disabled. They point to the widespread use of computers in the work world that has made it easier for disabled persons to gain access to information and to work at home. "All the predictors seem to indicate that [by 1990] disabled people are going to be able to participate in the job market to an extent never known before," said George Conn. Others have warned, however, that not all disabled persons will be helped by the computer revolution. "The shift from manufacturing base to a service-oriented industry causes problems with some handicapped people who are working in industry sweeping floors — the mentally retarded," said Paul Hippolitus, an employment adviser with the President's Committee on the Employment of the Handicapped. "Some jobs are being lost because of the new technology. . . . It's a double-edged sword; it helps some and it hurts some."

Federal Help for Handicapped Students

Another landmark piece of legislation credited with opening up opportunities for the handicapped is the Education for All Handicapped Children Act of 1975. Following the lead of legislation enacted in several states, the 1975 law mandated that public schools provide "free appropriate public education" to all disabled children. [14] President Gerald R. Ford and others criticized the law, saying it set up unnecessary administrative controls, involved the federal government in state and local affairs and cost too much. But the law has enjoyed enthusiastic sup-

---

[12] U.S. Department of Labor, Employment Standards Administration, "A Study of Accommodations Provided to Handicapped Employees by Federal Contractors," Final Report, Vol. I, June 17, 1982, p. i.

[13] E.I. du Pont de Nemours and Co., "Equal to the Task: 1981 Du Pont Study of Employment of the Handicapped," 1982, p. 4.

[14] See "Mainstreaming: Handicapped Children in the Classroom," *E.R.R.*, 1981 Vol. II, pp. 533-552 and Congressional Quarterly's *Congress and the Nation Vol. IV*, (1977), pp. 389-391.

port in Congress and among disabled-rights groups who credit the measure with enabling many more of the nation's disabled children than ever before to take part in public education. "You know, 93 percent of these kids are in classrooms — they're in schools with 'regular, normal' companions, normal students," Sen. Lowell P. Weicker Jr., R-Conn., said two years ago. "In the past they were left in the corner of an institution . . . just maybe a meal thrown at them, left there to grow fat with their tongue lolling in their head. Today, they're a part of our society." [15]

The Reagan administration proposed a series of amendments in August 1982 that would have loosened the federal regulations on local schools under the 1975 law. Among the suggested changes was a plan to end the requirement that schools work with parents to develop instructional plans for handicapped children and another that would have made it easier for schools to remove disruptive handicapped children from a classroom for disciplinary reasons. Seven weeks later, in the face of heavy criticism from Congress and disabled-rights groups, Education Secretary T. H. Bell withdrew some of the proposed changes, including the proposal that would have allowed schools to keep handicapped children out of regular classrooms if they were considered disruptive.

Bell refused to withdraw the entire set of proposed regulation changes, however, and the administration undertook a review of all the regulations implementing the 1975 law. On Nov. 28, 1983, in a White House speech following the proclamation of the National Decade of Disabled Persons, President Reagan announced that the review was completed and that the administration would propose no changes. "The regulations are fine the way they are," the president said. "No changes will be made and the program will be protected."

A recent Supreme Court ruling, however, has cast some doubt on the program. The court ruled Feb. 28 that a 1972 law prohibiting federal funding to educational institutions that practiced sex discrimination (Title IX of the Education Act Amendments) did not apply to all programs at a recipient institution but only to the particular program receiving federal aid.[16] William Bradford Reynolds, assistant attorney general in charge of the Civil Rights Division, said at a news conference

---

[15] Appearing Sept. 8, 1982, on PBS-TV's "The MacNeil-Lehrer Report." According to the latest available statistics (covering the 1981-82 school year) from the federal Office of Special Education, about 70 percent of school-aged handicapped children were being taught in regular public school classes, 24.5 percent in separate classes within public schools and the rest in separate schools or other educational institutions. Overall, there are some four million disabled schoolchildren in the United States.

[16] *Grove City College v. Bell.* In another ruling, *Consolidated Rail Corporation v. Darrone,* handed down the same day, the Supreme Court held that Section 504 prohibited job discrimination against the disabled in all federally funded programs, not just those created to provide jobs.

Photo courtesy of Courage Center

Preschool student in physical therapy

that day that he believed that the Section 504 regulations cutting off federal funds to schools for failing to provide equal educational opportunities to disabled students "would have the same interpretation. . . ." Several members of Congress quickly proposed legislation to overrule the Supreme Court decision and apply the fund cutoff provisions of Title IX and Section 504 institutionwide.

While nearly all observers agree that great strides have been made in public secondary and elementary education for the handicapped, the picture in higher education is not as rosy. In 1977, regulations were implemented under Section 504 of the 1973 Rehabilitation Act giving disabled college students the same opportunities as able-bodied students. Since then, most physical barriers on campuses have been removed, and hundreds of colleges have taken specific steps to help disabled students. Still, many colleges have yet to implement comprehensive programs for disabled students, and few institutions actively recruit the disabled. As a result, although there are more disabled undergraduates than ever before, the number has not increased significantly in recent years.

"We're making small gains, not big gains," said Paul Hippolitus. "Colleges and universities could do more in terms of accessibility — not just physical plant accessibility, but probably more importantly program accessibility: [helping with] note taking in the classroom, support services, the kind of things that facilitate the processing of information. Using a library is very difficult. . . . Getting from one class to another

33

with only 10 minutes in between. . . . It's a little bit complex."
Hippolitus' observations concur with a 1981 survey of college
and university disabled student programs conducted by the
Academy for Educational Development, an educational consult-
ing group. The survey concluded: " . . . Most colleges and
universities today are unprepared to fully serve handicapped
students." [17]

There has been one bright spot for the disabled in higher
education; the handicapped have made significant gains in the
legal, medical and science professions. "The success stories are
everywhere," said Dr. Martha Redden, director of the American
Association for the Advancement of Science's project on the
handicapped. "There are deaf students in dental school and
quadriplegics in medical school." Some 1,200 disabled scientists
belong to a special resource group sponsored by the association,
Dr. Redden said. The prestigious Columbia-Presbyterian Medical Center in New York, for example, recently awarded a residency in neurological surgery to Dr. Karin Muraszko, a 28-
year-old surgeon who has a mild form of spina bifida that forces
her to wear a leg brace. "Dr. Muraszko is the most outstanding
person I've met in medicine," said Dr. Bennett M. Stein, chairman of Columbia-Presbyterian's neurological surgery department. "Because neurological surgery is one of the most demanding residency programs, we did a lot of soul-searching before we
admitted her, because we were concerned that her handicap
might prevent her from doing the work. We have found, though,
that her intelligence, tenacity and motivation have enabled
her to make a remarkable contribution to the care of our patients." [18]

Reagan Administration and the Disabled

Since 1981 the Reagan administration has worked to cut back
federal domestic spending programs, including those that deal
with the handicapped.[19] One reason is the administration's belief that federal funds encourage the disabled to depend on
governmental largess. The aim, the administration says, should
be for disabled persons to try to become functioning members of
society. "Too often," Reagan said Nov. 28, 1983, "federal programs discourage full participation by society. Outmoded attitudes and practices that foster dependence are still with us.
They are unjust, unwanted and non-productive. Paternalism is
the wrong answer. . . ." The administration also claims that the
federal effort to help the disabled is inefficiently administered.

[17] S. G. Ticton, *et al.*, "Educational Opportunities for Handicapped Students: 1981 Idea
Handbook for Colleges and Universities," Academy for Educational Development, September 1981, p. i.
[18] Drs. Redden and Stein were quoted in *The New York Times*, July 18, 1983.
[19] See "Social Welfare Under Reagan," *E.R.R.*, 1984 Vol. I, pp. 189-208.

New Opportunities for the Disabled

Concerns among some disabled-rights groups over budget cutbacks have eased somewhat since the administration decided to use Section 504 of the Rehabilitation Act to protect the rights of severely handicapped newborns. The case that prompted the action occurred in April 1982 when a child in Indiana, known only as Baby Doe, died six days after it was born with Down's syndrome and a detached esophagus. The parents had opted against surgery that might have repaired the esophagus. Had the baby lived, he still would have suffered some degree of impairment from Down's syndrome. Public outcry encouraged the Department of Health and Human Services to notify the nation's 7,000 hospitals a month later that Section 504 specifically prohibits hospitals from discriminating against the handicapped. That notice and a subsequent federal regulation that later was declared invalid sparked a controversy over federal intervention in what had been considered private matters to be resolved between parents, doctors, hospitals and, occasionally, the courts. A compromise regulation went into effect in January 1984. But there are still questions about whether Section 504 authorizes such federal intervention.[20]

Meanwhile, some observers say that the government's use of Section 504 in the Baby Doe case has forced the administration to change its position on the other federal handicapped programs. "Prior to [1982] the programs protecting the rights of the handicapped people were sort of not looked favorably upon by the administration," an official familiar with the situation said. "In fact, we were very much fearful they would be wiped out. When the Baby Doe situation came up, the administration ... turned around 180 degrees on handicapped issues in general ... from being very antagonistic toward the current programs that exist for handicapped to now being very supportive."

Pioneering Advances

S CIENTIFIC advances and new attitudes toward the disabled have not only produced technological breakthroughs but also new patterns of living. These are embodied in the Independent Living movement. The first Independent Living center, set up in 1972 in Berkeley, Calif., was "based on the concept that disabled people should have the same choice or opportunity to live like anybody else in the community," said Michael Winter, the center's executive director. "We offer the

---

[20] See "Medical Ethics in Life and Death," *E.R.R.*, 1984 Vol. I, pp. 145-168.

disabled person a chance to be a productive member of society, to live as independently as anybody else. The key concept is not that a person do everything for themselves, but that the person has a choice to do what they want to do with their life. It doesn't [necessarily] mean that they be able to dress themselves or be able to drive, but that they be able to get a job and maybe hire somebody that can help them do what they can't do themselves."

Today there are hundreds of such centers that either provide or arrange for many services for the disabled — from hiring attendants and finding housing, to getting a driver's license and maintaining a balanced checking account. Some centers even provide housing. The idea is to free the disabled from depending on relatives or institutions. "You do not necessarily have to build a large brick and mortar structure and staff it with a great number of people," said Rehabilitation Services Administration Commissioner Conn. The centers, he said, "establish those independent living skills that disabled people need to exist within their community. . . . The primary form of assistance there is peer group support. Other disabled people are quite often on the staff and provide whatever independent living skills they have gained through their experiences and their interrelationships with agencies at the state and local level." [21]

Independent Living exponents predict that the concept will continue to gain many new adherents. The success of established centers has spurred more and more disabled persons to adopt the Independent Living philosophy. "As the opportunities become known and available to physically disabled persons to seek employment, improve their education and get involved in the community, then [other] physically disabled persons want to become more involved because they see that the opportunity is there," said Jim Norgard of Minnesota's Courage Center.[22]

Treatments for Spinal Cord Injuries

While Independent Living is providing new opportunities for many disabled persons, others are pinning their hopes on scientific research. Some of the most encouraging developments have been the advances made in treating paralysis caused by spinal cord damage. Every year 15,000-20,000 Americans — usually young, active persons — bruise, cut or otherwise damage their

---

[21] Independent Living centers receive their funds from three main sources: the federal government's Rehabilitation Services Administration, state and local agencies and private organizations.

[22] The Courage Center is one of the most extensive organizations fostering the Independent Living concept. The center, which provides more than 70 different programs for physically disabled adults and children, began in 1928 as the Minnesota Association for Crippled Children.

spinal cords, most often as a result of motor vehicle accidents, sports mishaps, falls or gunshot wounds. Injuries to the spinal cord impair the passage of electrochemical signals between the brain and the muscles. The result: paralysis, the extent of which depends on where the spinal cord is injured and the severity of the damage.

Some 500,000 Americans have spinal cord injuries, and the number seems to be growing. "I think there are far more injuries than there used to be simply because we have hang gliding and surfing and skateboards and the cars go faster," said Louise McKnew, director of the National Spinal Cord Injury Association. "Women are taking more and more risks; they're more athletic. [This] new physical freedom is going to result in devastating accidents. It used to be that 80 percent of them were young men. We still estimate that most of them are young men, but I think that the incident rate for women is going through the roof. ... "

Photo courtesy of Courage Center

Driver education

Before World War II most spinal cord injuries caused death. After the war, with the development of antibiotics and improved rehabilitative techniques, the death rate dropped sharply. The medical community began concentrating on helping spinal cord patients cope with their injuries. New discoveries in neurological research and pioneering types of aggressive therapy and treatment now make it possible in some cases to minimize the extent of paralysis. Moreover, some researchers are talking about the possibility of developing a cure in the not-too-distant future for paralysis caused by spinal cord injuries. "If you look at the work across the world in neuro-regeneration and general spinal cord research, I don't think anybody in a wheelchair should just sit there thinking, 'I'll never walk again,'" said Dr. Jerrold S. Petrofsky, director of biomedical engineering laboratories at Wright State University in Dayton, Ohio.[23]

A broad range of spinal cord research is taking place in this country and overseas. Researchers at Jackson Memorial Hos-

[23] Appearing on PBS-TV's "NOVA," broadcast Feb. 28, 1984.

pital in Miami are testing new types of surgical techniques using laser technology. New York University Medical Center researchers are trying to find out exactly what happens to nerve cells following a spinal cord injury. Their goal is to discover the exact point at which nerve-cell damage impairs functioning. Doctors at the British National Institute of Medical Research are studying nerve cell regeneration, focusing on what causes central nervous system cells to fail to reconnect after an injury. Dr. Jerald Bernstein at the George Washington University Medical Center in Washington, D.C., has been experimenting with spinal cord grafts in an effort to induce chronically injured spinal cord nerve cells to regrow. Experiments with the sheaths surrounding nerves are taking place at McGill University in Montreal under Dr. Albert Aguayo. A team of researchers led by Dr. Richard Sidman at Harvard University's Department of Neuropathology is studying the possibility of reconnecting damaged nerve cells.

Meanwhile, medical practitioners have put some of the knowledge gained in the laboratories to use in treating spinal cord injuries. The most advanced treatment is offered at special acute care trauma centers, including one at Jackson Memorial. "We're one of the largest spinal cord injury care centers in the world and every week we have new injuries arrive here," said Dr. Barth Green, a surgeon on the faculty of the University of Miami Medical School. "Several times ... every month I have to tell a patient that there is very little chance that by natural means they're going to walk again. And unless I genuinely felt there was some hope for the future, it would be very difficult for me to cope with this situation.... Right now, the hope is more than hope. It's based on concrete scientific information. So what I do tell them is, 'by natural means there is little chance that you may walk again, but there is hope through research.' " [24]

Biofeedback and Electrical Stimulation

Jackson Memorial Hospital also offers a newly developed technique that uses biofeedback to help spinal injury patients learn how to control their muscles.[25] Medical science does not know exactly why patients have regained control over muscles after working with the biofeedback machine, which was developed by Dr. Bernard Brucker of the University of Miami biofeedback laboratory. One theory is that the patient learns how to send signals through the healthy parts of the spinal cord, circumventing the damaged sections. One patient who had been

---

[24] Appearing on "NOVA," Feb. 28, 1984.
[25] Biofeedback is a technique in which information about physiological functions is fed back to a patient through machines that measure minute bodily changes such as muscle contraction and temperature.

diagnosed as completely paralyzed after a motorcycle accident was able to stand after 10 biofeedback sessions. He later walked with the aid of a walker, and eventually progressed to the point where he needed only a cane. "Brucker has had kids who were diagnosed as complete injuries walk out of his office," Louise McKnew said.

One of the most exciting successes in treating spinal cord injuries has taken place at Wright State University under the direction of Dr. Petrofsky, a biomedical engineer. Since 1971 Petrofsky has been working on a computer-based system of electrical stimulation that attaches to paralyzed muscles and stimulates movement. This functional electrical stimulation, as it is called, does nothing to restore the damaged spinal column. It simply uses electrical signals to force movement. The first success with the system came on April 28, 1982, when a quadriplegic was able to pedal an exercise bicycle. By getting the patient's legs moving, the doctors were able to stimulate his muscles as well as his cardiovascular system. "We can take people who were thought to be hopeless — people who have been in wheelchairs for five or 10 years, who have had deteriorated bones, muscles, heart, every other part of their body — and bring these folks, at least in the laboratory, back to health again," Dr. Petrofsky told producers of the PBS-TV program "NOVA."

Last year, 22-year-old Nan Davis, injured four years earlier in an automobile accident, became the first paraplegic to "walk" under her own power when she took a few steps with the aid of functional electrical stimulation developed in Petrofsky's laboratory. Although this breakthrough was widely publicized, researchers are quick to point out that much more needs to be done before the techniques are perfected and are available for widespread use. "It is not *the* answer," said Louise McKnew. "But it is an answer and a step toward maintaining body health. It doesn't do any good for people to come up with a cure [for spinal cord injuries] if their bones and muscles and cardiovascular capability are not kept up to full strength. And that's the kind of thing that Petrofsky is doing."

The success with functional electrical stimulation and the growth of the Independent Living concept are but two examples of new opportunities for the disabled. Technological innovations and attitudinal changes should continue to make life easier for many of the disabled in the future. Still, even with all the progress, myriad physical and psychological barriers are likely to linger in society, making it difficult for many disabled persons to live full, rewarding lives.

Selected Bibliography

Books

Burgdorf, Robert L. Jr., ed., *The Legal Rights of Handicapped Persons*, Brookes, 1980.

Articles

Cherry, Laurence, and Rona Cherry, "New Hope for the Disabled," *The New York Times Magazine*, Feb. 5, 1984.

DeJong, Gerben, and Raymond Lifchez, "Physical Disability and Public Policy," *Scientific American*, June 1983.

Fessler, Pamela, "Congress Pressed to Revamp Disability Review Procedures," *Congressional Quarterly Weekly Report*, June 4, 1983.

Johnson, William G., and James Lambrinos, "Employment Discrimination," *Society*, March-April 1983.

Marwick, Charles, "Wheelchair Calisthenics Keep Patients Fit," *Journal of the American Medical Association*, Jan. 20, 1984.

Singer, Peter, and Helga Kuhse, "The Future of Baby Doe," *The New York Review of Books*, March 1, 1984.

Reports and Studies

Courage Center, "The Challenge of Change: Courage Center's Fifty Years," 1979.

Editorial Research Reports: "Medical Ethics in Life and Death," 1984 Vol. I, p. 145; "Multiple Sclerosis," 1983 Vol. II, p. 573; "Chronic Pain: The Hidden Epidemic," 1983 Vol. I, p. 393; "Mainstreaming: Handicapped Children in the Classroom," 1981 Vol. II, p. 533; "Rights of the Handicapped," 1974 Vol. II, p. 885.

E.I. du Pont de Nemours and Co., "Equal to the Task: 1981 Du Pont Survey of Employment of the Handicapped," 1982.

National Center for Health Statistics, "Health Characteristics of Persons with Chronic Activity Limitation: United States, 1979," December 1981.

Tickton, S. G., *et al.*, "Educational Opportunities for Handicapped Students: 1981 Idea Handbook for Colleges and Universities," Academy for Educational Development, September 1981.

U.S. Commission on Civil Rights, "Accommodating the Spectrum of Individual Abilities," September 1983.

U.S. Department of Labor, "A Study of Accommodations Provided to Handicapped Employees by Federal Contractors, Final Report," June 17, 1982.

Graphics: Cover illustration by Art Director Richard Pottern.

RISING COST OF HEALTH CARE

by

Mary H. Cooper
and Sandra Stencel

Apr. 8
1983

Editor's Note: Detailed rules outlining a new system for re- imbursing hospitals for treating Medicare patients were made public by the Reagan administration on Aug. 31, 1983. The prospective reimbursement plan, which uses predetermined rates for all patients with the same illness or injury, was approved by Congress in March 1983 *(see p. 46)*. The administration sup- ported the measure as a means of bringing health care costs under control.

Another of Reagan's cost-containment proposals was rejected later that year by the Advisory Council on Social Security, a year-old committee set up by the Department of Health and Human Services to study proposals aimed at keeping Medicare's hospital insurance trust fund afloat in coming years. The panel, chaired by former Indiana Gov. Otis R. Bowen, a Republican, rejected the president's proposal to make employers' contribu- tions to group health insurance plans, now a tax-free fringe benefit, taxable to participating employees *(see p. 48)*.

Another administration proposal, which would increase the amount the program's elderly beneficiaries must pay for short- term hospital stays, is widely viewed as too hot a political issue for Congress to tackle — or the White House to push — before the 1984 presidential election *(see p. 49)*.

RISING COST OF HEALTH CARE

FOR Americans hard pressed by double-digit unemployment and high interest rates, one of the few encouraging developments during the current recession has been a fall in the rate of inflation. In 1982, the Consumer Price Index (CPI) rose by a relatively low 3.9 percent, five points below the 1981 figure.[1] But one component of the index continued to climb at a faster rate than other consumer prices. The amount Americans spent on health care in 1982 rose 11 percent over the previous year to a record $321.4 billion; hospital costs alone rose 12.6 percent last year. And while consumer prices actually fell by 0.2 percent in February 1983, medical costs went up 0.8 percent. The portion of the nation's gross national product (GNP) spent on health care has risen from 6 percent in 1965 to 10 percent today.

The federal government's contribution to the nation's health care bill also continues to climb, as rising hospital and physicians' charges are reflected in the cost of Medicare, Medicaid and other public health programs. Combined outlays for Medicare, the federal health care program for the elderly, and Medicaid, the state-federal program for the poor and disabled, are projected to reach $75 billion in fiscal 1983, accounting for 9.5 percent of the federal budget.

President Reagan has described the rate of increase in health care costs as "excessive," undermining "people's ability to purchase needed health care." [2] To help bring health costs under control, the administration has proposed a series of reform measures reflecting the president's often stated goal of reducing government influence and restoring public services to the private sector. One of these measures — a plan to set up a new system for reimbursing hospitals for treating Medicare patients — was approved by Congress March 25 as part of the Social Security rescue bill (see p. 46). [3]

Among the other cost-containment proposals Reagan sent Congress was one to set up a voucher system expanding "oppor-

---

[1] Published monthly by the Department of Labor's Bureau of Labor Statistics, the CPI follows a "market basket" of goods and services and determines the rate of price variation for each over the previous month.

[2] Message on his proposed budget for fiscal 1984, delivered to Congress Jan. 31, 1983.

[3] For background on the Social Security system's financial problems, see "Social Security Options," E.R.R., 1982 Vol. II, pp. 929-948.

tunities for Medicare beneficiaries to use their benefits to enroll in private health plans as an alternative to traditional Medicare coverage." Reagan also asked Congress to begin taxing employer-sponsored health insurance benefits *(see p. 48)* and to require Medicare beneficiaries to pay more out of their own pockets for short-term hospital stays. This plan would be coupled with "catastrophic" coverage for long illnesses *(see p. 49).* Reagan also proposed that Medicaid beneficiaries be required to pay nominal fees of $1 to $2 for each visit to a doctor or hospital. Under current law, states may impose such "cost-sharing" requirements, but are not required to do so.[4]

While the administration's health care reform package was presented as a cost-control initiative, the projected savings would be relatively small, at least in the short term. The Department of Health and Human Services estimated that the package would save $4.2 billion in fiscal 1984. But even if all the proposals are enacted, federal outlays for health would increase nearly 10 percent in fiscal 1984, to $90.6 billion, from the 1983 level of $82.4 billion, according to the budget.

The Factors Behind Health Care Inflation

The reasons for mounting health care costs are varied and complex. They include such things as the growing size and age of the elderly population, higher salaries for nurses and other hospital workers, and the increase in the number of malpractice suits, which many believe has caused doctors to overtreat their patients in an effort to protect themselves from possible legal action.

Consumer expectations were regarded as a primary cause of the problem in a recent survey of health experts conducted by Yankelovich, Skelly and White, Inc., for *Prevention* magazine.[5] One reason for consumers' "nearly limitless expectations of the system," the report said, was the fact that the cost of medical treatment has to a great extent been shifted to third parties. Patients pay only 29 percent of the nation's health care bill out of their own pockets, not enough, critics say, to make them cost-conscious. Public funds, including Medicare and Medicaid, pay 42 percent of the nation's medical costs, while private insurance companies cover 27 percent *(see box, p. 47).* Both private and public insurance plans reimburse health care providers on a fee-for-service basis for "reasonable" costs incurred in the treatment of beneficiaries, a system that many believe offers neither

---

[4] For additional information on Reagan's proposals, see *Congressional Quarterly Weekly Report,* Feb. 5, 1983, pp. 275-278.
[5] "The American Health System: A Survey of Leaders and Experts," March 1983. Copies of the report may be obtained from the Market Services Dept., *Prevention Magazine,* Rodale Press, Inc., 33 East Minor Street, Emmaus, Pa. 18049.

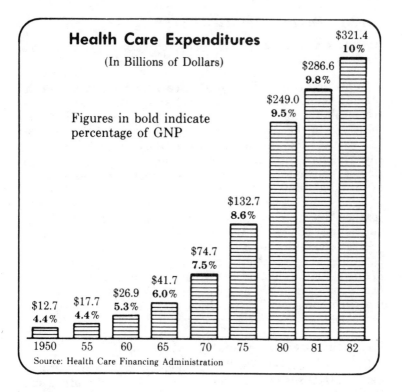

Health Care Expenditures

(In Billions of Dollars)

Figures in bold indicate
percentage of GNP

Year	Expenditure	% of GNP
1950	$12.7	4.4%
55	$17.7	4.4%
60	$26.9	5.3%
65	$41.7	6.0%
70	$74.7	7.5%
75	$132.7	8.6%
80	$249.0	9.5%
81	$286.6	9.8%
82	$321.4	10%

Source: Health Care Financing Administration

physicians nor hospital administrators any incentive to control costs; essentially, the more they charge, the more they make.

Another factor behind rising health care costs has to do with advances in medical technology that entail expensive equipment, such as the sophisticated X-ray device called a computerized axial tomography (CAT) scanner, or complicated surgical procedures such as coronary bypass operations and organ transplants. Other innovative hospital services, such as intensive care units and kidney dialysis machines, also entail high per-patient charges. The suggestion that such services be used with greater discretion in the interest of controlling costs has stirred intense debate over the moral implications of applying "cost-benefit" analysis to decisions regarding human life.

Administration's 'Free-Market' Strategy

Throughout the 1970s, much of the debate over reform of the health care delivery system centered on various proposals for national health insurance (see p. 54). After the election of Ronald Reagan, however, the focus of debate shifted to the president's calls for a "pro-competitive" or "free-market" health policy.[6] The president's goal was to make health care

---

[6] For background, see "Reagan Seeks 'Competition' in U.S. Health Care System," *Congressional Quarterly Weekly Report*, Feb. 20, 1982, pp. 331-333.

providers and their patients more cost-conscious by making them more aware of the full costs of medical care.

In his first two years in office, Reagan succeeded in reducing federal spending for health programs and in turning over responsibility for many of them to the states. Cost-reduction measures in the budget reconciliation laws of 1981 and 1982 included (1) a 25 percent increase in the amount elderly Medicare recipients had to pay for medical care; and (2) consolidation of funding for such programs as community health centers, drug and alcohol abuse centers, and maternal and child health programs into four block grants. The states then assumed responsibility for allocating the funds according to federal guidelines. The administration's changes allowed the states greater flexibility in the administration of Medicaid, and according to a recent article in *The New England Journal of Medicine,* more than 30 states have cut back spending on this health care assistance program for the poor by reducing benefits, tightening eligibility standards or simply cutting reimbursements to health care programs.[7]

Prospective Reimbursement for Medicare

On Dec. 28, 1982, the Department of Health and Human Services (HHS) sent Congress a report outlining the administration's plan for replacing the existing Medicare reimbursement system, under which charges are calculated after services have been rendered, with a "prospective" system that would set prices in advance. The administration was required to come up with the plan under the terms of the 1982 tax bill, approved by Congress on Aug. 19 of that year, which also placed caps on the overall amount of Medicare reimbursement.[8]

The HHS report outlined a method of using medical and financial data to assign an average price for treating 467 specific medical conditions or combinations of conditions, known as "diagnosis related groups" or DRGs. By providing for fixed payment rates in advance, the new system would end the existing policy of paying hospitals whatever it costs them to treat beneficiaries. The idea is to encourage hospitals to minimize use of expensive procedures, equipment and personnel so that their operating costs do not exceed the set prices. Hospitals that provide treatment for less than the set amount can keep the difference.

According to President Reagan, this plan will "establish

---

[7] John K. Iglehart, "The Reagan Record on Health Care," *The New England Journal of Medicine,* Jan. 27, 1983.
[8] For details on the Medicare provisions of the 1982 tax bill, see *Congressional Quarterly Weekly Report,* Aug. 21, 1982, p. 2042.

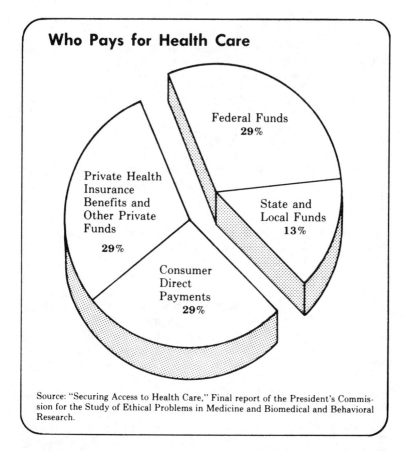

Who Pays for Health Care

Federal Funds
29%

Private Health
Insurance
Benefits and
Other Private
Funds

29%

State and
Local Funds
13%

Consumer
Direct
Payments
29%

Source: "Securing Access to Health Care," Final report of the President's Commission for the Study of Ethical Problems in Medicine and Biomedical and Behavioral Research.

Medicare as a prudent buyer of services and will ensure for both hospitals and the federal government a predictable payment for services. . . . Medicare traditionally paid hospitals . . . whatever they spent. There were, therefore, weak incentives for hospitals to conserve costs and operate efficiently." Under the new plan, he said, " hospitals with higher costs will not be able to pass on extra costs to Medicare beneficiaries and thus will face strong incentives to make cost-effective changes in practices." [9]

The administration's plan, with some modifications, was approved by the House Ways and Means Committee on March 2. To help speed its approval, the committee attached the plan to a bill for overhauling the Social Security system. That bill was approved by Congress March 25 and sent to the president for signing.

Unlike the administration's original proposal, which called for setting one national price for each ailment, the bill approved by Congress allows for regional cost differences and differences between rural and urban hospitals. The bill also would provide

[9] Message sending his health incentives reform program to Congress, Feb. 28, 1983.

exceptions for special high-cost hospitals, such as research and teaching hospitals, and would allow Medicare to make extra payments in special cases where people required extra care.

One reason the bill passed so quickly was that it had the support of influential hospital lobbyists and two major hospital groups, the American Hospital Association (AHA) and the Federation of American Hospitals. Both preferred it to the stringent Medicare payment caps enacted as part of the 1982 tax bill. "Prospective payment will change the incentives in the health system and allow hospital administrators to better manage their payments," a spokeswoman for AHA said in a recent interview.

The main objection to the proposal was that it would apply only to Medicare payments. Critics, including the American Association of Retired Persons and the Health Insurance Association of America,[10] claimed that in order to be effective, the DRG-based prepayment system should apply to Medicaid, private health insurance plans and individuals, as well as Medicare. Otherwise, they said, hospitals might shift the cost of providing services for Medicare recipients to private insurance companies, which would then pass on the higher charges to their subscribers through higher premiums. "Until we can solve the cost-shifting problem," said John K. Kittredge, executive vice president of The Prudential Insurance Co., "we will not have cost containment."

Officials are not sure exactly how much money will be saved by the prospective reimbursement program, which will be phased in over a three-year period, but they do not expect it to solve Medicare's mounting financial problems. A recent study by the Congressional Budget Office predicted that Medicare's Hospital Insurance Trust Fund, which is part of the Social Security system, could go broke as early as 1987.[11] The main reason for the projected deficits, according to the study, is the fact that "hospital costs are growing much more rapidly than the earnings to which the Hospital Insurance tax is applied." From 1982 to 1995, costs incurred by Medicare recipients are projected to increase by an average of 13.2 percent, while covered earnings are expected to rise by an average of only 6.8 percent over the same period.

Opposition to Health Insurance Tax Plan

President Reagan's other proposals for curbing health care costs are more controversial than the Medicare reimbursement plan. Particularly controversial is his plan to tax part of em-

---

[10] Both the American Association of Retired Persons and the Health Insurance Association of America are located in Washington, D.C.
[11] Congressional Budget Office, "Prospects for Medicare's Hospital Insurance Trust Fund," February 1983.

ployer-provided health insurance benefits. The administration contends that under current law neither employees nor employers have much incentive to hold down costs. Company-sponsored benefits represent tax-free income to employees and tax-deductible business expenses to employers.

The administration wants to change this arrangement by putting a ceiling on the amount of insurance premium payments that would continue to receive preferential tax treatment. It would require employees to pay taxes on employer contributions to their health insurance in excess of $175 a month for family coverage or $70 a month for individual coverage. The administration believes this would encourage employees to pressure employers for less comprehensive insurance coverage. The average yearly income tax increase for each of the 16.5 million Americans currently receiving employer-provided health insurance benefits above the proposed ceiling would be about $140, according to administration estimates.

Reagan's proposal elicits stiff resistance from organized labor. The AFL-CIO Executive Council said the proposed tax would constitute "an unprecedented intrusion in collective bargaining" that would "turn back the clock on decades of progress by workers in winning comprehensive health care protection." [12] Organized labor is not alone in its opposition. Representatives of about 50 groups, ranging from the Chamber of Commerce of the United States and the National Association of Manufacturers to the National Council of Senior Citizens, met with Sen. Bob Packwood, R-Ore., in early January to voice their opposition to the plan. Packwood told them there was "no constituency" for the tax scheme and predicted its defeat. He said such a plan would erode the health of working Americans and set a precedent for taxes on other fringe benefits.

Controversy Over Other Reagan Proposals

Also controversial is Reagan's suggestion that Medicare beneficiaries pay more for short-term hospital stays. Under current law, Medicare recipients pay a deductible ($350 in fiscal 1984) for the first day of every hospital stay, but are fully covered by Medicare for the next 59 days. Coverage is only partial for the next 30 days, during which time the patient must pay 25 percent of the deductible ($87.50 per day). If the patient is hospitalized longer than three months, he has only 60 remaining "lifetime reserve days," for which he must pay one-half the deductible ($175 per day). Thereafter, the patient is personally liable for all hospital costs.

Under Reagan's plan the emphasis of Medicare coverage

---

[12] *AFL-CIO News,* March 5, 1983.

Recession's Impact on Access to Health Care

When workers are laid off or fired, they frequently lose more than just their jobs. They may also lose company-provided health insurance benefits. The Congressional Budget Office estimated that 10.7 million unemployed Americans and their families had no health insurance coverage last year.

As Congress debates the Reagan administration proposals for containing health care costs, support is building for some kind of health benefits program aimed at the unemployed. While business interests are opposed to extending health insurance benefits to the unemployed beyond the usual 30-day limit after layoff, the AFL-CIO has called for their extension for at least 65 weeks. Senate Finance Committee Chairman Robert Dole, R-Kan., has suggested that medical benefits for the unemployed could be financed with revenues collected through the administration's proposed tax on employer-provided group health insurance *(see p. 48)*.

would shift to long-term hospital stays. In addition to the full first-day deductible, Medicare recipients would pay 8 percent ($28 per day) through day 15, then 5 percent ($17.50 per day) through day 60, but receive full and unlimited coverage after that time. While the administration proposal would seem to satisfy previous calls for "catastrophic" insurance to cover long-term hospitalization, it would in fact save the government an estimated $2 billion a year, since most Medicare recipients would end up paying more for hospital care. Only about 200,000 of the 7 million Medicare recipients hospitalized each year stay longer than 60 days. The average stay is 11 days. If Reagan's plan is enacted, an 11-day hospital stay would cost Medicare beneficiaries almost twice as much as it does now.

Critics say Reagan's proposal violates the federal government's commitment to the elderly embodied in Medicare legislation. According to Janet Myder of the National Council of Senior Citizens,[13] it would impose "a very, very heavy burden" on the elderly "which is not going to be alleviated by [Reagan's proposal for] catastrophic protection. This is not catastrophic insurance. What is catastrophic for the elderly is the cost of a nursing home, the cost of any long-term care, the cumulative cost of all the things that Medicare doesn't pay for, like prescription drugs." Myder and other critics also fear that the proposed changes would lead private insurance companies to substantially increase premiums for "Medigap" policies, which pay the difference between public coverage and hospital

---

[13] The National Council of Senior Citizens, located at 925 15th St., N.W., Washington, D.C. 20005, represents over 4.5 million elderly people in all the states.

charges. While 60 percent of those eligible for Medicare now subscribe to private "Medigap" policies, many could no longer afford such coverage if premium prices sharply increased.

Spokesmen for groups representing the elderly also are unhappy about the administration's new interpretation of Medicaid laws, which gave states the go-ahead to require adult children of nursing home patients to pay part of the cost of their parents' care. A few states already have adopted such "family responsibility" laws, but they have delayed enforcing them awaiting federal guidelines. Rep. Henry A. Waxman, D-Calif., chairman of the House Energy and Commerce Subcommittee on Health, which has jurisdiction over Medicaid, says the administration's directive is contrary to the intent of Congress and he plans to hold hearings on the matter.

Past Approaches to Problem

THE PUBLIC and private health insurance arrangements that are partly to blame for today's health care inflation are a product of the progressive monopolization of the health care delivery system. This trend began in the latter years of the 19th century with the licensing of physicians. With fewer doctors authorized to practice medicine, fees began to rise until, by the 1920s, physicians' incomes began to far outstrip those of other workers.

Growing recognition of the impact of rising medical costs led to the formation in 1926 of the privately funded Committee on the Costs of Medical Care, which provided the first analyses of the problem in the United States and which recommended in its final reports of 1932 an increase in access to medical care for the entire population and an increase in resources to fund it. The committee's recommendations of fostering group practice and group payment for medical care were, however, condemned by the increasingly influential American Medical Association (AMA) as a dangerous challenge to the private physician's control over services provided — and fees charged — to patients. The controversy that ensued led President Franklin D. Roosevelt to exclude health care reform from the New Deal social legislation that culminated in the Social Security Act of 1935.

During the same period, both the American Hospital Association and the AMA introduced their own private insurance mechanisms, Blue Cross and Blue Shield, respectively, in response to growing demand from consumers for some form of protection from debilitating health care expenses and also to prevent single-hospital plans and prepaid group practices from weakening their monopoly of the health care delivery system. In 1934, commercial insurance companies began offering health insurance on the same fee-for-service basis, which posed few, if any, limits on the amount physicians or hospitals could charge. In this way, wrote Paul Starr, "the structure of private health plans, it seems fair to say, was basically an accommodation to provider interests." [14]

By 1958, almost two-thirds of the population was covered by hospital insurance. But while more and more Americans came under various insurance plans, only half of those aged 65 or older were covered, even though they were the most vulnerable to disease and generally the least able to pay for health care services. Awareness of the plight of the aged and poor grew throughout the 1950s and early 1960s and led to the enactment in 1965 of the Medicare and Medicaid programs.

With Medicare, all Americans, regardless of income level, are entitled upon reaching age 65 to hospital benefits as well as a voluntary supplemental policy covering 80 percent of physicians' fees. Unlike Medicare, which is funded entirely at the federal level, Medicaid was introduced as a joint state-federal program. Coverage is less uniform under this program, as the federal government may only establish standards for the types of services offered, but not the payment levels provided by the states.

Statistics indicate that Medicare and Medicaid have succeeded in greatly increasing the access of elderly and poor Americans to health care. The frequency of physician visits by people whose family incomes were below $7,000 increased by almost 50 percent between 1964 and 1980.[15] The elderly have benefited from both programs; 95 percent of them are entitled to Medicare hospital insurance, while Medicaid helps the elderly poor pay for services not covered by Medicare, such as nursing home care. In 1978, the latest year for which official statistics have been compiled, elderly Americans incurred an average annual health bill of $2,026, 63 percent of which was covered by public funds.[16]

The number of health care providers greatly increased in the 1960s, thanks largely to federal grants, scholarships and loans for medical research and education. The number of active physicians increased by 70 percent between 1965 and 1975, while the number of dentists rose by 50 percent and the number of

---

[14] Paul Starr, *The Social Transformation of American Medicine* (1982), p. 309.
[15] Department of Health and Human Services, Public Health Service, "Health, United States, 1982," p. 90.
[16] *Ibid.*, p. 152.

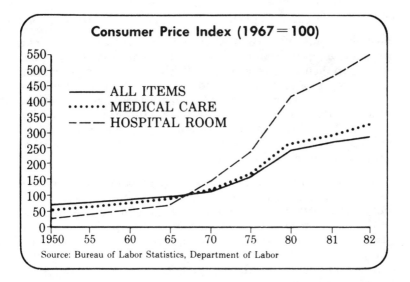

Consumer Price Index (1967 = 100)

ALL ITEMS
MEDICAL CARE
HOSPITAL ROOM

Source: Bureau of Labor Statistics, Department of Labor

nurses doubled.[17] The same period saw a burst of hospital construction and expansion, with the help of federal funds provided through the Hill-Burton program, which began in 1946.

The portion of health care expenditures paid by third parties also increased during this period, rising from 45 percent in 1965 to 65 percent in 1970. In addition to Medicare and Medicaid, a major contributing factor to this trend was the inclusion of health insurance benefits in labor contracts. These group health insurance schemes benefited not only American workers, but also the health care industry itself, which no longer had to wait long periods for payment of fees.

'70s Health Care 'Crisis'; Turn to HMOs

Growing awareness of the medical inflation problem in the early 1970s led the Nixon administration to speak of a "crisis" in health care financing. Liberals and conservatives alike agreed on the need for reform of the health care system, but they disagreed on the best way to approach the problem. While liberals like Sen. Edward M. Kennedy, D-Mass., tended to favor some form of national health insurance, the Nixon administration lent its support to the increasingly popular prepaid group health plans, or health maintenance organizations (HMOs), which had first appeared as a radical alternative to the traditional control exercised over the industry by hospitals and private physicians.

The HMO evolved along two principal models. So-called "group models" operate their own facilities and employ their

[17] Louise B. Russell, "Medical Care," in *Setting National Priorities: Agenda for the 1980s*, ed. Joseph A. Pechman (1980), p. 175.

own physicians, nurses and other personnel. Subscribers select a primary care physician from the staff and are required to go to the group facility to receive care. With the exception of certain emergency procedures, any medical care obtained outside the facility is not covered. "Individual practice associations," on the other hand, are more decentralized. Subscribers choose a participating physician in the community, often on the basis of geographical proximity, and go to his or her office for treatment rather than to a central facility.

The HMO, by operating on a strictly prepaid basis, was seen as an effective means of encouraging physicians and hospitals to hold down costs. Since they have to work within a fixed budget, HMO physicians are unlikely to extend their patients' hospital stays beyond the time necessary for treatment. In New Jersey, for example, the average hospital stay for surgical patients enrolled in HMOs is three days, compared to four days for the general population.

Nixon's support for HMOs led to passage of a 1973 law requiring all businesses with more than 25 employees to include at least one HMO among the health benefits offered to employees. Partly as a result of this measure, the number of HMOs in the country rose from 30 in 1971 to 268 by mid-1982. The main benefit of the HMO has been a reduction in health care costs through reduced utilization of hospital services. But while effective in the communities where they exist, HMOs have yet to have a significant impact on the national health care system, as only 5 percent of the U.S. population are currently enrolled in this type of program.

National Insurance Debate; State Plans

Advocates of national health insurance were bolstered by the election of Jimmy Carter in 1976. During the presidential campaign Carter promised to introduce a "comprehensive national health insurance system with universal and mandatory coverage." But when Carter finally unveiled his plan in 1979, it turned out to be a much more limited plan to protect Americans against catastrophic medical costs. By focusing on catastrophic coverage, Carter alienated Sen. Kennedy, who was still pushing for a more comprehensive national health program similar to those available in Britain, Canada and other industrialized countries.[18]

Neither Carter's nor Kennedy's bill was approved by Congress, however, in part because of an intense lobbying campaign against them by groups representing health care providers and

---

[18] For background, see Edward M. Kennedy, *In Critical Condition: The Crisis in America's Health Care* (1972).

also because of concern in Congress over their costs. The concept of national health insurance continues to find support, particularly among organized labor and groups representing the poor and elderly. But budgetary considerations appear to have pushed this option to the back burner for the foreseeable future.

While the federal government was having trouble coming up with ways to control rising health care costs, a number of states introduced their own cost-control schemes. Some set up public agencies to review hospital budgets and/or rates, while others set up systems to regulate hospital reimbursements. Under these plans, hospitals are reimbursed prospectively in one of two ways. Either they are paid a certain rate per case of a certain type of ailment or a general budget constraint is imposed. Six states — Connecticut, Maryland, Massachusetts, New Jersey, New York and Washington — introduced prospective payment plans in 1976 or earlier. These state plans were the subject of a study that found them to be effective in containing hospital costs.[19]

It was in New Jersey that the "diagnosis-related group" (DRG) basis for calculating hospital costs was first implemented in 1980. The New Jersey plan served as the model for the new Medicare reimbursement plan recently adopted by Congress as part of the Social Security rescue bill *(see p. 46)* Under the plan, each New Jersey hospital was required to break down all business into the 467 DRGs contained in a classification system developed at Yale University, and assign an average charge for each DRG. Patients were then billed according to their illnesses instead of the services actually received. On the basis of the hospitals' own estimates, the state of New Jersey established working annual budgets for each institution. Hospitals were encouraged to save money, as they pocketed all funds saved by working within the budget limits. But unlike the new federal program, the New Jersey plan does not just apply to Medicare, which prevents hospitals from shifting the costs incurred by some payers to other groups.

Prospects and Alternatives

C ORPORATE executives are also getting more involved in attempts to hold down health care costs. In fact, according to the report prepared by Yankelovich, Skelly and White for *Prevention* magazine, "large corporations will lead the way" in

---

[19] Brian Biles et al., "Hospital Cost Inflation Under State Rate-Setting Programs," *The New England Journal of Medicine*, Sept. 18, 1980.

solving the problem.[20] The reason for their concern is obvious. The corporate contribution to payments for health benefit plans was an estimated $60 billion in 1980. "Since World War II the employer, through negotiated benefits, has been paying more and more of the health care costs of this country for their employees and their dependents," Boyd Thompson, executive vice president of the American Association of Foundations for Medical Care, said in a recent interview. "This money was managed by insurance companies and Blue Cross-Blue Shield with no incentive on their part to hold down costs. The more the premium went up, the more money they made. Now the employers, individually and collectively, are telling the insurance companies and the Blues: 'Get out of our way, we're going to handle this ourselves by dealing with the provider directly.' "

"Since World War II the employer, through negotiated benefits, has been paying more and more of the health care costs of this country for their employees and their dependents."

Boyd Thompson, executive vice president, American Association of Foundations for Medical Care

In some communities corporations are banding together to form "preferred provider organizations." Under this arrangement, groups of physicians or hospitals are enlisted by employers to provide services at competitive prices. In return, the companies encourage their workers to use the services of the "preferred providers." Other companies are encouraging workers to join health maintenance organizations *(see p. 53)* ing to a newsletter published by the Group Health Association of America, Chrysler Corp. in Detroit has taken "the unprecedented step" of providing direct financial incentives to its workers enrolled in an HMO to sign up their friends. Under the plan, current members of the Health Alliance Plan of Michigan were given savings bonds of up to $250 for signing up fellow workers in the HMO.[21]

The Business Roundtable, a group made up of the chief executive officers of some 200 large U.S. companies, issued a report in February 1982 on the "appropriate role for corporations in health care cost management." Among other things, it

---

[20] "The American Health System," *op. cit.*, p. 13.
[21] See *Group Health News*, April 1983, p. 4.

recommended greater "corporate involvement in community coalitions established to address specific local health cost management problems," as well as programs to improve employee health. Many corporate executives have already discovered that it is cheaper to keep workers healthy than to pay to treat their illnesses. Thousands of companies have set up some type of physical fitness program for employees. Often these include not only exercise facilities, but also programs on nutrition, smoking, weight-control, stress management, alcohol and drug abuse, and similiar topics.[22]

Growth of Clinics; For-Profit Hospitals

An increasingly popular alternative to traditional care in hospitals and private doctors' offices is the emergency clinic, frequently set up in suburban shopping centers. It is designed to provide quick and inexpensive service for people who are willing to pay directly for the treatment of non-life-threatening emergencies. The advantages of these "emergicenters," hundreds of which have sprung up over the past few years, include immediate service, low-cost, 24-hour access, convenient location, and no need for appointments. They are not, however, a viable substitute for the hospital emergency room, where the presence of advanced support technology is required for serious emergency situations.

Despite the rise of such alternatives, the traditional, full-service hospital remains the basic structure for delivering medical care in this country. But while the number of non-profit and public hospitals has declined in recent years, the number of for-profit hospitals has rapidly increased, often by acquiring non-profit and public facilities. According to a recent article by Teresa Riordan in *The Washington Monthly,* "the for-profit hospital industry ... grew faster during the 1970s than the computer industry." [23]

Most public and non-profit hospitals were built with the help of federal funds provided through the Hill-Burton program, which required them to admit and treat charity and "bad-debt" cases as well as insured patients. But if such facilities are acquired by a for-profit chain, such as Humana Inc., Hospital Corporation of America or National Medical Enterprises, they are freed from this requirement. Critics have accused for-profit chains of favoring privately insured patients, whose policies usually reimburse the greatest amount of hospital expenses, while dumping Medicaid and non-insured patients on public

---

[22] See "Physical Fitness Boom," *E.R.R.*, 1978 Vol. I, pp. 271-273.
[23] Teresa Riordan, "The Wards Are Paved With Gold," *The Washington Monthly*, February 1983, p. 41.

and non-profit institutions. "This setup drains the already anemic philanthropic resources of publics and non-profits and often forces them to close or sell out to the for-profits," Teresa Riordan wrote.

Corporations have also taken over about half of the nation's nursing homes for the elderly. One-third of the nursing homes in this country are now owned by just 20 chains, including Beverly Enterprises and ATA Services, each of which owns 250 homes around the country. Some fear this trend may discourage the development of at-home or other community-based services for those whose conditions are not serious enough to warrant institutionalization.[24]

Providing health care for the elderly is likely to be a dominant concern for many decades. It has been estimated that the number of Americans aged 65 and older will rise steadily from the current level of 11.4 percent of the population to 21.7 percent by 2050, and that the ratio of workers to non-workers will drop from 5.4-to-1 to 2.6-to-1 over the same period.[25] This "graying of America" is expected to increase the portion of the nation's wealth allocated to health care from 10 percent today to 11 or 12 percent by the end of the century.

Ethical Issues and Budgetary Constraints

While nearly everyone agrees that more must be done to hold down increases in health care costs, some fear that cost-containment initiatives may adversely affect the quality of health care in the United States. Among those expressing this concern were the members of a presidential commission on medical ethics, whose recently released final report concluded: "Efforts to contain rising health costs are important but should not focus on limiting the attainment of equitable access for the least well served portion of the public. The achievement of equitable access is an obligation of sufficient moral urgency to warrant devoting the necessary resources to it." [26]

> The commission recognizes that efforts to rein in currently escalating health care costs have an ethical aspect because the call for adequate health care for all may not be heeded until such efforts are undertaken [the report continued]. . . . But measures

---

[24] For background, see "Housing Options for the Elderly," *E.R.R.*, 1982 Vol. II, pp. 569-588.

[25] Jerome A. Halperin, "Forces of Change in Health Services," address delivered to the College of Pharmacy, University of Arizona at Tucson, Nov. 12, 1982. Halperin is acting director of the Office of Drugs in the Food and Drug Administration.

[26] President's Commission for the Study of Ethical Problems in Medicine and Biomedical and Behavioral Research, "Securing Access to Health Care: A Report on the Ethical Implications of Differences in the Availability of Health Services," Vol. I, March 1983, pp. 5-6. Copies of the report can be obtained, at a cost of $6, from the Government Printing Office, Washington, D.C. 20402. The 11-member commission was established by Congress in 1980. Its chairman was Morris B. Abram, former president of Brandeis University.

designed to contain health care costs that exacerbate existing
inequities or impede the achievement of equity are unacceptable
from a moral standpoint. Moreover, they are unlikely by themselves to be successful since they will probably lead to a shifting of
costs to other entities, rather than to a reduction of total
expenditures.

The report did not comment on specific legislative proposals
to reduce health care expenses, but it did address some of the
current controversies. For example, it was critical of proposals
to charge Medicaid recipients a nominal fee for each day in the
hospital or each visit to a doctor's office. "Even a small out-of-
pocket charge can constitute a substantial burden for some
Medicaid participants," it said. The report also came out
against reductions in federal funding of Medicaid, saying this
"would worsen existing inequities in the distribution of the cost
of care." However, the commission did express support for the
idea of reducing federal tax subsidies of health insurance, as the
Reagan administration has proposed *(see p. 48)*. *"If properly*
designed, it is unlikely that such measures would compromise
access to adequate health care [nor would they have] a dis-
proportionate impact on the most economically vulnerable people...,'' the commission stated.

Bringing medical inflation under control without jeopardizing
the quality of health care in the United States will not be an
easy task. But some experts see reasons for optimism.
Yankelovich, Skelly and White, in their report for *Prevention*
magazine, predicted that consumers will become less deferential
in dealing with physicians, challenging doctors' judgments
about diagnosis, treatments, costs, etc. Not only will this help
control costs, the report stated, but it could change the nature
of the medical profession, since physicians will be forced to
become more people-oriented. At the same time, U.S. corporations are likely to continue their efforts to hold down medical
costs. "In sum," the report concluded, "all of the key actors are
either poised for change or will be unable to resist the pull of
change. And, given the way these groups are assessing the
problems and formulating strategies, there is no reason to think
that either the quality of care or the equity of its distribution
will diminish. They could even improve."

Selected Bibliography

Books

Davis, Karen and Cathy Schoen, *Health and the War on Poverty: A Ten-Year Appraisal*, Brookings, 1978.

Kennedy, Edward M., *In Critical Condition: The Crisis in America's Health Care*, Simon & Schuster, 1972.

Maxwell, Robert J., *Health and Wealth*, Lexington Books, 1981.

Pechman, Joseph A., ed., *Setting National Priorities: Agenda for the 1980s*, Brookings, 1980.

Pauly, Mark V., ed., *National Health Insurance: What Now, What Later, What Never?* American Enterprise Institute, 1980.

Starr, Paul, *The Social Transformation of American Medicine*, Basic Books, 1982.

Thompson, Margaret C., ed., *Health Policy: The Legislative Agenda*, Congressional Quarterly Inc., 1980.

Articles

Keisling, Phil, "Radical Surgery: Let's Draft the Doctors," *The Washington Monthly*, February 1983.

The New England Journal of Medicine, selected issues.

Seidman, Bert, "Bad Medicine for Health Care Costs," *AFL-CIO American Federationist*, April-June 1982.

Starr, Paul, "The Laissez-Faire Elixir," *The New Republic*, April 18, 1983.

"Treating the Ailing Health Care Dollar," *Journal of American Insurance*, winter 1981-82.

Reports and Studies

Congressional Budget Office, "Prospects for Medicare's Hospital Insurance Trust Fund," February 1983.

Editorial Research Reports: "Controlling Health Costs," 1977 Vol. I, p. 61; "Health Maintenance Organizations," 1974 Vol. II, p. 601; "Health Care in Britain and America," 1973 Vol. I, p. 437; "Future of Health Insurance," 1970 Vol. I, p. 61.

President's Commission for the Study of Ethical Problems in Medicine and Biomedical and Behavioral Research, "Securing Access to Health Care," March 1983.

U.S. Department of Health and Human Services, Public Health Service, "Health, United States, 1982," 1982.

Cover illustration by Staff Artist Robert Redding.

HUNGER IN
AMERICA

by

Marc Leepson

**Sept. 30
1 9 8 3**

Editor's Note: The debate over the extent of hunger in the United States and what the federal government should do about it continued during the winter of 1983-84. The President's Task Force on Food Assistance *(pp. 76-78),* in its final report released Jan. 9, 1984, found that "allegations of rampant hunger simply cannot be documented." The report recommended that states be allowed to drop out of the food stamp and other federal food aid programs and instead receive a block grant to distribute as they see fit. A 42-member coalition of religious groups, labor, civil rights and elderly groups criticized the report, saying it "tells us little more than that hunger exists — and then proposes recommendations that would, on balance, make this tragic problem worse."

HUNGER IN AMERICA

IN OUR AFFLUENT society, there are always millions of people unable to feed, clothe or house themselves adequately. During hard economic times — such as the recession and period of high unemployment that started in 1981 — the problems of the poor are compounded. And now, with the approach of winter, conditions of life for Americans living below the poverty line *(see p. 67)* will become even harsher.

The main problem today for the nation's poor appears to be hunger. In the last year evidence has accumulated from a variety of sources, including church groups, charitable organizations, city and county officials, congressional investigators and the media, that hunger is a significant and growing problem in the United States. Reagan administration officials and others say that reports of hunger in America are exaggerated, arguing that all the people crowding into food kitchens may not be destitute, but may simply want to take advantage of free meals. Others are convinced, however, that the problem is real.

"However we define it, there are apparently growing numbers of people in the United States who are experiencing both hunger and malnutrition over the last two years," said J. Larry Brown, professor of health policy at Harvard University's School of Public Health. Said Robert Greenstein, director of the Center on Budget and Policy Priorities, a Washington, D.C., non-profit research and analysis organization: "My sense is very much that hunger is a major problem and it has been growing over the last couple of years. With the combination of the recession and budget cuts, the problem has definitely grown." [1]

There are no reliable statistics measuring the extent of hunger in the United States. Most of the evidence indicating that hunger is a growing problem comes from reports and surveys that show that soup kitchens, food pantries *(see box, p. 65)* and other types of emergency feeding centers have been overwhelmed by significantly larger numbers of requests for food, especially in the last two years. For example, a study by the United States Conference of Mayors released in June found "a recent and significant increase in the demand for emergency

---

[1] Remarks by Brown, Greenstein and others in this report were, unless otherwise identified, made in interviews with the author between Sept. 1 and 8, 1983.

food assistance" in cities across the nation.[2] In Cleveland, where the unemployment rate is well above the national average,[3] emergency food requests increased 112 percent from 1981 to 1982. Detroit had a nearly fivefold increase in the number of households served by emergency food programs from 1980-82. Nearly twice as much free food was distributed in Denver during that period, and in Rochester, N.Y., the number of soup kitchens increased by 75 percent from 1981-82. According to New Orleans Mayor Ernest N. Morial, chairman of the conference's committee on health, education, unemployment and human services, "hunger is probably the most prevalent and the most insidious" problem facing the nation's cities.[4]

County government officials this year joined the big-city mayors in expressing concern about the hunger issue. At the National Association of Counties' annual meeting in Milwaukee July 17, the membership passed a resolution calling on the federal government to expand surplus food distribution programs and to make more funds available to states and counties to help distribute government surplus food. "There seems to be unanimous agreement [among county officials] that the incidence of demand for food assistance has grown tremendously," said NACo's director of human resources, Pat Johnson Craig. "Our officials are careful not to relate it automatically to budget cuts. It seems to be the economy as much as anything." Another factor adding to the hunger problem, Craig said, is the large number of persons who have been released from mental institutions under the "deinstitutionalization" policy that began in the 1950s.[5] "A lot of the hunger-food kitchen problems seem to be in response to the deinstitutionalization of folks who otherwise would be living in a mental hospital or a halfway house or some community care treatment center," she said. "Basically, people have fallen through all the systems that are there to support them."

Surveys By Private Groups and Government

The Center on Budget and Policy Priorities issued a report May 24 that examined 181 private, non-profit emergency food distribution programs across the country. It found "a dramatic increase in the number of people coming into soup kitchens and food pantries between February 1982 and February 1983 (the

---

[2] United States Conference of Mayors, "Hunger in American Cities, Eight Case Studies," June 1983, p. 5. The report focused on hunger problems in Cleveland, Denver, Detroit, Nashville, New Orleans, Oakland, Rochester and San Antonio.

[3] In June 1983, the last month for which statistics are available, the unemployment rate in Cleveland was 17.9 percent; the national rate that month was 10 percent. The national unemployment rate in August was 9.5 percent.

[4] Testifying Aug. 3, 1983, before the House Agriculture Committee's Subcommittee on Domestic Marketing, Consumer Relations and Nutrition.

[5] For information on the impact of deinstitutionalization, see "Mental Health Care Reappraisal," *E.R.R.*, 1982 Vol. II, pp. 609-632.

Soup Kitchens and Food Pantries

Soup kitchens serve meals on a regular — usually daily or weekly — basis. Often located in churches, temporary shelters or community centers, food kitchens typically are staffed by volunteers who prepare and serve meals. Food kitchens serve young and old adults, runaway children and families. Meals usually consist of a main dish (often soup), salad, dessert and coffee. Sometimes meals consist of sandwiches and coffee given away at the back door of a church rectory.

Food pantries, also usually run by churches or social service agencies, provide groceries to families in need. Although there are many different types of food pantry distribution systems, many provide a three-day supply of non-perishable groceries such as crackers, cereal, powdered milk, peanut butter, rice and canned soup. Food pantries typically obtain their food from local food banks, churches and community groups.

period of the survey)." [6] More than half of the emergency food programs taking part in the survey reported at least a 50 percent increase in the number of free meals or food baskets they provided during the 12-month period. Some 25 percent of the agencies were forced to turn people away during that time, and two-thirds had to limit the number of times the same person could receive food. "This survey documents dramatic increases in the number of Americans needing food aid and suggests that hunger and inadequate nutrition may again be a growing problem in this country," said the center's director, Robert Greenstein, who directed the U.S. Department of Agriculture's nutrition program during the Carter administration.

Another survey assessing the hunger problem was released June 23 by the U.S. General Accounting Office, Congress' investigative arm. Although an "official national 'hunger count' does not exist" and no one knows "precisely how many Americans are going hungry or how many are malnourished," the report said, many food assistance programs throughout the country report "significant increases in the numbers of people seeking food assistance in the past few years." [7]

Food distribution centers, which in the past had primarily served chronic derelicts, are now helping growing numbers of the "new poor" — formerly employed persons who in recent years have lost their jobs and run out of money.[8] "As contrasted

---

[6] "Soup Lines and Food Baskets: A Survey of Increased Participation in Emergency Food Programs," Center on Budget and Policy Priorities, May 1983, p. 1.

[7] U.S. General Accounting Office, "Public and Private Efforts to Feed America's Poor," June 23, 1983, pp. i, 6-7. The report documented increases in food assistance programs run by the Salvation Army, the United Church of Christ-World Hunger Action and emergency food centers in Washington, D.C., California, Ohio and Maryland.

[8] For background information on the new poor, see "The Homeless: Growing National Problem," E.R.R., 1982 Vol. II, pp. 793-812.

with the chronically poor," the GAO report said, "more of them are members of families, young and able-bodied, and have homes in the suburbs. They now find themselves without work, with unemployment benefits and savings accounts exhausted, and with diminishing hopes of being able to continue to meet their mortgage, automobile and other payments which they committed themselves to when times were better."

Rep. Leon E. Panetta, D-Calif., chairman of the House Agriculture Committee's Subcommittee on Domestic Marketing, Consumer Relations and Nutrition, inserted a report into the June 6 *Congressional Record* summarizing a series of hearings his subcommittee held earlier in the year in Washington, D.C., Cleveland, Birmingham and Los Angeles. Everywhere, Panetta said during House floor debate June 13, the subcommittee "heard the same story. The use of soup kichens, food pantries and hunger centers is up dramatically in the past two years; in some areas by 400 to 500 percent." Panetta said that "anyone who participated in our hearings or reads the record of the hearings will not dispute that there is a serious problem of hunger in the country today. Everywhere we went we saw and heard that the suffering was very real and more widespread than any time in recent memory."

Government Food Giveaways for the Poor

The reports of widespread hunger come at a time when — despite the summer's severe drought — American agriculture is awash in surplus food and the government is paying farmers under the PIK (Payment-in-Kind) program to stop growing more.[9] The government began giving away large amounts of its surplus cheese and butter to aid poor persons in December 1981. In 1982 the U.S. Department of Agriculture donated 166 million pounds of cheese and 18.9 million pounds of butter to the poor; 11 million pounds of surplus dried milk also were distributed in an experimental program. Still the U.S. larder continues to grow. The government currently has in storage about one billion pounds of cheese, 500 million pounds of butter and 1.3 billion pounds of powdered milk.

In May of this year the Reagan administration cut the distribution of surplus cheese from 60 million pounds a month to 25 million to 35 million pounds per month. The primary reason: the cheese giveaways were adversely affecting retail sales of cheese. But on Aug. 2 the Agriculture Department, under pressure from Congress and others, announced that surplus food distribution to the poor would be stepped up to about 40 million

---

[9] For information on the PIK program, see "Farm Policy's New Course," *E.R.R.*, 1983 Vol. I, pp. 233-252.

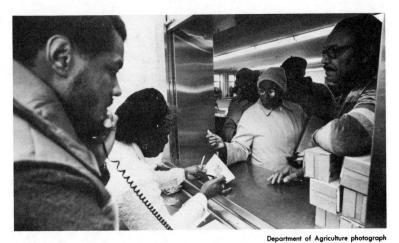

Surplus cheese distribution program in Washington, D.C.

pounds of cheese per month for up to two years. "I'm convinced there is a need," Agriculture Secretary John R. Block said that day.[10] Two days after the USDA announcement, Congress unexpectedly cleared a piece of legislation authorizing $50 million a year for the next two years to help states and charitable organizations distribute the government's surplus food. In the past the states and private groups had to pay the distribution and transportation costs.

All those who work with feeding the hungry favor using the surpluses. But most also agree that commodity distribution programs, soup kitchens and food pantries are at best temporary measures that cannot solve a widespread hunger problem. The problem of hunger "will never be solved ... with giveaways of cheese or corn meal," said Ellen Haas, executive director of Public Voice for Food and Health Policy, a Washington, D.C., consumer group. "Commodity distribution programs may help ease the pain. But they don't get at the underlying reason of it. Nor do they, like the existing food assistance programs — such as food stamps and child nutrition — attempt to provide balanced nutrition in an ongoing systematic fashion to all those who need it." [11]

Number of Americans Living in Poverty

In 1982 the national poverty rate rose for the fourth straight year to 15 percent of the population — the highest percentage in 17 years. The official poverty rate, announced by the Census Bureau Aug. 2, 1983, increased 1 percent from 1981 to 1982 *(see table, p. 68)*. Some 34.5 million Americans fit the official definition of poverty in 1982: an annual cash income of less than

---

[10] Appearing Aug. 2, 1983, on PBS-TV's "The MacNeil-Lehrer Report."
[11] Testifying Feb. 15, 1983, before the Senate Agriculture Committee's Subcommitte on Nutrition.

U.S. Poverty Rate, 1966-82*

	Black	White	Total
1966	41.8%	11.3%	14.7%
1967	39.3	11.0	14.1
1968	34.7	10.0	12.8
1969	32.2	9.9	12.1
1970	33.5	9.9	12.6
1971	32.5	9.9	12.5
1972	33.3	9.0	11.9
1973	31.4	8.4	11.1
1974	30.3	8.6	11.2
1975	30.3	9.7	12.3
1976	31.1	9.1	11.8
1977	31.3	8.9	11.6
1978	30.6	8.7	11.4
1979	31.0	9.0	11.7
1980	32.5	10.2	13.2
1981	34.2	11.1	14.0
1982	35.6	12.0	15.0

* Percentage of the population with incomes below the poverty level.
Source: Census Bureau

$9,862 for a family of four. The percentage of black Americans living in poverty was nearly three times greater than the percentage of whites.

Some observers blame the Reagan administration's economic and budgetary policies for the increase in the number of people living in poverty. Frank Farrow, deputy director of the Center for the Study of Social Policy in Washington, for example, singled out the administration's changes in eligibility rules for welfare and food assistance programs. "What seems to have been in the administration's mind when these policies were designed was to get rid of the relatively few high-income cases on [welfare]," Farrow said. "They've not only done this, but they have reached much further down into the income scale and taken off many people ... who were below the poverty line and who fell further below poverty." [12]

Others quarrel with the Census Bureau's definition of poverty, particularly because in-kind subsidies such as food stamps, housing subsidies and Medicaid benefits do not count as income. "The poverty statistics are overstated in that we don't include in-kind subsidies," said economist Walter Williams of George Mason University in Fairfax, Va. "I understand from people who have studied the area that if you did that, you're talking about poverty being no more than 2 or 3 percent of the population, which is very, very low."

[12] Appearing Aug. 18, 1983, on PBS-TV's "The MacNeil-Lehrer Report."

Questioning Extent of Problem

NOT EVERYONE accepts the proposition that hunger is a growing, widespread problem in this country. The Reagan administration and its supporters, for example, say the problem has been blown out of proportion by the news media and those who oppose the president's policies. "Reagan has done more to *help* the poor than Carter," wrote Michael Novak, resident scholar in philosophy, religion and public policy at the American Enterprise Institute, a conservative think tank in Washington, D.C. "Inflation has come down more quickly, more steeply and (so far) more steadily than anyone dared to hope on inauguration day. Whatever dollars the poor receive under Reagan, they are more honest dollars than they were under Carter, when even the practice of indexing welfare benefits to the rate of inflation could not prevent all other costs from leaping beyond reach." [13]

Sen. Robert Dole, R-Kan., chairman of the Senate Agriculture, Nutrition and Forestry Committee's Subcommittee on Nutrition, said recently that most reports of hunger in the United States were based upon anecdotal evidence. "There has been no documentation of nationwide 'hunger' problems, unless one accepts frequently biased media reports . . . ," Dole wrote in a column appearing in *The Washington Post* on Aug. 17. "The reality of the 'hunger' problem has been distorted by media in response to complaints by 'hunger' critics who seldom offer constructive ideas. They are, by and large, liberal Democrats who will always be 'anti-Reagan' — a point never made by the writers or commentators."

Economist Walter Williams of George Mason University agrees with Dole and others who say there is no widespread hunger problem in this country. "I have traveled all around the country and I have not seen people lying in the streets, dying of starvation," Williams said. "I used to live in the poor ghettos of North Philadelphia where poverty is rife . . . and the people there are not starving. They may not have very good nutrition, but that's because they'd rather use their money for potato chips rather than something else they could buy." Reports that increasing numbers of persons are showing up at soup kitchens do not necessarily mean there are more hungry Americans, Williams said. "When you make it easy for people to get soup or get food without having to spend money, you can expect to see more people" on food lines, he said.

Others question the supposition that the government should

[13] Writing in *Commentary*, August 1983, p. 29.

69

be the dominant provider of food for the hungry. "There seems to be a fairly widespread misunderstanding that the sole source of food assistance for the poor in the United States is, or should be, provided by the federal government in the form of various federal food and nutrition programs," Senate Agriculture Committee Chairman Jesse Helms, R-N.C., said at a Sept. 14 hearing. Helms said he favored "creative approaches" by private individuals and groups such as churches and food kitchens. "These individuals and groups have identified problems specific to their communities," Helms said, "and they have developed successful, varied approaches to address these problems. . . . I read the Bible's instruction to feed and care for the poor as addressed to individuals, not the federal government or taxpayers collectively."

Parker T. Williamson, minister of the First Presbyterian Church in Lenoir, N.C., which runs several food distribution programs, told Helms' committee that government programs are not as effective as privately administered ones. "Government programs, however well intended, when left to themselves, tend to institutionalize themselves until a great deal of the money which you appropriate feeds the service machinery and only a trickle reaches those for whom the appropriation was intended," he said. "Partnerships with local philanthropic organizations reduce this cost significantly." Williamson went on to say that government food and nutrition programs also "tend to become faceless and impersonal. Client families become numbers and needs are categorized into abstractions. This putrefication of government programs encourages a 'dole mentality' among the recipients and fertilizes a seedbed for graft. Partnerships with local philanthropic organizations tend to personalize assistance."

Government's Role in Food Distribution

Reagan administration officials respond to accusations that cutbacks in social services have aggravated hunger problems by pointing to the enormous size of the government's food distribution and nutrition programs. In recent congressional testimony, John W. Bode, deputy assistant secretary for food and consumer services for the U.S. Department of Agriculture, said the administration is "very concerned about the nutritional well-being of those Americans who are unable to provide an adequate diet for themselves." Bode cited what he termed "an impressive array of food assistance programs" that are "responsible for the subsidy — in part or in whole — of some 95 million meals a day." [14] Agriculture Secretary Block spoke recently of

[14] Testifying July 12, 1983, before the Senate Agriculture, Nutrition and Forestry Committee's Subcommittee on Nutrition. See also Elizabeth Wehr, "Congress, Administration Debate Need for More Help to Fight Hunger in America," *Congressional Quarterly Weekly Report*, May 7, 1983, pp. 881-886.

Funding for Government Food and Nutrition Programs

(in millions of dollars)

Fiscal Year	Food Stamps	Child Nutri-tion*	Food Dona-tions**	Women, Infants and Children	Total
1969	$ 228.9	$ 313.8	$ 601.8	$ 0	$ 1,144.5
1970	549.7	419.5	558.5	0	1,527.7
1971	1,522.7	663.1	580.4	0	2,766.2
1972	1,797.3	892.4	586.1	0	3,275.8
1973	2,131.4	1,065.3	559.5	0	3,756.2
1974	2,718.3	1,270.9	548.3	11.1	4,548.6
1975	4,385.5	1,593.2	434.1	89.3	6,502.1
1976	5,326.5	1,926.6	500.9	155.5	7,909.5
1977	5,067.0	2,196.1	641.2	256.5	8,160.8
1978	5,139.2	2,424.3	775.5	387.7	8,726.7
1979	6,480.2	2,660.2	855.6	527.3	10,523.3
1980	8,685.4	2,843.1	1,151.8	739.4	13,419.7
1981	10,632.8	3,238.5	1,208.4	888.0	15,967.7
1982	10,409.0	2,775.1	1,237.1	957.6	15,378.8
1983#	11,858.0	3,028.0	1,750.5	1,160.0	17,796.5
1984#	11,054.0	3,183.0	1,304.0	1,060.0	16,601.0

* Includes school and breakfast, child care, summer food and special milk programs.
** Includes commodities distributed under school lunch, summer food, child care, needy families, supplemental food, charitable institutions, Indian, elderly nutrition and cash-in-lieu of commodities programs. Years 1978-84 include Agriculture Department purchases for agricultural price support programs and/or programs to remove perishable commodity surpluses from the market.
# Estimates

Source: U.S. Department of Agriculture Food and Nutrition Service records compiled by U.S. General Accounting Office.

the "mammoth" federal food and nutrition effort. "One out of 10 people are on food stamps; one out of six people receive some kind of food assistance," Block said. "We are working with states; we are working with private institutions that are going out and making food available.... I just submit that there is a lot being done." [15]

Some 22 million Americans receive food stamps today, at a monthly federal cost of about $1 billion. In 1981 the Reagan administration changed the food stamp eligibility rules, limiting eligibility to households with total incomes below 130 percent of the federally defined poverty level. Previously families with incomes at or below the poverty level qualified for the program, but recipients were allowed to deduct items such as housing costs. This made the cutoff income limit for many recipients much higher than the federal poverty level.

[15] Appearing Aug. 2, 1983, on PBS-TV's "The MacNeil-Lehrer Report."

The government's Special Supplemental Food Program for Women, Infants and Children (WIC) provides monthly food packages to pregnant women, infants and young children up to four years old. The $1.1 billion program serves about 2.5 million Americans. To be eligible for WIC, a family's income must be at or below 185 percent of the poverty line — $17,210 for a family of four. There must also be some indication of nutritional need, such as anemia or history of low-birthweight babies. The government will distribute some 2.1 billion pounds of food to needy persons this year through WIC and other food and nutrition programs. These include:

School Lunch — a $3 billion-a-year program that will provide government-subsidized lunches to 22.9 million eligible schoolchildren in 1983.

School Breakfast — a $327 million-a-year program that will provide government-subsidized breakfasts to 3.4 million eligible schoolchildren this year.

Nutrition Education — a $7 million program that will provide nutrition education to three million children, 118,000 teachers and 60,000 school food service personnel this year.

Summer Food Program — a $99 million program that provided lunches to 1.4 million children in needy areas this summer when school was not in session.

Child-Care Food Program — a $334 million endeavor providing federal funds for meals served to some one million children in day-care centers.

Commodity Supplemental Food Program — a $32 million program that will provide monthly food packages to about 135,000 pregnant women and young children this year. The program is similar to WIC, but provides the actual food rather than a voucher and distributes a greater variety of food than is available through WIC.

Special Milk Program — a $20 million program that provides cash assistance to states to reimburse schools, child-care institutions and summer camps for milk served to children. Some 210 million half-pints a day are expected to be given out this year.

Food Distribution — Provides commodities for the programs listed above plus $52 million to serve some 90,000 needy persons on Indian reservations and $100 million to provide 184 million meals for the elderly.

There have been some cutbacks in these food assistance programs in the last two years. According to an Aug. 25 report by the Congressional Budget Office, federal government outlays for 1982-85 on 26 human resources programs (including retirement, disability, health, education, employment and training) will be reduced by 7 percent compared to what they would have been

Nearly 23 million schoolchildren will receive government-subsidized lunches in 1983.

under the laws existing at the beginning of 1981.[16] For food stamps, the CBO report said there will be a 13 percent decrease in program outlays and for the various child nutrition programs a 28 percent reduction in outlays. For WIC, there will be a 4 percent increase over the period. The study concluded that changes in eligibility rules for the food stamp program will eliminate about 4 percent of the program's recipients — about one million persons — in the next two years. The report said that participation in the school lunch program fell by some three million last year after new eligibility rules went into effect.

Reaction to Proposed Program Cutbacks

The Reagan administration proposed more cutbacks in social programs, including reductions for food stamps and the child nutrition programs, in its fiscal 1984 budget proposal. Under the proposed changes, food stamp outlays would be cut by $1.1 billion and child nutrition programs by $103 million. The administration also called for changes in food stamp eligibility rules, including a requirement that states institute "workfare" programs, requiring able-bodied persons to work as a condition for receiving food stamps. The CBO estimated that the proposed changes would reduce the food stamp benefits of about 4.9 million households.

The president's proposals ran into strong opposition on Capitol Hill. First, both the House and Senate passed non-binding resolutions opposing any further cuts in food programs. Then the House, on June 8, passed a fiscal 1984 appropriations bill providing $13.8 billion for domestic food programs, $29.7 mil-

---

[16] Congressional Budget Office, "Major Legislative Changes in Human Resources Programs Since January 1981," Aug. 25, 1983. The report also found that 40 percent of the cutbacks in government benefit programs in the last two years affected households with annual incomes below $10,000.

lion more than the administration had requested, but $232.5
million less than fiscal 1983. The House bill also provided $10.9
billion for the food stamp program. The Senate passed a similar
bill June 29.[17] Since House and Senate conferees are not likely
to reconcile the two appropriations measures before the beginning of the 1984 fiscal year on Oct. 1, funding for the food
programs will probably be temporarily continued at fiscal 1983
levels.

Administration officials and their supporters defend the past
and proposed changes saying that they ensure that federal
funds and food go only to those who really need it. "The food
stamp program now goes to a whole lot of people who are not
poor," said economist Walter Williams. "Food stamps should be
allocated just based on income and current assets." Special
presidential assistant Robert Carleson, one of the architects of
the administration's social services policies, said: "The changes
that were made in the food stamp program and in other nutrition programs were all aimed at people who were in the upper
end of the income levels that were eligible for food and nutrition
assistance at the time. . . . The food stamp program is actually a
finitely appropriated program. So the changes that were made
were not across-the-board cuts in benefits or anything like that.
They were aimed at people in the higher income areas of
eligibility."

Critics of the changes have a different view. The proposed
cutbacks "show how totally out of touch the president is with
the reality of the lives of millions of people," said Robert
Liberatore, staff director of the U.S. Senate Democratic Policy
Committee. "The president's commitment to wringing inflation
out of the economy through higher interest rates and thus high
unemployment, together with his budget cuts in the area of food
and nutrition have contributed significantly to the increase in
hunger in America."

Attacking Hunger Problems

THE DEBATE over the extent of the hunger problem and
the effectiveness of federal food and nutrition programs
comes at a time when the United States has an abundant supply
of surplus food *(see p. 66)*. In that respect what has been called
the "rediscovery" of hunger in America[18] recalls the events of

---

[17] See *Congressional Quarterly Weekly Report*, June 11, 1983, pp. 1151-1152 and July 2,
1983, pp. 1375-1377.
[18] See, for example, the story by Robert Pear in *The New York Times*, Aug. 5, 1983.

The Block Experiment

On July 28, 1983, the news media gathered at a Safeway supermarket in Bethesda, Md., to watch Agriculture Secretary John R. Block and his wife Sue spend $54.14 on groceries — $3.86 less than the maximum weekly amount the government provides to eligible families in the food stamp program. The Blocks, their 19-year-old daughter and a family friend then spent the next week eating only that $54.14 worth of food. "As the U.S. government official responsible for food programs in this country, it made good common sense to spend some time living within the food stamp program allotment," Block told the press. "I don't expect people to do anything that I won't do myself."

Not unexpectedly, the experiment was not universally praised. For example, an editorial in *The Washington Post* on Aug. 1 said that the Blocks might find their food-stamp diet "a good deal harder to accept if they had to put up with it for 52 weeks a year with no time out for parties or even a trip to McDonald's."

the late 1960s when reports began to surface of widespread hunger and malnutrition in the midst of plenty.

President Johnson had launched his war on poverty in 1965, but two years later there were still persistent reports of hunger and malnutrition in many parts of the United States. On April 28, 1967, the Senate Labor and Public Welfare Committee's Subcommittee on Employment, Manpower and Poverty called for emergency measures to fight hunger in America. In a letter to President Johnson, subcommittee members said they had uncovered "conditions of malnutrition and widespread hunger in the delta counties of Mississippi that can only be described as shocking and which we believe constitute an emergency." The subcommittee reported evidence of children with "distended stomachs, chronic sores of the upper lip" and other "tragic evidence of serious malnutrition." The subcommittee said the food stamp program, which had been permanently established three years earlier, was not helping alleviate hunger.

In June 1967, a panel of doctors who had studied hunger in the South under a grant from the Field Foundation[19] provided the panel with more evidence of widespread hunger and malnutrition among the rural poor in that area of the country. One of the doctors, Joseph Brenner of the Massachusetts Institute of Technology, told the subcommittee that conditions in the South were as bad or worse than those he had seen working for a year with primitive tribes in East Africa. A documentary on hunger broadcast on CBS-TV on May 21, 1968, helped provide publicity to the hunger issue, as did the Poor People's Campaign —

[19] Founded in 1940 by Marshall Field III, the Field Foundation primarily funds children's organizations, including the Children's Defense Fund and the Children's Foundation, both in Washington, D.C.

featuring a "Resurrection City" of poor people camped out on the Mall in the nation's capital — in the spring and summer of 1968.

These events were important factors in influencing Congress to expand existing federal food programs and enact new ones. The Senate created a Select Committee on Nutrition and Human Needs in 1968 to look into the problems of hunger and malnutrition.[20] And on Dec. 2-4, 1969, President Nixon convened a highly publicized White House Conference on Food, Nutrition and Health. Nixon told the conference that he planned to expand the food stamp and other food assistance programs to "virtually eliminate the problem of poverty as a cause of malnutrition." Nixon said it was "embarrassing and intolerable" that hunger remained in the "world's richest nation."

In the intervening 14 years the nation has spent tens of billions of dollars in federal food assistance programs. In April 1979 a follow-up study by the Field Foundation found "far fewer grossly malnourished people in this country than there were 10 years ago." And, at least until two years ago, most observers agreed that the massive federal effort to feed the poor had, as Sen. Dole put it in his recent column, "a dramatic, positive impact on hunger and malnutrition in this country." But recent reports of increased requests for food assistance prompted the following comment in a *New York Times* editorial on April 10, 1983: "Presidents Johnson, Nixon, Ford and Carter could take rightful pride in the findings of the team of physicians studying hunger in 1979. Given what's happening to the hungry in America, this administration has cause only for shame."

Reagan's Task Force on Food Assistance

On Aug. 2 President Reagan announced he was forming a presidential task force to look into the hunger problem. "I have seen reports in the press in the past week of Americans going hungry," President Reagan said in a memorandum to White House counselor Edwin Meese III made public that day. "I am deeply concerned by these stories, because I know the suffering that each of these incidents presents. At the same time, I admit to being perplexed by these accounts. . . ." The president asked the task force to conduct a "no-holds-barred study." "If the food assistance programs are being mismanaged, I want to know that," he said. "If certain aspects of our food assistance programs require more funding, I want to know that, too."

[20] The Senate Select Committee on Nutrition and Human Needs, chaired by Sen. George McGovern, D-S.D., (1963-81), held a series of hearings and issued numerous reports on hunger, nutrition and health. Its most famous report, "Dietary Goals for the United States," issued in January 1977 and revised later that year, said that Americans did not eat enough fresh fruit, vegetables, grains and other natural foods. The committee was abolished in 1977 and most of its functions were given to the Senate Agriculture Subcommittee on Nutrition.

World Food Problems

While debate continues in the United States over the extent of hunger and malnutrition problems, there is no question that food shortages are endemic elsewhere in the world. The United Nations Food and Agricultural Organization (UNFAO) keeps track of world food problems. UNFAO's monthly report for August 1983 listed "abnormal food shortages" in 29 countries. They were: Angola, Bolivia, Botswana, Chad, Cuba, Djibouti, El Salvador, Ethiopia, Ghana, Haiti, Kampuchea, Lesotho, Mauritania, Mozambique, Nepal, Nicaragua, Panama, Peru, Ruanda, São Tomé and Principe, Somalia, Swaziland, Tanzania, Togo, Uganda, Vietnam, Yemen Arab Republic, Zambia and Zimbabwe.

According to Agriculture Secretary Block, the Task Force on Food Assistance was set up "to find out the facts. . . . I've sent teams to cities across the nation . . . trying to find out if there is something that should be done that we're not doing. And that's what the president wants his task force to find out." [21] Presidential assistant Robert Carleson told Editorial Research Reports that the task force will examine one basic question: "Is there and to what extent is there hunger? By 'hunger' we mean people who are hungry for no fault of their own." The task force, Carleson said, also will make "an assessment of all the [government's food and nutrition] programs to see where there might be duplication or where there might be gaps." The panel will submit a report to the president the last week in December.

The White House officially named the 13-member panel on Sept. 9. Economist James Clayburn La Force Jr., head of the school of management at the University of California at Los Angeles, will chair the task force. Other members include Dr. George Graham of Johns Hopkins University, former Massachusetts Gov. Edward J. King, economist Kenneth W. Clarkson, and former Phoenix Mayor John Douglas Driggs, who is now board chairman of Second Harvest, a group that helps distribute food to food banks and other emergency food centers around the nation.[22]

Some members of the task force have publicly criticized the food stamp program and government welfare programs. Clarkson and Graham have been particularly outspoken opponents of government food and nutrition programs. Clarkson, the director of the law and economics center at the University of

---

[21] Appearing Aug. 2, 1983, on PBS-TV's "The MacNeil-Lehrer Report."
[22] The other members are: Richard L. Berkley, mayor of Kansas City; Sandra Smoley, president of the National Association of Counties; Erma Davis, director of the George Washington Carver Association in Peoria; Midge Decter, executive director of the Committee for the Free World in New York; Betsy Brian Rollins, director of St. Philip's Community Kitchen in Durham, N.C.; John M. Perkins, founder of the Voice of Calvary Ministries; businessman J. P. Bolduc, chief operating officer of the President's Private Sector Survey on Cost Control; and Donna Carlson West, director of government relations for Crafco Inc., of Chandler, Ariz.

Miami in Florida, served as associate director for human resources with the Office of Management and Budget from April 1982 to April 1983. In that position he helped draw up Reagan's fiscal 1984 budget proposals that called for cuts in food stamp and child nutrition programs. In a 1975 book Clarkson said that the food stamp program was a "failure" because it did not help farmers or poor people. "In some cases," Clarkson wrote, "nutrition may be hindered rather than helped by the food stamp program. Recipients are able to substitute more palatable or more conveniently packaged foods ... for cheaper (but not necessarily less nutritious) foods. The presence of malnutrition among families well above the poverty line clearly indicates that income supplementation in the form of food stamps will not automatically eliminate malnutrition." [23]

While under contract to OMB, Dr. Graham, in a July 31, 1981, letter to Vice President George Bush, termed the WIC program "very popular but wasteful and unneeded." Graham has been widely quoted as saying that there is no widespread hunger or malnutrition in the United States. In testimony April 6 before the Senate Agriculture Committee's Subcommittee on Nutrition, for example, Dr. Graham characterized the "nutritional status of our people including low-income groups" as "very good and continually getting better." In a recent interview he said: "From all the evidence I've seen, there is definitely not a growing malnutrition" problem. Those who claim that hunger is a problem "are probably making honest mistakes in the interpretation of statistics or don't know what they mean."

Graham also said that he believes government food assistance programs are not effective in helping alleviate hunger or malnutrition. "In the case of malnutrition," he said, "its causes in this country are very complex. But they're not that mysterious: social disruption of families, drugs, alcohol, jail, very young teenage mothers, when you talk about children. When you talk about the elderly, there's illness, isolation, fear to go out and buy, boredom of preparing their own food. ..." These problems, Dr. Graham said, "deserve our attention ... but I don't think that just throwing food at it is the solution. It's very appealing to think that you can solve complex social problems ... just by writing a check for food and not have the change of heart that's required to solve these problems. ..."

Criticism of Task Force's Members, Goals

Reaction from groups representing the poor to the president's decision to set up the task force was overwhelmingly negative. There was criticism of the membership and of the motivation for setting up the panel. "The task force is dominated by people

[23] Kenneth W. Clarkson, *Food Stamps and Nutrition* (1975), pp. 61-62.

who have been close allies of the Reagan administration and strong proponents of deep cuts in these programs," said Robert Greenstein of the Center on Budget and Policy Priorities. "I think beyond question that one of the task force's purposes is to exonerate Reagan administration policies and indicate that whatever [hunger] problems may exist out there, that the administration is not responsible for them." Greenstein called the decision to set up the task force "entirely a political one," and said, "the White House was very concerned about the fairness issue, saw hunger becoming the cutting edge of the fairness issue and decided they needed to act to deflect it quickly before it got out of hand."

"If the purpose of the task force is to determine whether or not there is a problem of hunger in this country, they're wasting their time," said Rep. Panetta. "If the purpose of the task force is to develop steps to deal with the problem of hunger, then there may be some merit to the task force. The reality is, all you have to do is look around at the facts. . . . You just don't have to look very far to find the facts supporting the conclusion that people are going hungry in our society." Nancy Amidei, director of the Food Research and Action Center, a privately funded interest group working to end hunger, said the decision to set up the task force was "a little bit late in the day. . . . The notion that anybody would be surprised, under the circumstances, that there is hunger in this country, given the budget and policy decisions of the last few years, is just astonishing to me." [24]

Some people believe the task force's findings could be politically embarrassing for President Reagan. If the task force's report concludes that the president's policies have not caused a hunger problem, "cries of disbelief may be deafening," *The Wall Street Journal* stated Aug. 19. If, on the other hand, the task force concludes that the president's budget cutbacks have hurt the poor, it would "confirm what Reagan's critics have said all along — but might not alter his stand much."

Robert Carleson, who oversaw the establishment of the task force, disagrees. "I would be surprised if that turned out to be a problem," he said. "But if it were a problem it would not be embarrassing. The president is the one that's creating the task force. He certainly didn't have to. And he did it because he wants to get to the bottom of the question." The task force's findings will not likely end the debate on the extent of hunger in the United States, nor will they likely eliminate the long lines at soup kitchens, food pantries and other emergency food distribution centers this winter.

---

[24] Panetta and Amidei appeared Aug. 2, 1983, on PBS-TV's "The MacNeil-Lehrer Report."

Selected Bibliography

Books

Auletta, Ken, *The Underclass*, Random House, 1982.
Brown, Roy E., *Starving Children*, Springer Publishing, 1977.
Coles, Robert, *Still Hungry in America*, World Publishing, 1969.
Eckholm, Erik P., *Losing Ground: Environmental Stress and World Food Prospects*, Norton, 1976.
Galbraith, John Kenneth, *The Nature of Mass Poverty*, Harvard University Press, 1979.
Levitsky, David A., *Malnutrition, Environment, and Behavior*, Cornell University Press, 1979.

Articles

Banks, Howard and Jayne A. Pearl, "Poverty in America," *Forbes*, Aug. 29, 1983.
Easton, Nina, "The Myth of the Safety Net," *Common Cause*, May-June 1983.
"Has Reagan Hurt the Poor?" *Fortune*, Jan. 24, 1983.
Novak, Michael, "The Rich, the Poor & the Reagan Administration," *Commentary*, August 1983.
Nutrition Week (published by the Community Nutrition Institute), selected issues.
Schoen, Elin, "Once Again, Hunger Troubles America," *The New York Times Magazine*, Jan. 2, 1983.
"Tabling Hunger," *The New Republic*, Sept. 5, 1983.
Wehr, Elizabeth, "Congress, Administration Debate Need for More Help to Fight Hunger in America," *Congressional Quarterly Weekly Report*, May 7, 1983.
Williams, Maurice J., "Prospects for Eliminating Hunger in the Face of Worldwide Economic Recession," *International Labour Review*, November-December 1982.

Reports and Studies

Center on Budget and Policy Priorities, "Soup Lines and Food Baskets: A Survey of Increased Participation in Emergency Food Programs," May 1983.
Clarkson, Kenneth W., "Food Stamps and Nutrition," American Enterprise Institute, 1975.
Congressional Budget Office, "Major Legislative Changes in Human Resources Programs since January 1981," August 1983.
Editorial Research Reports: "The Homeless: Growing National Problem," 1982 Vol. II, p. 793; "Nutrition in America," 1973 Vol. II, p. 581.
Overseas Development Council, "World Hunger or Food Self-Reliance? A U.S. Policy Approach for the 1980s," May 1982.
United States Conference of Mayors, "Hunger in American Cities: Eight Case Studies," June 1983.
U.S. General Accounting Office, "Public and Private Efforts to Feed America's Poor," June 23, 1983.
U.S. Senate, Democratic Policy Committee, "The President's Task Force on Hunger: Nothing to Bite Into," Aug. 4, 1983.

THE CHARITY SQUEEZE

by

Robert Benenson

Dec. 3
1 9 8 2

Editor's Note: The American Association on Fund-Raising Counsel, a leading authority on philanthropic trends, has reported that individuals, companies and foundations gave $60.4 billion to charity in 1982, more than ever before. Individual giving accounted for $48.7 billion of the total, an increase of 9.4 percent above the 1981 figure. However, this was below the 11.9 percent increase of the previous year. The amount of giving during 1983 had not been compiled at the time of this book's publication.

THE CHARITY SQUEEZE

I N THE WEEKS between now and Christmas, Americans will be asked to give a little more of themselves to help others. Community fund-raising drives will be making their final appeals. Charitable and other non-profit institutions will be asking for donations in the spirit of the season. Newspapers will remind people to "remember the neediest." Salvation Army bell-ringers and sidewalk Santa Clauses will ask passersby for their dimes and quarters.

The willingness of people to pitch in to build a better society has been an American trait since the birth of the nation. But President Reagan has made it part of his administration's domestic agenda. Using the catchall phrase "private sector initiatives," Reagan has encouraged businesses, churches, voluntary organizations and individuals to become more involved in improving communities and helping individuals.

Reagan and his supporters believe that growing federal involvement in such areas as welfare, community development, health care, education and even the arts has hampered local initiative and innovation, destroyed the willingness of different sectors of society to work together, and left the fate of many communities and individuals in the hands of distant federal bureaucrats. "The truth is we've let government take away many things we once considered were really ours to do voluntarily out of the goodness of our hearts and a sense of community pride and neighborliness," Reagan said in a nationally televised address Sept. 24, 1981.

To many in the private sector, especially those involved with non-profit organizations, the symbolism of the president's call for more volunteer help was negated by the impact of recent budget cuts in social welfare, community development and similar programs. "We are trying to walk a tightrope between being supportive of an administration ... that is encouraging more giving, more volunteering, more community initiative ... and [being] one of the sharpest critics of the budget cuts, because we're in a position to see that they are already impacting the already-vulnerable," said Brian O'Connell, president of Independent Sector, an umbrella organization for non-profit groups which is based in Washington, D.C.[1]

---

[1] The group acts as a liaison between the non-profit community and governmental bodies.

Many non-profit groups rely heavily on federal funds to carry out their programs *(see box, p. 93)* and they have accused the president of pulling the rug out from under them. At the same time, the recession, which has sent unemployment soaring to double digits, and cuts in such programs as Aid to Families With Dependent Children, food stamps, housing assistance and Medicaid have greatly increased demands on social service agencies — demands that many organizations say they are incapable of meeting. Consequently, many needy people are falling into the "gap" between what government is no longer doing and what the private sector is capable of doing.

White House Task Force on Initiatives

In 1981, during the first round of federal budget cuts, President Reagan was stung by charges that his administration was unfair to the needy. To help defuse this criticism, Reagan established the Task Force on Private Sector Initiatives.[2] According to Executive Director Jerry Guth, the task force's mission is to "uncover the very best in private-sector initiative, volunteerism, partnership, philanthropy" and to "package them, explain them, articulate them, share them with a whole host of institutions."

The task force, whose one-year authorization expires at the end of December, has 44 members from the business, philanthropic, religious and political communities. It is headed by C. William Verity Jr., chairman of Armco Inc., a Middletown, Ohio, steel company known for its philanthropy and community involvement. Other well-known members include Cardinal Terence Cooke, Roman Catholic Archbishop of New York; George Romney, former governor of Michigan and chairman of the National Center for Citizen Involvement;[3] and three current Republican officeholders, Rep. Barber B. Conable Jr. of New York, Sen. David Durenberger of Minnesota and Gov. Pierre S. du Pont IV of Delaware.

Guth, who is also on loan from Armco, where he serves as a marketing executive, says the task force is not trying to find ways to make up for all of the federal budget cuts. "That was never an expectation the president or we had," Guth said in a recent interview. "Anybody who looks at the numbers knows that is absolutely impossible. . . ." Instead, he said, the task force wants to foster greater cooperation between state and local governments, business interests, voluntary organizations and

---

[2] See Marvin N. Olasky, "Reagan's Second Thoughts on Corporate Giving," *Fortune,* Sept. 20, 1982, pp. 130-136.

[3] The center serves as a clearinghouse for information on volunteer programs and operates a network of Voluntary Action Centers which help communities and organizations coordinate and improve voluntary activities. The organization, formed in 1979 by a merger of the National Center for Voluntary Action and the National Information Center for Voluntary Action, is based in Boulder, Colo., but has a national affairs office in Washington.

individuals, in line with its motto "Building Partnerships USA." "We're asking people to cross borders and do some new things," Guth said. "For most people ... that is not the most comfortable thing on earth."

Urban Partnerships That Make a Profit

One of the achievements that task force executives are proudest of is the creation of a computerized data bank containing models of successful private sector programs. As of Oct. 29, there were 2,300 "success stories" in the data bank, many of which find their way into the task force's newsletter and press releases.

Among the programs applauded by the task force is the placement of business facilities in low-income or otherwise dilapidated neighborhoods. A pioneer of this strategy was Control Data Corp., a Minneapolis-based computer manufacturing firm. In 1968, with the full support of company Chairman William C. Norris, Control Data opened a plant in a mainly black, low-income section of Minneapolis. Despite having to provide special benefits for employees, including day-care facilities, the plant, which employs over 300 workers, has turned a profit that Norris described as "a handsome one." Control Data has since opened three more plants in similar Minneapolis-St. Paul neighborhoods, and has opened facilities in the inner cities of Washington, D.C., San Antonio and Toledo.

Control Data officials emphasize the need for a profit motive to get businesses involved in such job creation and community development projects. "The magnitude of the job to be done is far beyond any potential for sheer philanthropy to fulfill,"

Control Data President Robert M. Price said.[4] To encourage other businesses to get involved, Control Data in 1978 joined a consortium of corporations and churches called City Ventures Corp. The group has been slow in starting, but Control Data has established a plant in inner-city Baltimore as part of the City Ventures project.

Baltimore is also the site of another for-profit venture that task force officials use as a model. The Inner Harbor project, a hotel, office building, shopping and entertainment complex in a formerly decaying waterfront area of downtown Baltimore, was constructed by the Rouse Corp. in the late 1970s. The company's chairman, James W. Rouse, has been active in some of the country's most successful urban renewal projects, including a similar renovation of Boston's Faneuil Hall. In developing Baltimore's inner harbor, Rouse worked closely with the city government, local business and banks, and community groups. "One of the reasons that Inner Harbor works so terribly well is that all of these key institutions . . . have for the first time come together in a partnership," said Jerry Guth.

But opponents of the Reagan administration's budget policies point out that projects like City Ventures and Baltimore's inner harbor would have been impossible without federal seed money from the Urban Development Action Grant (UDAG) program.[5] The idea that federal incentives may be necessary to encourage profit-making, job-creating enterprises to move into inner cities is supported by another Reagan proposal. Last March the president submitted a plan to Congress under which businesses would receive substantial tax breaks and regulatory relief for locating in sections of inner cities designated by the secretary of housing and urban development as "enterprise zones." Although there is skepticism over the efficacy of tax incentives in luring businesses to the ghetto, many of the groups that oppose the overall thrust of Reagan's politics, including the National Urban League, support the enterprise zones plan.[6]

Debate Over Corporate Responsibilities

The most publicized endeavor of the Task Force on Private Sector Initiatives was a call last March for corporations to

---

[4] Price and Norris were quoted in *Newsweek*, Feb. 8, 1982, p. 69.

[5] The UDAG program provides grants for selected urban development projects. Although the grants make up only a small percentage of the projects' budgets, they do provide the credibility necessary to attract other sources of credit.

[6] The Senate Finance Committee passed the enterprise zones plan as part of an unrelated tax bill on Sept. 28, 1982, but the House has taken no action on it. Hearings have not even been held by the committees that have jurisdiction over the plan — Ways and Means, Judiciary and Banking. President Reagan made a new pitch for the plan in an address to the National League of Cities, meeting in Los Angeles on Nov. 29. But the House is still not expected to take action on enterprise zones in the lame-duck session that began Nov. 29, and the legislation probably will be resubmitted in the 98th Congress in January. For more information on the enterprise zone concept, see "Reagan and the Cities," *E.R.R.*, 1982, Vol. II, pp. 529-548.

double their total giving to philanthropy. Corporate philanthropy has averaged about 1 percent of pretax income. The task force called for corporations to increase that to 2 percent over the course of four years. Although the task force also called on individuals to double their giving, from an average of 2 to 4 percent of pretax income, it was the suggested corporate increase that created the greatest controversy, since it raised the whole issue of whether there was such a thing as "corporate social responsibility."

The nation has a history of corporate philanthropy that dates back at least a century, to the days when railroad industrialists funded the expansion of the Young Men's Christian Association (YMCA), which, in turn, provided good, cheap housing for workers in railroad towns. The tradition took firm root with the establishment of philanthropic foundations by such tycoons as John D. Rockefeller and Andrew Carnegie in the early part of this century.

Despite the billions of dollars invested by business in philanthropic causes, there are some businessmen and economists who are opposed to corporate philanthropy. Led by conservative economist Milton Friedman of the University of Chicago, this group believes that corporate philanthropists are playing games with other people's money. "It belongs to their workers, their employees, or their shareholders," said Friedman.[7] In fact, according to The Conference Board, a business research group in New York, only about 30 percent of American corporations contribute to philanthropy.

There are many who vehemently disagree with Friedman. The strongest protest comes from the philanthropic community. According to William Aramony, president of the United Way of America, "Friedman's in another world." Members of the White

---

[7] Quoted in *Fortune*, Sept. 20, 1982, p. 136.

House task force also take a strong stand in defense of their "doubling" proposal. Taking what economists would regard as a liberal view of corporate capitalism, Executive Director Guth said:

> There are those who say that the first task of business is to make a profit. That's wrong. . . . People organize themselves and their resources to respond to human needs and they create products and services of one kind or another to meet those needs. . . . The expectations of publics in communities where they have their economic life are equally valid as the whole host of other market needs that they have historically organized themselves to meet.

Others in the corporate community agree. One of the leaders in corporate philanthropy is the Minneapolis-based Dayton-Hudson Corp., which operates department stores in the Midwest. In 1947, Dayton-Hudson pledged to contribute 5 percent of its pretax income to philanthropy, and has since encouraged businesses in Minneapolis and other cities to form "5 Percent" or "2 Percent" clubs. In a speech to the Commonwealth Club in San Francisco last year, company Chairman Kenneth N. Dayton not only predicted that "increased corporate philanthropy is, indeed, an 'idea whose time has come,' " but also warned that if corporate philanthropy is not significantly increased, "we can count on a swift return to primary dependence on government for meeting all public needs, with all that implies." Dayton added, "The public's 'honeymoon' with business will come to a very abrupt end, indeed. And, given the raised expectations, the backlash could be severe enough to threaten the entire free enterprise system."

Business leaders point out that corporate philanthropy extends beyond cash donations. Some companies "lend" executives to non-profit organizations, to aid in such areas as accounting, fund raising, management and employee/volunteer training. Contributions of equipment constitute another form of corporate philanthropy and are especially popular among computer manufacturers. For example, International Business Machines Corp. (IBM), which gave $40 million in cash contributions in 1981, estimated that its contributions of equipment and loaned executives increased its philanthropic total to $80 million.[8]

Some observers credit the rise of "corporate social responsibility" to a new breed of corporate manager that has risen in recent years. "From the 1960s on, the new chief executive was much more socially conscious than we knew in the past," said Guth. However, social activists say they pressured corporations into becoming more socially responsible. "They have become

---

[8] See *The New York Times*, Sept. 22, 1982.

conscious of that because the work done by minority organizations, women's organizations, environmental organizations, public law advocacy organizations, and Nader's groups has forced them to focus on it," said Robert O. Bothwell, executive director of the National Committee for Responsive Philanthropy.[9]

Task Force Models of Voluntary Effort

The Reagan administration is counting on the voluntary, nonprofit sector to help some of the people affected by the recession or the budget cuts. The task force's computer bank is full of voluntary success stories, most of which predate the Reagan administration's advocacy of private sector initiatives. One of President Reagan's favorite examples of voluntary action is Sister Falaka Fattah's House of Umoja in Philadelphia. In an attempt to cut down on gang violence in her inner-city neighborhood, Sister Fattah began in 1968 to provide shelter and counseling for local youths. In 14 years, she worked with over 500 boys, reclaiming most from the streets. Her efforts earned her a meeting and a letter of praise from President Reagan.[10]

The task force gladly supplies examples of other praiseworthy volunteer programs. Members of the United Auto Workers local in Waterloo, Iowa, working with the Hawkeye Valley Area Agency on Aging, formed a group several years ago called Brown Baggers. Union workers contribute excess produce from their gardens for distribution to the elderly and shut-ins. A New York City organization known as J.O.B., for Just One Break, provides free job placement for handicapped men and women. Silver Key Senior Services provides homemaker services and meals to the low-income elderly in Colorado Springs.

Then there are efforts that the task force does not emphasize, but which illustrate the kinds of partnerships that the administration is advocating. In Philadelphia, for example, the Consortium for Human Services has brought state and local officials together with the business and voluntary communities to plan employment and human service strategies. The city government in Baltimore spearheads the "Blue Chip-in" campaign to raise funds from local businessmen. William Aramony of the United Way says his organization helped set up consortiums of local businesses, foundations and voluntary agencies in several cities.

---

[9] The committee, located in Washington, is a coalition of "non-traditional" non-profit organizations, mainly those involved in minority and women's causes.

[10] Ironically, the House of Umoja was almost caught up in the Reagan budget-cutting. During the Carter administration, Sister Fattah accepted her first federal grant in order to create an "urban boys' town" in Philadelphia. In the first round of budget cuts in 1981, the House of Umoja lost the equivalent of $250,000, most of it related to the loss of workers supplied under the CETA public-service jobs program, which was terminated. However, the loss was made up by a grant approved last summer by the U.S. Department of Health and Human Services. According to Sister Fattah, the project will now be completed, although her organization is one year behind in its construction schedule.

Impact of Budget Cuts

THAT WAS the good news. But according to many in the non-profit community, there is plenty of bad news for voluntary agencies and the people who depend upon them. At the same time that cuts in direct federal assistance to individuals and record-high unemployment have created a demand for voluntary relief unseen since the Great Depression, many voluntary agencies are taking deep cuts in the parts of their budgets supplied by federal grants. "It's ironic that at the time that needs are greatest, the capacity to generate resources tends to be more difficult," said Aramony.

The Reagan administration has gone to great lengths to attack the excesses of federal government programs while extolling the initiative of private sector and especially voluntary groups. However, many of these groups put much of their effort into carrying out government programs. According to an Urban Institute study,[11] non-profit groups received $40.4 billion from the federal government in 1980. That year, total philanthropic giving was $47.7 billion, and only $25.5 billion of that went to non-religious organizations. "The administration did not recognize the financial partnership and the service partnership that related government and many of these private groups," said Brian O'Connell of Independent Sector. "They assumed they were cutting public programs, when indeed much of that money was flowing to voluntary organizations."

Advocates of some of the small, minority-oriented charities paint the administration's actions in darker colors. "I think it's clear that the administration wanted to cut the budget, that it did not care about the neediest in our population," said Pablo Eisenberg, executive director of the Washington-based Center for Community Change.[12] "I don't think they gave a damn about the impact on the non-profits."

There are no exact figures on how much non-profit groups can expect to lose because Congress had completed action on only three of 13 appropriations bills before the campaign recess in October. The most quoted estimates are those in the Urban Institute study. Using the results of the fiscal year 1982 budget cuts along with President Reagan's proposals and early congressional action on the fiscal 1983 budget, authors Lester M. Salamon and Alan J. Abramson determined that the non-profit sector would lose $33 billion in federal funds between fiscal 1982

---

[11] Lester M. Salamon and Alan J. Abramson, "The Federal Budget and the Non-profit Sector," The Urban Institute, September 1982.
[12] Founded in 1968, the center provides technical assistance for its affiliate organizations, which are involved mainly in anti-poverty or community development activities.

and fiscal 1985. In addition, programs in areas in which the non-profit sector has an interest, including social welfare and community development, would lose $115 billion during that four-year period. Salamon and Abramson referred to these as "indirect cuts," since they would tend to increase demands for non-profit services.

Brian O'Connell of Independent Sector estimated that the total income for the non-profit sector over those four years would be $650 billion. Therefore, a $33 billion, or 5 percent, cut does not seem overwhelming. But as O'Connell pointed out, "The impact is not proportional. Some programs and organizations face not the 5 percent cut, but devastating slices of 50-100 percent." [13]

The hardest hit groups were the small, neighborhood organizations that were heavily dependent on federal money for their survival. But even those groups affiliated with established voluntary organizations are feeling the pinch. William Aramony of the United Way reported that United Way-affiliated organizations in large cities received an average of 47 percent of their funding from the federal government; in some cities, such as New York, the figure hit 75 percent.

The Reagan administration states optimistically that the success of the president's economic recovery program and the implementation of his "New Federalism" plan will enable worthy causes to turn to state and local governments for assistance. Advocates of some philanthropic groups, especially those in the social welfare and community development fields, are not thrilled about the prospect. "The history of increasing federal programs in the 1960s came as a direct result of the inattention of cities and states to problems of minorities and ultimately women," said Robert O. Bothwell.

Organizations Hardest Hit by Cutbacks

Although the budget cuts have pinched organizations across the voluntary spectrum, O'Connell drew a profile of the organizations most likely to be hurt. These include organizations that are most dependent on government funds, those least able to compete for block grants[14] and other government funding,

[13] "Briefing on Current Issues Impacting the Independent Sector," address presented at Independent Sector meeting, San Francisco, Oct. 25, 1982.
[14] As part of Reagan's "New Federalism" program, a number of federal programs are being combined into "block grants," with fewer regulatory strings attached for state and local governments, but with reduced funding levels. For background, see "Reagan and the Cities," *E.R.R.*, 1982 Vol. II, pp. 529-548; "Reaganomics on Trial," *E.R.R.*, 1982 Vol. I, pp. 1-20; and "Reagan's New Federalism," *E.R.R.*, 1981 Vol. I, pp. 249-268.

those least experienced at fund raising, and those that are least popular. According to James Castelli of Independent Sector, "Social welfare organizations, civic and political organizations, minority and newer organizations, and community organizations will feel the greatest impact."

The National Urban League has for years been involved in federally funded job training projects for minorities. In the fiscal year that ended last July, the Urban League funded 39 programs with a total of $34 million; in this fiscal year, $9 million will be spent on 22 projects. Other charitable organizations report similar troubles. Responding to a survey by Independent Sector, the National Council of La Raza, a Hispanic social welfare organization, said it had suffered a 40 pecent reduction in staff with a 45 percent reduction in services. Opportunities Industrialization Centers, a Philadelphia-based job training organization, lost $65 million, or 50 percent of its 1981 budget. The National Council of Churches reported that 25 domestic hunger projects with an annual average income of $142,000 in 1981 would average $72,000 in 1982.

Another problem for voluntary agencies was caused by the elimination of the Comprehensive Employment Training Administration (CETA) public service jobs program. Critics of the CETA jobs program complained that many of the jobs created were of the "makework" variety. But non-profit organizers say that CETA workers were vital to many of their functions. "Many organizations were taking advantage of the CETA program in a very useful way," said Robert O. Bothwell.

Also hindering voluntary organizations is the increase in the postal rate for non-profit groups. Last January Congress did not appropriate the full amount of an expected subsidy. As a result, the third-class bulk rate for non-profit organizations rose from 3.8 cents per piece to 5.9 cents. Although Congress restored part of the subsidy shortfall in July, the rate decreased only to 4.9 cents per piece. Since many organizations use direct mail to raise funds, or provide a magazine or newsletter to attract contributions, the increase in postal rates will cut into their capacity to provide services. O'Connell pointed out that the postal rate subsidy was one of the devices "developed by government to encourage private initiative to the public good."

Recent Increase in the Needy Population

Many social service agencies report that, as a result of the recession and federal budget cuts, they are being overwhelmed by demands for their services. In addition to requests for cash assistance to help pay rent or electricity bills, which social agencies typically receive during rough times, they have also

Reliance of Non-profit Groups
on Government Funding

Proportion of total revenue provided by government grants, contracts and other programs:

Civil and Social Action	44 percent
Health Services	43 percent
Human Services	43 percent
Culture	10 percent
Education and Research	9 percent

Source: "The Fiscal Capacity of the Voluntary Sector," a study prepared by Bruce L. R. Smith of the Brookings Institution and Nelson M. Rosenbaum of the Center for Responsive Governance for a Brookings Institution conference, Dec. 9, 1981.

seen a big increase in the number of people requesting the basic necessities: food, clothing and shelter. In 1981, when President Reagan first started pressing for budget cuts, he promised to provide a "safety net" for the "truly needy." But social welfare advocates are not convinced. "I don't think that there ever was a safety net," said Father Gary Christ of the National Conference of Catholic Charities. "Someone without food or without shelter and without clothing and without the possibility of getting a job is someone who is truly needy."

Leaders of black and Hispanic organizations say that minorities are generally the most needful people in the country and have been hit the hardest by the recession. "When you get right down into the streets where we operate, it's incredible, the needless suffering in this country," said Milton Bondurant of the National Urban League. But they also point out that the problem is not exclusively a minority one. The ranks of the "truly needy" have been swelled by the "newly needy": lower-middle and middle-class Americans whose lives have been drastically changed by the recession.

Much of the demand on social agencies from the middle class is in the form of counseling services. Many people are having a hard time dealing with the psychological consequences of unemployment. Christ reported that in Buffalo, N.Y., requests for the marriage counseling services of Catholic Charities affiliates are up 20 percent over last year.

But growing numbers of middle-class people are turning to charities for the basics. Christ said that a visit to a soup kitchen would belie the stereotype of aid recipients as all welfare cases. "We're seeing people who, a couple of years ago, would have never dreamed that they'd be coming anywhere for help," Christ said. With the onset of winter, social agencies also expect an upturn in requests for shelter.[15]

---

[15] See "The Homeless: Growing National Problem," *E.R.R.*, 1982 Vol. II, pp. 793-812.

Cutbacks Felt in Other Non-profit Areas

While most of the national attention has been focused on these social welfare issues, other areas of the non-profit sector have also been affected by budget cuts. The Urban Institute estimated that the area of health care and financing would take $8.1 billion in direct cuts and $19.9 billion in indirect cuts. Medicaid, community mental health centers, alcohol abuse, maternal child and health and immunization are among the programs included in this area.

According to the Urban Institute, education and research will lose $5.2 billion directly and $28 billion indirectly. Programs listed in this category include student loans, school nutrition, Title I aid for disadvantaged students, Social Security payments to college students and work-study programs. Although education agencies receive a relatively small part of their funding from the federal government — 9 percent — educators worry that the budget cuts could have significant impact. For instance, there is concern that cutbacks in student aid could force many middle-class students to forgo private colleges in favor of public schools, squeezing out low-income and minority students who have traditionally found opportunity in state institutions.

Even the arts and culture communities are feeling the effect of the budget cuts. The Urban Institute found that the Reagan administration's fiscal 1983 budget proposals would result, by 1985, in more than 50 percent reductions from 1980 budget levels for the National Endowment for the Arts and the National Endowment for the Humanities, which supply grants to theater, dance and music companies, museums and other cultural institutions. The Corporation for Public Broadcasting would lose 59 percent of its funding between 1980 and 1985.

Weathering the Changes

THE REAGAN administration says it never intended to create the impression that the private sector would be able to make up for all of the budget cuts. But leaders of the non-profit community complain that Reagan's tendency to mention federal budget reductions and private sector initiatives in the same breath has raised expectations to a level that they cannot come close to meeting. "The gap is there and it's getting wider," said John J. Schwartz, president of the American Association of Fund-Raising Counsel in New York City. "Philanthropy simply can't make up the difference."

Rise in Philanthropic Giving

Year	Total Giving (billions)	Year	Total Giving (billions)
1981	$53.62	1975	$29.68
1980	47.74	1974	27.71
1979	43.31	1973	25.60
1978	39.63	1972	23.30
1977	36.02	1971	22.84
1976	32.54	1970	20.75

Source: "Giving USA," American Association of Fund-Raising Counsel, Inc., 1982 Annual Report.

Philanthropy has been growing rapidly in recent years. Last year, despite the onset of the recession, philanthropic giving scored a record increase of 12.3 percent over 1980, for a total of $53.6 billion. But according to the Urban Institute study, non-profit organizations would have to increase their income from private sources by 30-40 percent per year, or 3-4 times the all-time record increase, in order to maintain their 1980 service levels. In order to make up for all the indirect cuts, giving to voluntary agencies would have to increase by 90-100 percent per year.

Those involved in non-profit organizations cite similar statistics. Father Gary Christ said that to make up for the budget cuts in its areas of interest, Catholic Charities would have to take its best year and multiply it 4-6 times. "Anybody who really thinks that anybody can make up for the budget cuts is frankly living in a fool's paradise," he said.

Others in the non-profit community say that corporate philanthropy cannot be counted on to "fill the gap." Even after a record increase of 11.1 percent last year, corporate philanthropy still only comprised 5.6 percent of all giving. And with corporate profits plummeting in the recession, even some fund-raisers think it is unfair to ask business to dramatically increase its contributions. "When corporations are also responsible to their stockholders and a lot of our good corporate friends have names such as International Harvester and Ford Motor Co. and Montgomery Ward, is that a practical thing to ask?" said Gary Bloom of the National Urban League.

It is uncertain what the overall picture will be for philanthropy this year. William Aramony of the United Way estimated that United Way's national fund raising would increase by 6-8 percent this year, a substantial increase but less than last year's record 10.3 percent. The amount varies from locality to locality. Aramony expected Buffalo to run behind last year's pace, and Cleveland's campaign, which ended in October, raised just 0.5 percent more than last year, a result Aramony called a "miracle" considering Cleveland's depression-like condition. Some cities are running way ahead of average, including Hartford, whose United Way enjoyed a 13 percent gain over 1981. But whatever the increase, most people within the philanthropic community do not think it will be enough. "A lot of people are obviously going to be hurt, and are being hurt," said Schwartz.

Finding Fault in the Voluntary Sector

Reagan administration officials believe that too many groups were getting federal aid, that there was duplication of effort and that the time was ripe for a "sorting out." And there are those in the non-profit sector who agree. According to William Aramony, "There are some programs that should not be continued. There's nothing sacrosanct about that. What every community has to do is look at its service needs, look at its resources that are now available."

Some non-profit leaders are concerned about the reliance of some groups on federal funds. "The organizations that have done their fund-raising homework are going to raise more money," said Schwartz. "The ones that have been relying very heavily on government grants are not doing well, and they're not going to do well." But leaders of smaller, newer, neighborhood-oriented groups, many of which have poor or minority constituencies, say they lack a broad base of support and need those federal dollars. "A whole generation of organizations, some of which would have grown up to be effective forces, has been wiped out by the federal budget cuts," said Bothwell.

Brian O'Connell of Independent Sector said that there could always be streamlining, but that he gets "impatient" with critics who claim that it is time for a "shaking out." According to O'Connell, many non-profit groups have been "doing more with less" for a decade, including the YMCAs, Boys' Clubs and the National Council of La Raza.

Strategies to Deal With the Budget Cuts

The idea of stretching dollars in these hard economic times is pervasive in the non-profit community. "There is a commitment to do more with less," said Barbara J. Oliver, executive director of the National Assembly of National Voluntary Health and Social Welfare Organizations.[16] One dollar-stretching strategy being used by many voluntary organizations is the replacement of paid staff personnel with volunteers. O'Connell noted that many agencies had become addicted to the idea of professional-

[16] Based in New York, the assembly encourages "intercommunication" and "interaction" between the nation's large voluntary health and social welfare agencies. Its members include The United Way of America, The American Red Cross, The Salvation Army, The National Conference of Catholic Charities and the Girl Scouts of the U.S.A.

ism, and had filled many positions with professionals, such as social workers, teachers and nurses, that could just have easily been handled by volunteers. "This is one favorable aspect of the problem, there's a whole new re-emphasis on volunteers," said O'Connell.

There is also a re-emphasis on fund raising. Some established organizations are looking to new strategies to help replace lost

revenues. The National Urban League has pinpointed 300,000 likely contributors for a direct-mail campaign, has revitalized its finance committee which will conduct a two-year, 16-city fund-raising tour, and is hoping to raise $1 million from an entertainment event, the first in the organization's history. Some groups that were highly dependent on government funds are beginning to look for independent sources

of revenue. O'Connell said that he tells these groups, "often to their utter consternation, that they must be prepared to devote a minimum of 25 percent of their efforts to building the kind of independent funding necessary to provide reasonable program continuity."

Some groups are either merging completely or are combining some administrative services. The Greater New York Fund/ United Way published a guide earlier this year entitled "Merger: Another Path Ahead — A Guide to the Merger Process for Voluntary Human Services Agencies." Many organizations are also intensifying their public relations and lobbying efforts to try to prevent further budget cuts. Barbara Oliver said the organizations in her assembly were committed to "do something to continue to raise the consciousness of the general public and the government of their responsibility for the greater welfare."

Task Force and Reagan Policies Assessed

To the White House Task Force on Private Sector Initiatives, most of the complaints of the voluntary community and the private sector stem from a resistance to change. "For all of our talk about change, none of us accepts it very well," said Jerry Guth. "I find a lot of skepticism...."

As the task force approaches its planned termination date of Dec. 31, there is also skepticism within the private sector about its role and accomplishments.[17] Some people, especially those involved with organizations that have been hard hit by the recession, see the task force as a public relations gimmick meant to divert attention from the president's budget cuts. "[Reagan] appointed a highly visible task force that could go out and talk about what the issues were and what private philanthropy ought to do with them, at the same time as he was lopping off very substantial monies to them," said Robert O. Bothwell.

"There is no responsible individual in the private, non-profit community today who will even suggest that there is a way for private giving to make up for the federal budget cuts."

Robert Bothwell, executive
director, National Committee
for Responsive Philanthropy

Pablo Eisenberg of the Center for Community Change said that the task force would have been unnecessary if it had not been for the budget cuts: "The Reagan administration and the task force talk about public-private sector partnerships, but what they're talking about is such a small drop in the bucket compared to the ... partnerships that already existed, and which the administration killed." Another problem, Eisenberg said, is that the task force is split between members who sought to be independent and others who maintained primary allegiance to the president. The task force "has never been able to get away from that tension," he said.

Others view the task force more positively. Aramony of the United Way indicated that Reagan and the task force played a useful role in encouraging more private sector activity. "[Reagan] created the climate in which corporations and individuals say, 'Uncle Sam's not there anymore, I've got to do something,'" he said. Brian O'Connell of Independent Sector praised the task force for "keeping the president focused on this area" and for putting "a new emphasis on community groups working together to solve problems." Even Bothwell was obliged to credit the task force for a "guts call" for its suggestion that corporations double their philanthropic contributions.

---

[17] Although the task force is likely to go out of business as scheduled on Dec. 31, the White House plans to continue its "Office of Private Sector Initiatives," which was established along with the task force last December. The office, which is headed by Jay Moorhead, special assistant to the president for private sector initiatives, will be in charge of carrying out the task force's recommendations to the president, which are scheduled to be submitted on Dec. 8, 1982.

The Charity Squeeze

There is also debate over the future direction of Reagan's economic policies. Some believe that the social programs that have already carried most of the burden of Reaganomics will continue to be victimized by budget cuts. "The meanness and the willingness to put the burden on those who can't afford it continue," said Eisenberg. However, others in the non-profit community see a trend away from the budget cuts in the administration and in Congress. "I think there's a strong sentiment against further cuts," said Aramony. Some political observers foresee greater difficulty for Reagan in pushing domestic budget cuts through a House that picked up 26 Democratic members in the recent elections.

There is one thing that virtually everyone, from the task force leadership to corporations to voluntary organizations, agrees on: whatever the incremental gains made through private sector initiatives, partnerships and belt-tightening, there is no way for the private sector to make up, dollar-for-dollar, for the federal budget cuts. How society adjusts to help the thousands of individuals and communities caught up in the transition may be the decisive issue of the next two years of Reagan's tenure.

Selected Bibliography

Books

Meyer, Jack A. (ed.), *Meeting Human Needs: Toward a New Public Philosophy,* American Enterprise Institute, 1982.

Articles

"A Spurt In Voluntarism, But Is It Enough?" *U.S. News & World Report,* Sept. 20, 1982.

"A Triple Whammy on Charities," *Business Week,* March 23, 1981.

"Can Companies Fill the Charity Gap?" *Business Week,* July 6, 1981.

Kinsley, Michael, "Waiting for Lenny," *Harper's,* March 1982.

Kirschten, Dick, "Even If Charity Does Begin at Home, Government May Still Play a Key Role," *National Journal,* May 22, 1982.

Miller, William H., "Industry Isn't Rushing Into Social Activism," *Industry Week,* Feb. 22, 1982.

Olasky, Marvin N., "Reagan's Second Thoughts on Corporate Giving," *Fortune,* Sept. 20, 1982.

Pauly, David et al., "Doing Good — at a Profit," *Newsweek,* Feb. 8, 1982.

Tuthill, Mary, "Countrywide Call for Volunteers," *Nation's Business,* March 1982.

Reports and Studies

"Analysis of the Economic Recovery Program's Direct Significance for Philanthropic and Voluntary Organizations and the People They Serve," Independent Sector, April 1982.

Editorial Research Reports: "Volunteerism in the Eighties," 1980 Vol. II, p. 905; "American Philanthropy," 1974 Vol. I, p. 21.

"Giving USA," American Association of Fund-Raising Counsel, Inc., Annual Report, 1982.

Salamon, Lester M. and Alan J. Abramson, "The Federal Budget and the Non-profit Sector," The Urban Institute Press, 1982.

THE HOMELESS: GROWING NATIONAL PROBLEM

by

Marc Leepson

**Oct. 29
1 9 8 2**

THE HOMELESS:
GROWING NATIONAL PROBLEM

GEORGE ORWELL'S 1933 memoir, *Down and Out in Paris and London,* contains this rumination about the nature of poverty: "You have thought so much about poverty — it is the thing you have feared all your life, the thing you knew would happen to you sooner or later; and it is all so utterly and prosaically different. You thought it would be quite simple; it is extraordinarily complicated. You thought it would be terrible; it is merely squalid and boring. It is the peculiar *lowness* of poverty that you discover first; the shifts that it puts you to, the complicated meanness, the crust-wiping." [1]

With the nation mired in recession, more and more Americans are discovering firsthand the melancholy of poverty. Even worse, increasing numbers are finding themselves at the bottom rung of the poverty ladder — penniless and homeless. Highly visible evidence of the large numbers of homeless Americans is easy to find in nearly every city. Disheveled, dirty men and women can be seen huddled with their meager belongings in city parks, on street corners, in alleyways and abandoned buildings, and in airport, bus station and railway waiting rooms. In the last two years homeless persons have crowded emergency shelters in record numbers. Although exact numbers are impossible to come by, experts estimate that there are between 250,000 and one million homeless persons in the United States today.

"We are seeing the phenomenon all over the country," said Mitch Snyder of the Community for Creative Non-Violence in Washington, D.C., a group that works with the homeless in the nation's capital and researches the problem nationwide. "In city after city across the country there's at least a growing awareness of the added dimension and seriousness of the problem of homeless people, of destitute people, of marginal people who are slipping quietly and quickly through the cracks."

Snyder worries that the coming winter will bring especially serious problems. "There's probably one-and-a-half to two times as many people on the streets now as there were a year ago," he said. "Forecasters are saying that it's expected to be the worst winter of the century.... Folks are going to be dying all over the place in large numbers." Kim Hopper, a researcher

---

[1] George Orwell, *Down and Out in Paris and London* (1933), pp. 16-17.

with New York's Community Service Society, a non-profit social welfare agency, agreed. "From the looks of things in New York and what we're hearing elsewhere it'll be worse than last year, which was the worst since the Depression."

Effects of '60s Deinstitutionalization

One thing that has changed since the 1930s is the sociological makeup of the homeless population. Some say as much as half of this group is made up of former mental patients. The reason: drug therapy enabled large mental institutions to begin releasing patients in large numbers in the 1950s. Few were "cured" but many were released — often without provision for adequate follow-up medical and social services.[2] "In the early Thirties most of the people on the streets were without jobs or victims of the stock market crash," said the Rev. John J. McVean of New York City's St. Francis of Assisi Church. "Even when I came to New York in 1969 the homeless tended to be older alcoholics in their 40s and 50s. But ever since the early 1970s, the most dramatic shift has been in the numbers of released mental patients."[3]

The number of patients in U.S. mental hospitals dropped to 150,000 in 1978 — the last year for which complete statistics are available — from a peak of about 650,000 in the mid-1950s.[4] Many of the deinstitutionalized patients have been placed in nursing homes or community mental health centers. But there are only about 800 local mental health facilities across the country — not nearly enough to accommodate the need. Many former mental patients are therefore either under-served or unserved by community outpatient facilities. Often they wind up on the streets.

"The lack of services for mentally disabled people in the community, particularly for the chronic mentally ill people who have been institutionalized ... is a contributing factor" in the increasing number of homeless Americans, said Lee Carty, administrator of the Washington-based Mental Health Law Project. "They simply don't connect up with the services in the community." A 1976 survey of homeless men conducted by the New York City Human Resources Administration found that more of them suffered from psychiatric problems than from alcoholism; 31 percent of those interviewed were former mental patients.

The fact that the mental institution population is at a record low suggests that the deinstitutionalization problem has peaked.

---

[2] See "Mental Health Care Reappraisal," *E.R.R.*, 1982 Vol. II, pp. 609-632.
[3] Quoted by Randy Young in "The Homeless: The Shame of the City," *New York* magazine, Dec. 21, 1981, p. 27.
[4] Unofficial statistics put the number of persons in mental institutions today at 138,000.

But this is not the case. The reason is that admissions criteria for mental institutions have been tightened significantly, and thousands of persons who in former years would have been sent to mental institutions are no longer eligible to be admitted. Many of those persons have wound up on the streets. "There are an estimated 8,000 people a year in New York who aren't admitted [to state mental institutions] who would have been admitted, say, in the mid-60s," Kim Hopper told Editorial Research Reports. "Nobody knows what they're doing. It's clear that some of them are going to municipal hospitals. It's also clear that a lot of them are going begging."

The Impact of Social Service Cutbacks

Those who work with the homeless say the problems of the mentally disabled homeless have been worsened by recent cutbacks in federal social service programs undertaken by the Reagan administration. Many deinstitutionalized and other homeless persons subsist on Social Security Disability Insurance — payments made to persons unable to work because of physical or mental disability. But in 1980 Congress ordered the Social Security Administration to review the eligibility lists. The Reagan administration, some say overzealously, complied with that order by taking about 158,000 persons off disability rolls in a stepped-up review process that began last year. It is estimated that one-third of those persons will be reinstated after lengthy appeals, but they still will have had to face a long period in which their benefits were disrupted.[5]

[5] See *Congressional Quarterly Weekly Report*, Sept. 11, 1982, p. 2242.

The impact of Reagan administration cutbacks in social services was discussed in a report issued recently by the Urban Institute. The report said that non-profit, private organizations such as hospitals, universities and social service agencies stand to lose about $33 billion in federal funds in the next three years. During the same period the government is expected to cut back an additional $115 billion in funds for federally run social service programs. "Most hard hit by these changes will be non-profit social service agencies and community organizations," the report said, "which will lose one-fourth to one-third of their total revenues." [6]

Those who lose federal benefits often turn to state and local governments for help, but those jurisdictions are also reducing their budgets for social service programs. "One source after another of service or financial support for the disadvantaged has been withdrawn," said Jennifer R. Wolch, assistant professor and associate dean of the University of Southern California's School of Urban and Regional Planning. "As programs have been dismantled, the disadvantaged are tracked less by the health and mental health services system. They drift and are generally less well off. Some find temporary refuge in transient-renter areas or the remaining group homes. But more and more are ending up on the streets." [7]

Lack of Housing Options for the Poor

Another underlying cause of the rising number of homeless Americans is the deteriorating supply of housing for the poor. A 1982 report by the Community Service Society of New York estimated that every year about two-and-a-half million Americans are involuntarily displaced from their residences because of renovation, redevelopment or rent increases — victims of housing restoration projects in inner cities. "At the same time," the report said, "a half-million units of low-rent dwellings are lost each year through the combined forces of conversion, abandonment, inflation, arson and demolition.... When it is added that the major victims of mass development are the poor, those with the fewest resources to absorb new hardships or to recover in its wake, it is no mystery that the ranks of the homeless continue to swell." [8]

The problem of housing the very poor has been compounded by the nationwide shortage of public housing. In Washington,

---

[6] Lester M. Salamon and Alan J. Abramson, "The Federal Budget and the Non-profit Sector," 1982, p. xvii.

[7] Quoted in the Gardena, Calif., *News Tribune*, April 22, 1982.

[8] Community Service Society of New York, "One Year Later: The Homeless Poor in New York City, 1982," June 1982, p. 3. Also see National Housing Law Project, "Displacement: How to Fight It," 1982, and "Housing Restoration and Displacement," *E.R.R.*, 1978 Vol. II, pp. 861-880.

Choosing the Streets

A young drifter at the Men's Shelter in Manhattan told *New York* magazine late last year what he thought of the city-run facility. "This is a bad place to be," he said. "The guards beat you up for no reason at all. You never know what the guy next to you is going to pull. You're much better off in the streets."

No one knows how many homeless persons choose to sleep outdoors rather than inside private and public shelters or skid-row flophouses. Some avoid the shelters because they fear violence; some stay away because they distrust any sort of organized activity. Some private groups have reacted to this situation by implementing special programs to try to reach out to the homeless who refuse to come to them. Some groups deliver food and clothing directly to the homeless. Some tailor their operations so that they do not resemble institutional, government-run facilities.

The Community for Creative Non-Violence in Washington, D.C., has taken the concept one step further. The group, which claims that government-run shelters for the homeless are "destructive and dehumanizing," will not accept funds from government agencies. "You can't get government money and not become a replication of the government," said spokesman Mitch Snyder. "We are not about to replicate institutions and approaches which we consider to be utterly bankrupt, morally and in every other way."

D.C., where the apartment vacancy rate is very low, some 8,500 families are on a waiting list for public housing. Many are forced to live in motel rooms at public expense while they wait for available housing. Analysts say there also is a growing shortage of cheap rooming houses and hotels, "flophouses," in the nation's big cities. Some have been abandoned, others are being converted into luxury apartments. Rising unemployment has compounded the situation. "The single male who used to pick up enough casual labor to pay for a low-cost room cannot even do that anymore," said City Commissioner Margaret Strachan of Portland, Ore. "Those jobs have dried up, too." [9]

Nationwide Emergence of the 'New Poor'

These factors — deinstitutionalization, budget cuts, the housing shortage, high unemployment — have brought about a fundamental change in the makeup of the nation's homeless. "Fifteen years ago we used to see the classic Bowery bum — the white, middle-aged alcoholic," said Bonnie Stone, an assistant deputy administrator for New York City's Human Resources Administration. "This has radically changed. The people who show up are quite mixed. Now there are a large number of mentally ill people and younger people who have a variety of

---

[9] Quoted in *U.S. News & World Report*, March 8, 1982, p. 61.

problems." [10] According to the Community Service Society of New York, "At no time since the Depression has the homeless population represented so wide a cross-section of American society as it does today." [11]

Included in this cross-section are the so-called "new poor" — formerly employed persons who have lost their jobs, run out of money and unemployment benefits and lost their homes. The group includes more persons under age 40, more blacks, more women and more children than ever before. Social service workers say it is not uncommon for entire families to live in automobiles or in tents pitched alongside highways or in park campsites.

"There's probably one-and-a-half to two times as many people on the streets now as there were a year ago."

Mitch Snyder, Community
for Creative Non-Violence

Newspaper accounts have described families living in county, state and national parks from Maryland to California. Jean Forbath, director of Share Our Selves, an emergency center in Costa Mesa, Calif., recently described the plight of a family living in their car in a California campground. "The father worked in a factory days and the mother worked in a fast-food restaurant at night. They had four children and they made $30 a month too much to get welfare help. Welfare told them if they continue to keep their children in a car in the park, they would take the children from them. It's a horrible situation, a Catch-22." [12]

Severe economic problems are even hitting once prosperous families. "We're getting calls from people out in the suburbs who own their own homes, who are very well established and settled who have been out of work for months and months and want us to take them out early in the morning and show them how to scavenge food out of [grocery store] trash bins," said Mitch Snyder of the Community for Creative Non-Violence, which this year successfully lobbied Washington-area supermarkets to donate, rather than dump, their leftover food to soup kitchens and other charities.

---

[10] Quoted in *The New York Times,* Sept. 23, 1982.
[11] Community Service Society of New York, *op. cit.,* p. 6.
[12] Quoted in *Safety Network,* the newsletter of the New York Coalition for the Homeless, national edition, September 1982.

Past American Experiences

THE HOMELESS have always been part of the American scene. At all times in the nation's history there have been vagrants, drifters and mentally and physically disabled persons surviving as well as they could without permanent housing. The first skid rows — rundown sections of cities with cheap hotels ("flophouses") — began appearing across the country in the decade following the Civil War. They got their name from Seattle's Skid Road, a wide, hilly street along which horses skidded logs to a saw mill. "The street was inhabited by lumberjacks who lived in a community of saloons, brothels and flophouses — all the institutions regularly associated with the homeless man," wrote Harvey A. Siegal and James A. Inciardi.[13]

Skid rows were in existence in most American cities by the Panic of 1873.[14] Many thousands of men thrown out of work by that economic depression took to the road, following the railroads out West to look for work as loggers, miners, farmhands, or in oil fields, construction sites and canneries. Much of this work was temporary, and the workers were forced to move from town to town to gain employment. These migratory workers, some of whom were skilled laborers, came to be known as *hobos* — as opposed to *tramps* who migrated along the rails but had no desire to work, and *bums* who did not migrate and did not look for work.

Devastating Effect of Great Depression

During the economic prosperity of the 1920s the number of homeless people declined. But the next decade plunged the nation into its worst depression in history and "made transience a national way of life."[15] By 1933 nearly a quarter of the labor force — from 12 to 15 million Americans — was out of work. Many of the unemployed faced extraordinarily grim living conditions. "Millions stayed alive by living like animals," wrote historian William Manchester. "In the Pennsylvania countryside they were eating wild weed-roots and dandelions; in Kentucky they chewed violet tops, wild onions, forget-me-nots, wild lettuce, and weeds which heretofore had been left to grazing cattle.... Whole families were seen plunging into refuse dumps, gnawing at bones and watermelon rinds...."[16]

---

[13] Harvey A. Siegal and James A. Inciardi, "The Demise of Skid Row," *Society*, January-February 1982, p. 39. Siegal is an associate professor in the Department of Medicine in Society at the Washington State University School of Medicine. Inciardi is professor of criminal justice at the University of Delaware.

[14] The best-known skid rows at the turn of the century were the "Main Stem" in Chicago and New York's infamous Bowery.

[15] Siegal and Inciardi, *op. cit.*, p. 40.

[16] William Manchester, *The Glory and the Dream: A Narrative History of America, 1932-1972* (1974), p. 42.

Thousands of Americans found themselves on bread lines, in soup kitchens or otherwise dependent on charities for food, clothing and shelter. In the cities, many wound up living in subway corridors, abandoned construction sites, or "Hoovervilles," makeshift shantytowns derisively named for President Hoover. Hoovervilles sprang up on the edges of cities across the nation. Two were located in New York City, one below fashionable Riverside Drive, and the other in Central Park, within easy view of the stately buildings bordering the park on Fifth Avenue and Central Park West. A New York *Daily News* photograph of the time showed a woman "at home" in a cardboard box on Park Place near City Hall.

The number of homeless and unemployed dropped significantly as the United States began pulling out of the Depression in the late 1930s. Those who remained homeless in the economic boom years during and after World War II tended to be middle-aged male alcoholics and persons with deep emotional and psychological problems. Alcoholism continued to be the dominant characteristic of skid-row men until the late 1950s when deinstitutionalization of mental patients began changing the character of the homeless population *(see p. 104)*

Sociologists now say that skid rows are largely things of the past. " 'Skid Row' is no longer a geographically confined way of life," noted a recent report by the Community Service Society of New York. "The subways, train and bus depots, doorways and abandoned buildings, public parks and loading docks, alleyways and sidewalks of the entire city are home for thousands of New Yorkers each night." [17]

Spread of Problem to Sun Belt States

The homeless are showing up in large numbers in places where they never made much impact in the past — in the Sun Belt states. Unemployed workers and their families have flocked to cities in the Southwest and West in search of work. Many have ended up broke and homeless. "Austin [Texas] officials cope daily with transients living in cars, looking through garbage cans, hanging around in office buildings," according to the report issued by the U.S. Conference of Mayors. "In Houston, transients are living in their cars on freeways and in the parks.... It is estimated that in Tulsa ... there may be up to 1,000 people living in cars, trailers and tents, in camping grounds or in the woods.... There are now between 200 and 300 people living under bridges in the city." [18]

The problem is that the Sun Belt states are finally feeling the

---

[17] Community Service Society of New York, *op. cit.*, pp. 1-2.
[18] U.S. Conference of Mayors, *op. cit.*, p. 18.

effects of the recession. In Texas, for example, the unemployment rate was 8.4 percent in September 1982, up from 5.5 percent in November 1981. The 8.4 rate is the highest since the state began keeping such figures in 1970, and may be the highest in the state since the Depression. The Texas Department of Human Resources reported a 22 percent increase in the number of applications for AFDC (Aid for Families with Dependent Children) payments and a 26 percent increase in the number of applications for food stamps last summer compared to the previous summer. State welfare officials do not keep tabs on the impact of out-of-state job seekers on these totals, but they believe that newcomers are a significant factor in the increase in persons seeking welfare.

"At no time since the Depression has the homeless population represented so wide a cross-section of American society as it does today."

Community Service Society
of New York

Even though the number of applications for state welfare and food stamps has risen greatly, the number of persons on Texas welfare rolls has not increased significantly. This is due to the state's strict eligibility standards. The state's AFDC program, which is funded solely by the Texas Legislature, allows payments only to children of low-income families without the support of one or both parents due to the parent's absence or disability. The average monthly payment for families on AFDC in Texas is only $104. The national average is $277.

The state Department of Human Resources recently issued a pamphlet trying to dissuade job seekers from coming to Texas. Entitled "Dead Broke in Texas," it has been sent to welfare agencies in other states. "People are pouring into Texas seeking jobs, but here, as in other states, jobs may not be easy to find," the pamphlet warned. "Too often these people's savings run out before work is found.... The Texas Department of Human Resources wants to help.... But the fact is that DHR doesn't have the money, staff or authority to give all these people all the help they need." The pamphlet pleaded with local communities to help those the department could not reach. "Desperate people are in need of more aid than DHR can furnish," it concluded.

Sources of Homeless Relief

DOES GOVERNMENT have an obligation to feed, house and shelter the homeless? If not, should the task be left to private, volunteer efforts? Those questions have not yet been fully answered by American society. A few states and localities have increased public spending to help the homeless. But the national trend is in the opposite direction. The Reagan administration is leading a movement to cut back government social service programs and encourage private, voluntary efforts on behalf of the poor, including the homeless (see p. 105)

Federal cutbacks have placed an added burden on local and state governments. Robert Trobe, New York City's Human Resources Administration's deputy commissioner in charge of shelters for the homeless, said local and state governments are "up against a very clear federal policy to limit the number of people eligible for assistance. It seems clear that they [the federal government] want to reduce their responsibility for these people as much as possible." [19]

One response to the decline in public funds has been the formation of private groups that work in a variety of ways to implement humane programs for the homeless. The National Coalition for the Homeless, which gives legal assistance to the homeless and their advocates, was formed last April. The coalition's headquarters in New York City serves as an information clearinghouse and gives assistance to local social service agencies, private charities, churches, community shelters and others interested in working with the homeless.

Recent Improvements in New York City

The New York City Coalition for the Homeless has been instrumental in getting that city to do significantly more for the homeless. Robert M. Hayes, a lawyer who heads the coalition, began working with homeless persons four years ago, shortly after graduating from law school. What prompted a Wall Street securities lawyer to get involved with the homeless? "Idle curiosity," Hayes said. "I went into the flops and the shelters and was shocked. I started talking to the bureaucrats and the legislators and got absolutely nowhere. So I began researching the law and finally turned to the third branch of government as the court of last resort for these folks." [20]

Hayes filed a lawsuit in the fall of 1979 on behalf of six homeless men alleging they were forced to live in unsafe, over-

---

[19] Quoted in *The New York Times*, May 3, 1982.
[20] Quoted by Randy Young in *New York* magazine, Dec. 21, 1981, pp. 28-29.

Profile of Homeless Men*

Age: Median age: about 40
    About 75 percent under 50
    Newly homeless: average age mid-30s
            25 percent below 30

Ethnicity: About 60 percent black
    20-25 percent white
    About 10 percent Hispanic

Education: 28 percent completed high school

Residence:
    38 percent native to area
    75 percent lived in area for at least one year

Drinking Problem:
    14 percent admit to alcoholism
    25 percent show evidence of alcoholism

Reasons for Seeking Shelter:
    25 percent recently unemployed
    14 percent displaced from housing
    10 percent released from mental institutions

*Data taken from surveys of homeless men in city shelters commissioned by New York City's Human Resources Administration. Source: Community Service Society of New York.

crowded and unsanitary conditions in New York's city-run shelters. Hayes maintained that the city shelter system was not living up to a provision in New York's state constitution that guarantees "aid, care and support of the needy." The upshot of the suit was an August 1981 consent order issued by the New York State Supreme Court in which New York City agreed to provide clean and safe shelter to all homeless persons who desired it, and to alleviate overcrowded conditions at its homeless shelters.

The city's shelters now have more than 4,000 beds for the homeless, compared to about 1,800 beds in 1978. The seven city-run shelters provide three hot meals a day, showers, delousing equipment, clean clothing, as well as mental health, medical and social services on a 24-hour-a-day basis. New York City now spends about $27 million a year to care for its homeless, compared to about $8 million in 1978. But the Coalition for the Homeless maintains that city shelters still are too large — some have rooms with 50 or more beds — and dangerous. The overcrowded conditions breed violent crimes; knifings, beatings and muggings are common occurrences. The coalition wants the city to invest in smaller, neighborhood shelters where the homeless can be treated individually and with dignity.

Last July, New York Gov. Hugh L. Carey signed a bill into law that could help make available more beds in smaller facilities. The new law provides about $4 million for the renovation of single-room occupancy hotels into residences for the very poor and homeless. Two million dollars goes directly to nonprofit organizations to do the renovation. The other $2 million will come in matching funds from municipalities. About half of the renovation work is expected to take place in New York City.

The state also will provide $1 million in matching funds to go toward acquiring and renovating shelters for the homeless. Carey also announced a $276,000 grant to the Vera Institute of Justice to develop an apartment hotel demonstration project for low-income housing and a $244,000 grant to the Community Services Society for a technical center to help other non-profit groups set up shelters for the homeless.

Examples of Successful Local Efforts

Private groups around the nation are running successful programs to help the homeless. One of the most widely praised is the St. Francis Residence in New York City, a 103-bed facility set up not as a shelter, but as a permanent residence for the very poor. The residence, a former run-down welfare hotel, was purchased two years ago by the St. Francis Friends of the Poor. It spent $550,000 for the building and $300,000 for renovations. Nearly all of the building's residents are former mental patients who receive Social Security and welfare payments. They pay $140 a month rent. The residence provides some meals, and has a professional staff to help the residents deal with financial problems and the Social Security system.

The biggest problem with the residence, said program director Al Pettis, is that all its rooms are filled and the staff must turn away prospective guests daily. "We spend the days turning people away and we don't often have an alternative because there are so few places where people can live on $300 a month in New York," Pettis told Editorial Research Reports. St. Francis soon will open another facility, a 125-bed residence. "Our second building is a little bigger," Pettis said, "but it'll get full and we'll be in the same position."

The Detroit Coalition on Temporary Shelter (COTS) is another group that works with the homeless. Last July, COTS — a consortium of churches, civic groups, social agencies and business leaders — opened an emergency 40-bed shelter in property donated by the Episcopal Church. The shelter, which is staffed by Franciscan friars, was filled 48 hours after it opened its doors. COTS officials are meeting with city leaders to try to set up plans to open a second shelter to house about 1,000 homeless adults.

"We spend the days turning people away and we don't often have an alternative because there are so few places where people can live on $300 a month in New York."

Al Pettis, program director,
St. Francis Residence
in New York City

Another successful local effort on behalf of the homeless is the Pine Street Inn in downtown Boston, which is run with state funds as well as voluntary contributions. The original Pine Street Inn opened in 1916 as a low-income housing facility. Today's inn, a short distance away from the original site, is a shelter for the homeless managed by the Association of Boston Urban Priests. The inn, which operates round the clock, has 55 full-time, paid staff members and provides nightly shelter for 300 men and 50 women.

Pine Street Inn opens its doors every evening, and gives out rooms on a first-come, first-served basis. The inn provides laundry facilities where clothing is cleaned and fumigated during the night. Donated clothes also are available. There are showers and clean beds in a dormitory-like setting. Volunteer groups provide hot evening meals, and the inn serves breakfast.

Persons with medical problems are permitted to stay at the inn during the day, as are those who make appointments to see counselors or volunteer nurses. "Our counselors are, in a non-threatening way, available to guests just to talk to them and find out what's going on with them, why they're in our shelter, what their problems might be and ... to tie them up with existing services in the community," said Paul Sullivan, Pine Street's director since 1969.

During winter months when Pine Street's beds are filled, overflow guests are permitted to sleep on the floors, benches or tables. The inn also runs a program in which guests are given the chance to take jobs in the building under the supervision of counselors. Working guests are paid a dollar an hour, given shelter, allowed to eat in the staff dining room, and provided job counseling. "I'd like to say it [the job program] was a perfect program," Sullivan said. "Some people do make it and others don't make it. But it allows for human nature. Some people will be here for a long while. And others will use it for a short while and be able to get out."

At last count there were about 60 food pantries and soup kitchens run by religious groups and other private organizations in Washington, D.C. SOME (So Others May Eat), a private, charitable group which provides free health care and counseling, has a soup kitchen currently feeding about 600 persons a day. The group also runs Martha's Table, a special soup kitchen for children which provides about 100 evening meals daily. SOME recently opened a traveling soup kitchen called McKenna's Wagon, which is run by 12 volunteers and distributes donated and purchased food in areas of the city where homeless persons congregate.

The Community for Creative Non-Violence *(see p. 103)* began with a handful of student activists in the late 1960s and now has about 25 full-time volunteers working with the very poor and homeless. CCNV provides free meals of stew and salad to about 1,000 persons daily. The group distributes donated clothing to about 100 needy persons a week, runs a free medical clinic and has plans to open an infirmary for the homeless who are sick but not ill enough to be hospitalized. CCNV also runs a series of drop-in centers where the homeless can take showers, get cleaned up, pick up donated clothing, wash their clothes or simply rest.

CCNV also stages peaceful protests and hunger strikes to draw attention to the problems of the poor and homeless. Last year the group erected a small tent city called "Reaganville" in Lafayette Park across Pennsylvania Avenue from the White House. The tents served as shelter for as many as a dozen people, and on Thanksgiving Day CCNV volunteers served dinner there to about 600 homeless persons. The tent city also had a display of 539 crosses, each representing a homeless person who died of exposure or similar causes over the previous five years in 11 areas of the country where such figures are compiled by church groups.[21] The crosses were planted in the park on Dec. 28, Holy Innocents Day, the Christian feast day commemorating the biblical account of the slaughter of the children of Bethlehem at King Herod's orders.

---

[21] The areas are Atlanta, Baltimore, Chicago, Connecticut, Dayton, Ohio; Massachusetts, New York City and state, Philadelphia, Virginia, Washington, D.C., and Wisconsin.

**Protest organized last year by the Community
for Creative Non-Violence in Washington, D.C.**

Reaganville was torn down on March 20, 1982, at the end of winter. But CCNV plans to build two more tent cities this year — a group of 40 tents on the Mall between the Capitol and the Washington Monument, to be named "Congressional Village," and 20 tents in Lafayette Park called once again "Reaganville." CCNV member Mitch Snyder told Editorial Research Reports that the two villages are ways of "both communicating the raw increase in numbers" of homeless persons, as well as "the deepened complicity of Congress in the situation." The group has filed suit in federal court for permission to erect the villages on the first day of winter, Dec. 21.

On Oct. 24, 1982, tent cities called "Reagan Ranches" were erected in several cities by members of church, labor and action groups under the direction of the Association of Community Organizations for Reform Now (ACORN). The encampments, intended to call attention to the effects of President Reagan's economic policies, were erected in Lansing, Mich.; Columbus, Ohio; St. Louis, Atlanta, Houston, Pittsburgh, Philadelphia, Boston and New Orleans. More than two dozen additional encampments will be set up in the coming weeks.

Problem of Volunteer Worker 'Burnout'

More and more volunteers are coming forward to work with the homeless. They are motivated by compassion for the plight of the very poor, and usually begin their work with great expectations of providing significant help. But in many cases this early ardor quickly sours when volunteers see firsthand the size and complexity of the problem. Kim Hopper of the Community Service Society in New York told Editorial Research Reports that many of the volunteers exhibit "a growing sense of despondency" as they get involved with the homeless. "While their willingness to do something hasn't flagged, their understanding of what they can accomplish has been severely checked and chastened by what they've seen in the past year or so," he said.

A case in point is an aborted effort to feed and shelter homeless persons undertaken last winter by St. Paul's Episcopal Church in Washington, D.C. The church's effort began when a parishioner started delivering food to 15 homeless men who lived on steam grates near the U.S. State Department. The church soon expanded the program, taking some homeless into the parish hall for overnight shelter and starting a once-a-week sandwich line. The feeding effort soon became a nightly program. When the church started feeding the homeless in March, five persons showed up. By August, when the program ended, the church was feeding about 140 persons a night.

What caused the program to end? "It was not financial," said volunteer Beverly Reece. "It closed because we became victims of our own success." [22] The church's volunteer workers, who had expected to feed about 50 homeless persons a night, were overwhelmed by the number who showed up. "The crush of people meant that we could not reach out to individuals to find out who they were and what had brought them to our doors," Reece said. "There was no chance to do the personal ministry that had been part of the grate patrol and the shelter." Nor were the volunteers prepared to deal with the social misfits and mentally ill individuals who showed up at the church.

---

[22] Writing in *The Washington Post*, Aug. 19, 1982.

The Homeless: Growing National Problem

Despite such failures and the growing phenomenon of volunteer burnout, those who work with the homeless see a growing interest by the public in the problem. Robert Hayes of the New York Coalition for the Homeless said that he is encouraged by "the new swelling of public support for the homeless. Once people learn that there are so many homeless, and that they do not want to live on the streets, there is a strong insistence that they be sheltered. Americans are not willing to see old people living in cardboard boxes. That's true in New York, a place that Americans think of as being hard-hearted. But it's a response that I hear across the country today." [23] The question remains, though: Will public compassion translate into meaningful action to help the hundreds of thousands of homeless Americans make it through the winter?

[23] Quoted by syndicated columnist Neal Peirce in the *Los Angeles Times*, Sept. 24, 1982.

Selected Bibliography

Books

Auletta, Ken, *The Underclass,* Random House, 1982.
Bahr, H., *Skid Row: An Introduction to Disaffiliation,* Oxford, 1973.
Bogue, Donald J., *Skid Row in American Cities,* Community and Family Service Center, University of Chicago, 1963.
Donovan, James G., *The Politics of Poverty,* Bobbs-Merrill, 1976.
Halpern, Joseph, et al., *The Myths of Deinstitutionalization,* Westview Press, 1980.
Johnson, M. Bruce, ed., *Resolving the Housing Crisis,* Ballinger, 1982.
Rich, Richard C., ed., *The Politics of Urban Public Services,* Lexington, 1981.
Rousseau, Ann Marie, *Shopping Bag Ladies: Homeless Women Speak About Their Lives,* Pilgrim Press, 1982.
Salamon, Lester M. and Alan J. Abramson, *The Federal Budget and the Non-profit Sector,* Urban Institute Press, 1982.

Articles

Bruns, Roger, "Hobo," *American History,* January 1982.
Chaze, William L., "Street People: Adrift and Alone in America," *U.S. News & World Report,* March 8, 1982.
Hacker, Andrew, "The Lower Depths," *The New York Review of Books,* Aug. 12, 1982.
Morganthau, Tom, et al., "Down and Out in America," *Newsweek,* March 15, 1982.
"Off the Street and Out of the Cold," *Time,* Feb. 8, 1982.
Safety Network, newsletter of the N.Y. Coalition for the Homeless, selected issues.
Siegal, Harvey A. and James A. Inciardi, "The Demise of Skid Row," *Society,* January-February 1982.
Young, Randy, "The Homeless: The Shame of the City," *New York,* Dec. 21, 1981.

Reports and Studies

Community Service Society of New York, "One Year Later: The Homeless Poor in New York City, 1982," June 1982; "Public Lives/Public Spaces," March 1981.
Editorial Research Reports: "Mental Health Care Reappraisal," 1982 Vol. II, p. 609; "Housing the Poor," 1980 Vol. II, p. 801; "Housing Restoration and Displacement," 1978 Vol. II, p. 861.
Texas Department of Human Resources, "Dead Broke in Texas?" 1982; "A Matter of Facts: Confronting the Myths About Welfare in Texas," 1982.
United States Conference of Mayors, "Human Services in FY 1982: Shrinking Resources in Troubled Times, A Survey of Human Services Officials in the Nation's Cities," October 1982.

Cover illustration by Staff Artist Robert Redding; photos p. 105 and p. 113 by Barth Falkenberg, staff photographer, *The Christian Science Monitor;* photo p. 117 by Jim Wells.

HISPANIC AMERICA

by

Mary Barberis

July 30
1 9 8 2

Editor's Note: In 1984, for the third straight year, Congress is trying to enact a complete revision of the nation's immigration laws. But America's Hispanic community remains opposed, and its opposition — decisive in 1982 and 1983 — is expected to prevail in this presidential election year. The Senate in 1983 passed its version of immigration legislation, known as the Simpson-Mazzoli bill *(see footnote 37, p. 136)*. But Speaker Thomas P. O'Neill Jr. kept the bill from coming to a vote in the House. He contended that if it passed, President Reagan might veto the measure to win favor with Hispanic voters — a charge that the White House promptly denied.

Senate and House versions of the bill, though differing in some respects, would impose sanctions against employers who hire illegal aliens. Hispanics say they fear employers would stop hiring them to avoid hiring an illegal alien accidentally. Both bills would give legal status to many of the illegal aliens already in this country. The Congressional Hispanic Caucus — lawmakers of Hispanic descent — are reported to be developing a bill to offer in Congress as an alternative to the Simpson-Mazzoli bill.

HISPANIC AMERICA

THIRTY years ago the term Hispanic referred primarily to a few million Mexican-Americans residing in the southwestern United States. Today, Hispanics, with their distinctive heritages — Puerto Rican, Cuban, Mexican, and Central and South American — have settled in every state of the Union. While they are still concentrated in such states as New Mexico, Texas and California, the number of Hispanics in other parts of the country has grown substantially; for example, almost one in 10 people in New York and Florida are Hispanic. Having demonstrated their permanence as a distinct cultural group, Spanish-speaking Americans are becoming accepted as part of American society, creating their own neighborhoods and influencing the structure and development of the communities in which they live.

According to the 1980 Census, there are 14.6 million Hispanics in the United States, or 6.4 percent of the total population.[1] Hispanics are the second largest minority group, after blacks, and the fastest growing. While the total population of the United States increased by just under 50 percent between 1950 and 1980, the Hispanic population surged 270 percent. Part of this growth was fueled by high immigration — legal and illegal — and part by the large families typical of most Hispanic groups.

Perhaps most significantly, Hispanics constitute a youthful population, with much of its future ahead of it — schooling, employment, household formation and parenting — promising not only rapid numerical growth, but an increasingly important role in the economic and social structure of the United States. While precise projections are impossible, since they depend on how long the current high growth rate is sustained, some observers expect this collective group to surpass blacks as the country's largest minority, making them an even more visible element of Amerian society and further contributing to what is increasingly referred to as the "Hispanicization" of the United States.

---

[1] Due to difficulties in defining "Hispanics" and in estimating the number of illegal aliens of Hispanic origin, there is controversy over the number of Hispanics living in the United States. The 14.6 million figure refers to persons who identified themselves as Hispanic on the 1980 Census questionnaire.

It has only been during the last two decades that public attention has focused on "Hispanics." Before, people talked about Puerto Ricans in New York or Cubans in Miami, but the umbrella term Hispanic, which refers neither to race, nationality nor ethnic group, is a relatively recent invention, coined by the federal government, to encompass the myriad of Spanish-speaking people living throughout the United States. Concern in the 1960s for groups suffering disadvantages and discrimination in U.S. society brought "Spanish-Americans" to the national headlines as they were one of the minorities targeted by equal opportunity measures. When, for the first time, the 1970 Census questionnaire asked people about their "Spanish origin," Hispanics began to capture increasing attention in national and local statistics.

New Population Patterns of Hispanics

Spanish, the nation's second-most used language after English, is spoken by 11.1 million people, almost half of those who speak a language other than English at home.[2] While the various ethnic groups described as Hispanic usually do not overlap with each other and remain clustered in a few states, these patterns are changing. Today, every state has some Hispanic residents. They form over 5 percent of the populations of Arizona, Colorado, New York, Florida, New Jersey and Illinois; about 20 percent of the population in Texas and California; and over one-third in New Mexico. Fifteen states have Hispanic populations of at least 100,000 *(see map, p. 125)* and 25 U.S. cities contain 50,000 or more Hispanics *(see box, p. 127)*

About 60 percent of the Hispanic population is comprised of Mexican Americans who live primarily in the Southwest, but who, like other Hispanic groups, are spreading to states with little tradition of Spanish-speaking residents, such as Illinois. Since 1950, Mexican Americans have been primarily native born; those who are U.S.-born are known as Chicanos. California has the largest concentration of Chicanos of any state.

Although perceived by many as rural, nine out of 10 Hispanics live in cities. The urban lifestyle is particularly prevalent among Puerto Ricans and Cubans, but in no state are less than half the Hispanic residents city dwellers.[3] By 1970 there were more Puerto Ricans in New York City than in San Juan. Now totaling around 2 million nationwide, Puerto Ricans are still concentrated in the industrial Northeast, particularly New York City, but there are also substantial communities as far

---

[2] Refers to people over age 5. U.S. Bureau of the Census, "Provisional Estimates of Social, Economic, and Housing Characteristics," PHC80-S1-1, March 1982.

[3] "The Demographic and Socio-Economic Characteristics of the Hispanic Population in the United States, 1950-1980," Report to the Department of Health and Human Services, by Development Associates Inc. and Population Reference Bureau Inc., Jan. 18, 1982.

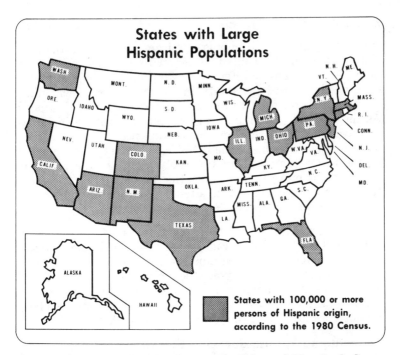

States with Large Hispanic Populations

States with 100,000 or more persons of Hispanic origin, according to the 1980 Census.

west as Chicago and in Rochester, Buffalo and Hartford, Conn. Across the United States today there are more than 30 cities with a Puerto Rican population of 5,000 or more.

Almost all the 1 million Cubans in the United States live in urban areas, chiefly in Florida and, to a lesser extent, New York. The Cuban impact on metropolitan Miami, their undisputed population center, has been credited with renewing the city's economy. Cubans have been largely responsible for turning Miami from a resort town to a year-round center of commerce with linkages throughout Latin America. Their cultural role has been just as important to Miami's transformation, although perhaps more controversial among the city's non-Hispanic population. Miami is an officially bilingual city and members of the tightly knit Cuban community are able to retain both language and traditions where they work, shop, bank and play. Cuban foods are readily available in the city, children are sent to Cuban-oriented private schools that have classes in Spanish, Cuban artists display their work, original plays in Spanish are performed by well-known Cuban actors, and a wide-ranging media serves the Spanish-speaking public. The arrival of the Cubans also has meant a tremendous expansion of the local Catholic Church.

Those Hispanics not of Mexican, Cuban or Puerto Rican origin (one in five of the total)[4] are more evenly distributed

---

[4] U.S. Bureau of the Census, "Current Population Survey Estimate," March 1980.

throughout the nation. Immigrants from every Latin American country live in the United States, with Dominicans, Colombians, Argentinians and Ecuadorans forming the largest groups. Continued political instability in Central America will likely increase the flow from El Salvador, Guatemala and Nicaragua. As the Hispanic community's geographical diversity increases, heterogenous mixes of Spanish-speaking peoples are becoming more common in some of the nation's cities. New York may still be the prime example, but Chicago's variety of Latino ethnic groups helps make Cook County the nation's fourth largest in terms of Hispanic population, after the counties of Los Angeles, Dade (Miami) and Bexar (San Antonio, Texas).

In San Francisco, the largest Hispanic group is from Nicaragua, followed by El Salvador, then Mexico. While different Hispanic neighborhoods within the same city usually retain their distinct national flavor, they may share some cultural experiences. For example, the Catholic Church is credited with drawing people together in the "Mission District," where a large number of San Francisco's 83,000 Hispanics have settled.

Marketing to Spanish-Speaking Groups

A common theme among Hispanic communities throughout the United States is the intention to retain the Spanish language, at least in the home setting, and, many times, in the business sector as well. Many Spanish-speaking Americans share the sentiment expressed in a 1980 *New York Times* survey of Hispanics that Spanish is a "guardian of their identity." [5]

A fast-growing broadcast media serves the Hispanic community, including 13 full-time Spanish language television stations and 107 full-time Spanish language radio stations.[6] The Spanish language SIN Television Network now has close to 200 affiliates across the country. In addition to the dozens of national or regional magazines and 22 Spanish language newspapers[7] in the United States, a number of metropolitan dailies have either daily or weekly supplements (or regular columns) to serve their local Hispanic customers.

The non-Hispanic economic community is beginning to realize that the best way to reach this large and growing segment of the U.S. population is to use Spanish. In 1979 J. C. Penney Co. introduced catalogues with Spanish-language directions for its Hispanic customers in U.S.-Mexico border towns and in

---

[5] See story by David Vidal in *The New York Times,* May 13, 1980.
[6] Figures provided by the National Association of Spanish Broadcasters in Washington, D.C.
[7] Number listed in *Editor and Publisher International Yearbook, 1982.* Although the Spanish language print media is dwarfed by the English language establishment, two newspapers of some influence are El Paso's *El Continental,* established in 1929, and *La Opinion* in Los Angeles, established in 1977.

Cities With Hispanic Populations of 50,000 or More*

New York, N.Y.	1,405,957	Hialeah, Fla.	107,908
Los Angeles, Calif.	815,989	Denver, Colo.	91,937
Chicago, Ill.	422,061	Santa Ana, Calif.	90,646
San Antonio, Texas	421,774	Laredo, Texas	85,076
Houston, Texas	281,224	San Francisco, Calif.	83,373
El Paso, Texas	265,819	Tucson, Ariz.	82,189
Miami, Fla.	194,087	Brownsville, Texas	71,139
San Jose, Calif.	140,574	Austin, Texas	64,766
San Diego, Calif.	130,610	Philadelphia, Pa.	63,570
Phoenix, Ariz.	115,572	Newark, N.J.	61,254
Albuquerque, N.M.	112,084	Fresno, Calif.	51,489
Dallas, Texas	111,082	Long Beach, Calif.	50,700
Corpus Christi, Texas	108,175		

*As of April 1980.

Source: U.S. Bureau of the Census, "Standard Metropolitan Statistical Areas and Their Central Cities by Race and Spanish Origin, 1980."

Southern California. Other companies, like Nabisco, Pepsi and Buster Brown Shoes, are advertising on such Spanish-language radio stations as WJIT-AM in New York. A growing segment of U.S. business is discovering that Hispanics are "prime consumers," who are young, have large families, spend a large proportion of their disposable income on groceries and clothing and display what advertising agencies call "brand loyalty."

Advertising expenditures in the Hispanic market total only $100 million to $150 million annually, or less than one-tenth of 1 percent of the overall U.S. advertising market. But *The New York Times* and *Newsweek* magazine recently ran articles describing the "boom" in Hispanic advertising and most ad executives predict that the courtship of Hispanic consumers will continue to grow.[8] Many companies have already made significant strides in meeting Hispanics' special needs. For example, when grocery chains like Safeway in California and Jewel in Chicago realized they were losing ground to neighborhood shops ("bodegas") they began to stock tropical fruits and vegetables, such as varieties of chilies, and special cuts of meat. Mattel, Inc. is even marketing a Hispanic version of the Barbie doll.

In recent years a number of Madison Avenue advertising firms have sharpened their Hispanic marketing talents. J. Walter Thompson has an "Hispania" unit, Young and Rubicam a "Bravo" unit, and other agencies are following suit. There are now at least 25 agencies in the country specializing in Spanish language advertising.[9]

[8] See story by Philip Dougherty in *The New York Times*, April 8, 1982, and "Learning the Hispanic Hustle," *Newsweek*, May 17, 1982. Also see "U.S. Hispanics — A Marketing Profile," National Association of Spanish Broadcasters and Strategy Research Corp., 1980.
[9] Greg Johnson, "La Administracion En Un Medio Ambiente Hispanico," *Industry Week*, Jan. 25, 1982.

A parallel development is the growth of Hispanic-owned businesses serving their own communities and, increasingly, the "Anglo" population. The *Dallas-Ft. Worth Bilingual Yellow Pages and Tourist Guide* lists about 2,500 Hispanic-owned businesses. "Originally we thought of the directory as a way of keeping Hispanic dollars in the Hispanic community," publisher Michael Gonzalez said in a recent interview. "But we have evolved, like the whole Hispanic community is evolving, to support those who support us. Many Anglo dollars depend on our dollars."

In all there are approximately 250,000 Hispanic-owned businesses in the United States, generating $12 billion in sales. However, more than 90 percent of these businesses are small retail or service operations with fewer than 5 employees.[10] Some Hispanics believe there is a great deal of catching up to be done in the business world, pointing to the fact that only one *Fortune* 500 company, Coca-Cola of Atlanta, is headed by a Hispanic.[11]

Continued Poverty and Discrimination

This lack of prominence in the U.S. business establishment is one indication that Hispanics have not gained the affluence proportionate with their numbers. Only about 9 percent are in higher paying professional occupations compared with around 17 percent of the non-Spanish-origin work force. The median income of Hispanic families hovers around $16,400 compared to $22,390 for all families, and 26.5 percent of Hispanics are below the official poverty line.[12] Even Cubans and others of Central and South American origin, who are typically older, better educated and economically more secure than Puerto Ricans or Mexicans, fall below the income average for non-Hispanic whites.[13] Unemployment among Hispanics is 60 percent higher, partly because many Spanish-speaking Americans are clustered in blue-collar and semi-skilled jobs in construction, manufacturing and agriculture that suffer high rates of seasonal and cyclical unemployment.[14]

Often language and educational disadvantages keep Hispanics on the lower strata of economic life. Well over 2

---

[10] Statistics cited in *La Vida Americana*, reprints of a 13-part series published by *The Dallas Morning News* in December 1981.

[11] Cuban-born Roberto Goizueta is head of Coca-Cola.

[12] U.S. Bureau of the Census, "Money, Income and Poverty Status of Families and Persons in the United States: 1981," *Current Population Reports*, P-60, No. 134, July 1982.

[13] Hispanics are doing better than black Americans, however, according to a number of statistical measures of economic well-being. For example, their median family income is higher than the $13,270 earned by blacks. Although 26.5 percent of Hispanics are below the poverty level, the figure is 34.2 percent of blacks (and 11.1 percent of whites). The poverty line is raised each year to reflect price increases. In 1981 it was $9,287 for a family of four.

[14] An estimated 50 percent of the migrant farm-worker population in the United States is Spanish-speaking. However, migrant farm workers represent only a small part of the U.S. labor force, and only 3 percent of the U.S. Hispanic work force are categorized as migrant farm workers by the Census Bureau.

million adult Hispanics speak no English at all or do not speak it well.[15] Only about 45 percent of Hispanic adults over 25 have a high school diploma, according to the 1980 Census, compared to about 70 percent of the Anglo population. Fewer than 8 percent have four or more years of college, less than half the rate for non-Hispanic whites.

Thirty or forty years ago it was not uncommon for Anglo teachers to consider their Hispanic students "retarded" when the only problem was their inability to speak English. Though school systems have demonstrated an improved sensitivity to Hispanic students in recent years, discrimination, condescending attitudes to low-income students and language barriers remain common problems. Thus, while younger adults show significant improvement over their elders in educational attainment, Hispanic youths have a high school dropout rate averaging about 40 percent. For Puerto Ricans in New York City, the dropout rate is double that, according to statistics compiled by the New York City Board of Education.[16]

The same educational and language handicaps that hinder Hispanics promise to have a growing impact on the U.S. business community as American corporations come to rely increasingly on the Spanish-American population — whose median age is just over 23 compared to 30 for the total population — to fill entry-level positions in the coming years. Already, programs such as BOLT ("basic occupational language training"), sponsored by the Puerto Rican Forum in New York City, have been established to give Spanish-speaking employees the vocabulary they need to communicate with non-Hispanic co-workers and supervisors. Westinghouse — wishing to hire more Hispanic engineers — has launched a campaign of advertising and seminars to motivate Spanish-American teen-agers to enter technical fields. In order to deal with day-to-day problems that arise when the work force has not had English training, some companies in heavily Hispanic areas are hiring bilingual personnel for on-the-job translations and making sure their plant safety signs and company rule books are printed in both English and Spanish.

---

[15] Refers to age 18-plus. See "Provisional Estimates of Social, Economic and Housing Characteristics," *op. cit.*, Table P-2.

[16] Puerto Ricans rate below other Hispanic groups in a number of key socioeconomic areas. A 1980 study of the Puerto Rican community by Puerto Rican Forum, Inc., found that Puerto Ricans were worse off than they were two decades before, with family income dropping from 71 percent of the national average in 1959 to 47 percent in 1979. The average Puerto Rican's income was lower than that of the average black and less than half the national average. For an overview of the socioeconomic dilemma faced by Puerto Ricans, see *Puerto Ricans in the Continental United States: An Uncertain Future*, Report of the U.S. Commission on Civil Rights, October 1976.

Roots of Hispanics in U.S.

THE HISTORY of Hispanics in the United States starts in the Southwest. Over 250 years before Mexico signed the 1848 Treaty of Guadalupe Hidalgo relinquishing the northern half of its national territory to the United States, Spaniards, and later Mexicans, had settled in what are now the states of Texas, New Mexico, Arizona, Colorado and California.[17] If asked, the inhabitants of these states will sometimes still distinguish themselves as either "Hispanos," Spanish-American descendants of the early settlers, "Chicanos," Mexican-Americans who were born in the United States but have close ties to Mexico, or "Mexicano" immigrants.

The first real Mexican migration, which began with the building of the railroads across the American Southwest, resulted in about 500,000 Mexicans living in the United States by 1900. The vast majority of today's Mexican-origin population is the result of migration in the 20th century. The immigrant waves of the first quarter of the century brought almost three quarters of a million registered immigrants between 1901 and 1930. It ended during the Great Depression with the systematic deportation of over 400,000 Mexicans (including many who were born in the United States) who became both scapegoat and safety valve for the economic ills of the Southwest.

While permanent immigration picked up again to 61,000 in the 1940s, wartime labor shortages spurred a series of agreements between the United States and Mexico known as the "bracero" program under which large numbers of temporary workers were transported north. The program, supposed to end with the war, lasted until Congress refused to renew it in 1964. Braceros — 4.8 million over the life of the program — worked in at least 38 states, with the majority picking fruit and vegetables in the Southwest.[18]

Of the 2.3 million Spanish surnamed people residing in the United States in 1950, 45 percent lived in Texas and 33 percent lived in California. Approximately 70 percent of the U.S. Hispanic population was of Mexican origin in 1950,[19] though legal

---

[17] After the war with Mexico, Hispanic landowners had difficulty protecting both their property and personal rights under the new government. The history of the Southwest is fraught with often bitter resentment among Hispanics about the methods used by unscrupulous "Gringos" to separate Spanish settlers from their land. See Bernard Valdez, "The History of Spanish Americans," *Selected Reading Materials on the Mexican and Spanish American* (1969).

[18] For background information, see Congressional Quarterly, *Congress and the Nation Vol. I* (1965), pp. 762-767.

[19] "The Demographic and Socioeconomic Characteristics of the Hispanic Population in the United States, 1950-1980," op. cit.

immigration from Mexico amounted to only about 6,800 a year. Comparatively high birthrates and increasing levels of immigration combined to keep the proportion of Mexicans high.[20] But because of postwar immigration from Puerto Rico and the large influx of post-revolutionary Cubans, the Mexican share of the total Hispanic population dropped to 60 percent by the late 1970s. It may well rise again, however, because their birthrates (especially for new arrivals from Mexico) remain high, and, at least for now, no other Spanish-speaking country sends such a large number of immigrants on a regular basis.

Unique Status of Puerto Ricans in U.S.

Puerto Rico was a territory of the United States from the time of the Spanish American War in 1898 to 1952 when it achieved the status of "Estado Libre Asociado" or Commonwealth, a unique relationship in which Puerto Rico remains part of the United States but governs itself.[21] In the 1950s, Puerto Ricans were responsible for America's first large-scale airborne migration as job opportunities and affordable plane travel attracted some 45,000 island residents annually to the mainland. They settled primarily in New York where this relatively poor, illiterate and unskilled group entered the low level and often exploitative jobs traditionally occupied by immigrants.

The U.S. Puerto Rican population has undergone a rapid transformation from being primarily of foreign birth to roughly equal proportions of native born and island born. While the wave of immigrants leveled off in the mid-1950s there continues to be a large movement of people back and forth from the island. Net migratory flows depend to a large extent on the relative buoyancy of the mainland and Puerto Rican economies and in some years, more Puerto Ricans move back to their native land than come to the United States.

The decline of immigration to the United States from its peak in the early 1950s has signaled Puerto Rico's transformation from a languishing agrarian society to a predominantly urban and, by Latin American standards, prosperous one.[22] This has altered the profile of the immigrant, who is now likely to be better schooled and an urban blue-collar or service worker

---

[20] By the late 1970s legal immigration from Mexico amounted to 50,000 or 60,000 people a year.

[21] Puerto Ricans are U.S. citizens. Residents of the island do not vote in presidential elections nor elect voting representatives to Congress but neither do they pay federal taxes. When Puerto Ricans come to the United States they enjoy full rights of citizenship, including the voting franchise, and they pay federal taxes. Unlike Mexicans and other Latin Americans, they need neither passport nor visa.

[22] Still, Puerto Rico's per capita income is only $3,000, compared to over $5,000 for the poorest state of the union (refers to $5,327 in Mississippi, according to the 1980 Census). The average unemployment rate is 18 percent, which helps explain the continuing lure of the mainland.

rather than a farm laborer. The stream of people moving from the urban mainland to Puerto Rico has no doubt contributed to social change on the island. In the United States, the ease with which Puerto Ricans can travel back and forth from the territory has been identified as a factor in reinforcing their cultural separatism from the U.S. mainstream and low economic status. The population has, at times, been characterized as having "one foot on the mainland and one on the island."

Growing Importance of Cuban Immigrants

The Cuban population for the most part has been in America less than 20 years and did not begin to exert a visible cultural and economic impact on American cities until the 1970s. Most Cubans in the United States are first generation. Cuban fertility, which has been lower than that of the non-Hispanic white population, plays a very small role in the growth of the Cuban community. Immigration — since 1959 — has been the key to the Cuban imprint on American society.

Little is known about the Cubans who were in the United States prior to the revolution, but they probably numbered not more than 50,000, about 5 percent of the current total.[23] With the fall of Fulgencio Batista at the end of 1958 and the rise of Fidel Castro, a major immigration of Cubans into Miami began, composed largely of upper- and middle-class professionals. This first large wave continued until air traffic between the two countries ceased temporarily following the 1962 missile crisis. A 1965 "memorandum of understanding" with the Cuban government signed by the Johnson administration established an airlift between Varadero and Miami that brought another 257,000 Cubans to U.S. shores before it ended in 1973. Thousands more left Cuba clandestinely by small boat or through Spain or Mexico.

The latest mass exodus of Cubans to the United States began in April 1980, when Castro announced that whoever wanted to leave the island was welcome to go. Over the next four months, about 117,000 Cubans left the port of Mariel, near Havana, in a "freedom flotilla" of small boats and landed at Key West, Fla. Many of those who came to this country were criminals or other undesirables. About 1,200 of the refugees remain in prison, according to the U.S. Office of Refugee Resettlement.[24]

---

[23] "Cubans" by Lisandro Perez, reprinted from *The Harvard Encyclopedia of American Ethnic Groups*, Stephan Thernstrom, ed., Harvard University Press, 1980.
[24] At the time of their arrival, the boatlifted Cubans would have been illegal aliens under existing law. They were considered political refugees, however, and gained legal status through enactment of a special Cuban-Haitian Entrant Program. For background see "Refugee Policy," *E.R.R.*, 1980 Vol. I, pp. 385-404, and *1980 CQ Almanac*, p. 430.

Illegal Immigration Issues

THE EMERGENCE of large numbers of arrivals from Latin America represents perhaps the most striking shift in the pattern of 20th century U.S. immigration, resulting in a sharp upturn in the proportion of Hispanics entering the country in comparison to other immigrants. Between 1820 and 1964, over 80 percent of immigrants were Europeans, predominantly Germans, Italians, Irish or British. Western Hemisphere immigration before 1965 represented only 15 percent of total immigration; 60 percent of that originated in Canada.[25] Now Latin Americans have replaced Europeans as the principal group seeking entry into the United States. By the late 1970s, Latin Americans made up 42 percent of total immigrants and Europeans were down to 13 percent.[26]

This transformation in the profile of the American immigrant reflects the change in U.S. policy occurring with the passage of the Immigration and Nationality Act of 1965,[27] which opened the doors to ethnic diversity and abolished the quota system that had given preference to certain European nationalities for the previous 40 years.[28] In place of the old system, the 1965 legislation substituted an overall annual ceiling of 170,000 immigrants for the Eastern Hemisphere plus a 20,000 annual per country limit based on a complicated visa preference system which stressed employment skills and close family ties with persons already in the United States. Countries in the Western Hemisphere became subject to a 120,000 overall annual ceiling, but no individual country limits or preference system requirements. Thus the admission of arrivals from Western Hemisphere countries remained essentially on a first come, first-served basis.

The effect of the 1965 act was threefold. First, it increased the percentage of immigrants from non-European countries. Second, the 120,000 ceiling for the Western Hemisphere was imposed just one year after Congress ended the bracero program which, at its peak, brought over 400,000 Mexicans to the U.S.

---

[25] Robert Warren, "Recent Immigration and Current Data Collection," *Monthly Labor Review*, October 1977. See also "Ethnic America," *E.R.R.*, 1971 Vol. I, pp. 45-64.

[26] Over 150,000 Hispanics immigrated to the U.S. in 1979, the latest year for which figures are available. See *1979 Statistical Yearbook of the Immigration and Naturalization Service*, and Leon F. Bouvier, "Immigration and Its Impact on U.S. Society," Population Reference Bureau Inc., September 1981.

[27] Signed into law by President Johnson on October 3, 1965, the act became fully operative July 1, 1968.

[28] The national origins quota system had been established during the 1920s when Congress, alarmed at the preponderance of Southern and Eastern Europeans during the peak immigration years of 1880 to 1920, established quotas for each country that favored the Northern and Western Europeans. The law also established an annual limit on the total number of immigrants allowed into the United States. Immigrants from the Western Hemisphere, however, were excluded from the ceiling. While the number of arrivals from countries such as Italy subsequently fell, immigration from Latin America grew.

annually. This had the effect of leaving many Mexicans without legal means of entry. Third, because the act failed to impose the visa restrictions of the preference system on Western Hemisphere countries, U.S. officials found they had little control over who was entering the United States from Latin America.

With the intention of gaining more control over new arrivals and putting Latin America on an "equal footing" with the rest of the world, the United States on Jan. 1, 1977, extended the visa preference system and the annual per country limit of 20,000 to the Western Hemisphere.[29] This imposed the most severe restrictions in history on Western Hemispheric immigration — and may well have increased illegal migration of persons who did not qualify for a preference or refused to submit to the often lengthy procedure.[30]

Dimensions of the Illegal Alien Problem

The flow of illegal immigrants has contributed substantially to the growth of the Hispanic population in the United States, but as with other clandestine actions, it is almost impossible to pinpoint with certainty the numbers involved. Estimates of illegal residents in the United States have ranged from 2 million to 12 million. However, there is now some agreement among U.S. government officials that the real number is lower than expected, somewhere between 3.5 and 6 million.[31]

Perhaps 50-60 percent of illegal aliens come from Mexico.[32] The circular flow of legal and illegal migration historically has been a normal part of the labor intensive segment of the Southwest's economy. While both the U.S. and Mexican governments saw the bracero program as a way to stop illegal immigration, the evidence suggests that it may have actually stimulated clandestine border crossings by highlighting the economic opportunities in America.

Illegal immigrants from Mexico do not confine their activities to agriculture but can also be found in industry and services. While it is commonly believed that the U.S.-Mexican border is porous and that undocumented workers usually spend part of the year with their families back in Mexico, research studies

---

[29] On October 5, 1978, hemispheric ceilings were abolished and a worldwide ceiling of 290,000 was established. The current worldwide ceiling is 270,000. An estimated 150,000 additional aliens enter the United States each year with virtually unrestricted rights of entry as close relatives of U.S. citizens. Country limits may also be exceeded in this manner. For example, Mexico, the largest single Western Hemisphere source country, was responsible for over 52,000 legal immigrants in 1979, more than double its 20,000 quota.

[30] Charles B. Keely, "Illegal Migration," *Scientific American*, March 1982, p. 41.

[31] Jacob S. Siegel *et al.*, "Preliminary Review of Existing Studies of the Number of Illegal Residents in the United States," U.S. Bureau of the Census, prepared for the staff of the Select Commission on Immigration and Refugee Policy, Jan. 30, 1981.

[32] Michael S. Teitelbaum, "Right Versus Right: Immigration and Refugee Policy in the United States," *Foreign Affairs*, fall 1980. See also "Mexican-U.S. Relations," *E.R.R.*, 1977 Vol. II, pp. 708-710, and "Illegal Immigration," *E.R.R.*, 1976 Vol. II, pp. 907-926.

Growth of the Hispanic Population

Year	Total U.S. Population (millions)	Hispanic Population (millions)	Percent Hispanic
1950	151.3	4.0	2.6
1960	179.3	6.9	3.8
1970	203.2	10.5	5.2
1980	226.5	14.6	6.4

Source: "The Demographic and Socioeconomic Characteristics of the Hispanic Population of the United States 1950-1980," report submitted to DHHS, January 18, 1982, by Development Associates Inc. and Population Reference Bureau Inc.

indicate that a large number stay in the United States — from several months to many years.[33]

A substantial portion of remaining undocumented immigrants are from countries such as Guatemala, El Salvador, the Dominican Republic, Colombia, Ecuador and Peru. The non-Mexican component of illegal residents typically overstay their visa periods or enter with fraudulent documents rather than entering clandestinely across the border. They are often found in large cities that afford cover from detection. Census Bureau officials speculate that this group may add to the permanent resident population of the United States to a proportionately greater extent than illegal Mexicans.[34]

One clue to the dimension of the illegal immigration problem is the number of deportable aliens apprehended each year by the Immigration and Naturalization Service. Between 1964 and 1974 the annual number of apprehensions increased steadily from 87,000 to 788,000.[35] Available statistics since 1977 indicate over 1 million apprehensions of illegal immigrants each year. Estimates of the net volume of unapprehended illegal migrants range from 250,000 to 500,000 annually.

Congress's Last Attempts at Reform

Although the vociferous charges by some Americans of a "silent invasion from the south" have receded in recent years, illegal immigration remains one of the most emotion-ridden issues touching the Hispanic community. On the one hand, undocumented aliens are frequently exploited in the U.S. labor market. Often uneducated, non-English speakers and strangers to the notion of civil rights, they fear apprehension and deportation and so will not avail themselves of the protection of U.S.

[33] *U.S. Immigration Policy and the National Interest*, Report and Recommendations of The Select Commission on Immigration and Refugee Policy to the Congress and President of the United States, March 1, 1981, p. 37.

[34] Siegal, *op. cit.*

[35] *1979 Statistical Yearbook of the Immigration and Naturalization Service*, Table 23.

laws. On the other hand, they compete for jobs with at least a part of the unskilled work force, which includes some Hispanic U.S. citizens or legal residents.

Because undocumented workers take a number of jobs that no one else wants, they generally do not displace U.S. workers on a one-for-one basis, although this may happen in certain locations during periods of high unemployment. The most important impact on U.S. employment may be that they tend to hold down wages, impede modernization of capital equipment, and hinder efforts to improve working conditions. They also make it easier for employers to break minimum wage and occupational safety laws.[36]

Each of the past four presidents has appointed a cabinet committee or task force to study the problem of illegal immigration, and shortly after taking office Ronald Reagan established his own 11-member task force headed by Attorney General William French Smith. The administration unveiled the outlines of its immigration reform plan at a July 30, 1981, joint hearing of the Senate Judiciary Immigration and Refugee Policy Subcommittee and the House Judiciary Immigration, Refugees and International Law Subcommittee.[37] Bills incorporating the administration's proposals were introduced on Oct. 22, 1981.

Congress, however, is now considering its own reforms which, if enacted would be the most comprehensive revision of federal immigration law in 30 years.[38] Although the House and Senate bills differ in some of their details, they have the same general provisions. These include civil and criminal sanctions against employers who knowingly hire illegal aliens; amnesty for most illegal aliens already in the United States; a revised temporary worker program to aid the agriculture industry;[39] streamlined procedures for exclusion, deportation and asylum claims; overall cap on legal immigration; and new restrictions on the categories of people allowed to immigrate.

---

[36] See *U.S. Immigration Policy and the National Interest, op. cit.,* p. 42.

[37] The administration's plan was based in part on the recommendations of the bipartisan Select Commission on Immigration and Refugee Policy set up by Congress in 1978. The commission's recommendations, released on Feb. 26, 1981, called for a modest increase in legal immigration, a program to legalize illegal aliens already in the United States and strict enforcement measures to stop border crossings and visa abuse as well as prevent employers from hiring illegal aliens. For details on the Reagan administration's plan, see *1981 CQ Almanac,* p. 422.

[38] The Senate bill (S 2222), sponsored by Sen. Alan K. Simpson, R-Wyo., was approved by the Judiciary Committee on May 27 and could come to the Senate floor by the end of August. See *Congressional Quarterly Weekly Report,* June 5, 1982, p. 1352 and July 24, 1982, p. 1761. A similar House bill (HR 5872), sponsored by Rep. Romano L. Mazzoli, D-Ky., was approved May 19 by the Judiciary Immigration, Refugees and International Law Subcommittee and is awaiting full committee action. See *Congressional Quarterly Weekly Report,* May 22, 1982, pp. 1232-1233.

[39] When the Bracero program was terminated in 1964, the H-2 provisions of the Immigration and Nationality Act became the only vehicle for the temporary admission of foreign laborers. Over the past decade, employers have used the H-2 provisions to bring about 18,300 alien laborers to the United States each year. These workers fill a wide variety of temporary jobs, but their greatest impact is in agriculture.

Virtually all these proposals have proven controversial and have been the subject of vigorous lobbying by an array of Hispanic, religious and civil rights groups, organized labor and business and agricultural producers. The provision to make illegal aliens eligible for permanent resident status has drawn the particularly vocal opposition of local government officials and such groups as the National Association of Counties, National Governors' Association and National League of Cities, who fear that a host of undocumented aliens, previously afraid of using public services or seeking public benefits, will suddenly emerge and put new financial strains on already hard-pressed communities.

Use of Public Services by the Illegals

The cost to local and state governments of accommodating large influxes of illegal residents — or refugees — has been an issue clouded in controversy and litigation for a number of years. The area of medical services is particularly controversial. A number of hospitals have estimated losses of millions of dollars in unreimbursed medical costs resulting from use of their facilities by undocumented aliens.[40] In reality, most studies indicate that illegal aliens make little use of cash assistance programs like welfare and Social Security, but do take some advantage of unemployment compensation, medical facilities and educational services.[41] While the financial burden may be great in some localities, two-thirds to three-quarters of illegal workers pay federal withholding income and Social Security taxes.[42] Those who use school facilities are usually well-established residents who tend to pay local taxes.

Increasingly, the issue of which public services illegal aliens are entitled to use is being resolved by the courts. For example, the U.S. Supreme Court ruled June 15 that illegal alien children have a constitutional right to a free public education. The 5-4 decision[43] struck down a Texas law that withheld state funds for the education of children who were not "legally admitted" into the United States and authorized local school districts to deny enrollment to such children or to charge them tuition. In their decision the justices declared for the first time that illegal aliens are among those to whom the 14th Amendment guarantees the "equal protection of the laws." Court analysts believe the ruling will give illegal aliens a new weapon with which to go to court to

---

[40] Department of Health, Education and Welfare, "Unpaid Medical Costs and Undocumented Aliens," March 1979.
[41] A 1976 report prepared for the U.S. Department of Labor found 27.4 percent of illegal aliens used hospitals or clinics; 3.9 percent collected unemployment insurance; 3.7 percent had children in schools; 1.3 percent used food stamps; and 0.5 percent received welfare payments. See David S. North and Marion S. Houstun, "The Characteristics and Role of Illegal Aliens in the U.S. Labor Market: An Exploratory Study," March 1976.
[42] Keely, *op. cit.*, p. 41.
[43] *Player v. Doe, Texas v. Certain Undocumented Alien Children.*

claim civil liberties sometimes denied them and may boost their claims to other types of state and federal programs such as food stamps and Medicaid.[44]

One reaction to the decision came from Los Angeles County Supervisor Deane Dana, who believes "the ruling will result eventually in illegal aliens' rights to all forms of public welfare." Dana asserted that Los Angeles County — home of an estimated 300,000 to 600,000 illegal aliens, overwhelmingly Hispanic — already is facing a shortfall of "a couple hundred million dollars" in providing medical and other services to illegal residents.[45] On the other side of the coin, John Huerta, an associate counsel with the Mexican-American Legal Defense and Educational Fund (MALDEF), the group that argued the Supreme Court case, estimated that illegal aliens in Los Angeles County pay $2.4 billion a year in federal, state and local taxes, well over what they take out in services.

New Areas of Concern

S OME Hispanic groups say the immigration reform bills now before Congress *(see p. 136)* reflect a general hostility to the Hispanic community. Sanctions against employers who hire illegal aliens and worker identification systems could simply provide an excuse for exacerbating traditional discrimination against their people, they charge. In particular, there is the fear that an identification system would cause the harassment of all "brown-skinned people" regardless of their legal status, or that employers might refuse to hire any "foreign-looking" Hispanics.

The extent to which there has been a public backlash against Hispanics has not been confined to illegal aliens. A 1980 Roper poll found that 91 percent of the U.S. public favored putting a stop to illegal immigration, and 80 percent favored reducing legal immigration. Some Americans may be concerned that the United States is importing a new "poverty class." Others are resentful of newcomers who speak little English and are fearful that the nation's rapidly growing Spanish-speaking minority will eventually force the United States into bilingualism or even lead to a separatist movement. In November 1980, voters in Dade County, Fla., overturned a countywide policy of bilingualism adopted in 1973. Sen. S. I.

---

[44] See Elder Witt, "Court Rules Illegal Aliens Entitled to Public Schooling," *Congressional Quarterly Weekly Report*, June 19, 1982, pp. 1479-1480.
[45] Quoted in *The Wall Street Journal*, June 16, 1982.

Hayakawa, R-Calif., has proposed a resolution to amend the U.S. Constitution to make English the country's official language.

Bilingual education is increasingly being attacked as a barrier to assimilation that some say could create an "Hispanic Quebec" in America. Such concerns, coupled with economic hard times and a conservative national mood, are beginning to force a pullback in bilingual programs. Secretary of Education Terrel Bell announced last March that the federal government was dropping the requirement that local schools must provide instruction in a child's first language. He also said that the administration wants to allow current bilingual funds to be spent on other teaching approaches.[46]

Efforts to Increase Political Impact

Since the 1960s militancy of farm workers' organizer Cesar Chavez and such groups as the "brown berets," Hispanic political activism has evolved into an increasingly sophisticated — and vocal — national force. The National Council of La Raza, Mexican-American Legal Defense Fund, American GI Forum, League of United Latin American Citizens, the National Puerto Rican Forum, and the Cuban National Planning Council are examples of the most prominent Hispanic organizations. An attempt to forge a coalition of these and other national Hispanic groups has been undertaken in the past five years by the Forum of National Hispanic Organizations.

Although Hispanics have not had political representation commensurate with their population — only six (of 435) voting U.S. representatives, no senators, and no governors are Hispanic — this pattern is changing.[47] Hispanics are key players in the latest realignment of political districts as the ballooning of the Hispanic population — confirmed by the 1980 Census — claims political power at all levels. The new congressional map may bring as many as four new Hispanic representatives to Washington.

Perhaps the overriding political problem for Hispanics today is a failure to register and vote. Under 60 percent of those eligible were registered to vote in 1980, compared to over 70 percent of all eligible voters. Only about 37 percent of eligible Hispanic voters actually cast their ballots, according to the Southwest Voter Registration Project in San Antonio, Texas. Hispanic organizations, led by the San Antonio group, have

---

[46] For background see "Bilingual Education," *E.R.R.*, 1977 Vol. II, pp. 617-636.

[47] The six representatives are Robert Garcia, D-N.Y., Henry B. Gonzalez, D-Texas, Edward R. Roybal, D-Calif., E. "Kika" de la Garza, D-Texas, Manuel Lujan Jr., R-N.M., and Matthew G. (Marty) Martinez, D-Calif.

launched a drive to get out the vote. In some areas with a high concentration of Hispanics, the political strides are apparent. Last year Henry Cisneros won a 62 percent victory to become San Antonio's first Mexican-American mayor. This year Mario Obledo was considered a strong — though ultimately unsuccessful — contender for governor of California.

Ethnic militancy seems to have subsided over the past decade, but the concern of Hispanics over their future has not dimmed. As America struggles to achieve a balance between the melting pot philosophy and cultural pluralism, the Hispanic influence shows every sign of growing.

Selected Bibliography

Books

Corwin, A. F., *Immigration and Immigrants: Perspectives on Mexican Labor Migration to the U.S.*, Greenwood Press, 1978.

Jaffe, A. J., *et al.*, *Spanish Americans in the United States — Changing Demographic Characteristics*, Academic Press, 1980.

Mindel, Charles H. and Robert W. Habenstein, eds., *Ethnic Families in America*, Elsevier, 1976.

Articles

Estrada, Leobardo, *et al.*, "Chicanos in the United States: A History of Exploitation and Resistance," *Daedalus*, spring 1981.

Haub, Carl, "The U.S. Hispanic Population: A Question of Definition," *Intercom*, November-December 1981.

Keely, Charles B., "Illegal Migration," *Scientific American*, March 1981.

Teitelbaum, Michael S., "Right Versus Right: Immigration and Refugee Policy in the United States," *Foreign Affairs*, fall 1980.

Reports and Studies

Bureau of Labor Statistics, U.S. Department of Labor, "Employment in Perspective: Minority Workers," Report 667, 1982.

Editorial Research Reports: "Refugee Policy," 1980 Vol. I, p. 385; "Illegal Immigration," 1976 Vol. II, p. 907; "Ethnic America," 1971 Vol. I, p. 45; "Spanish-Americans: The New Militants," 1970 Vol. II, p. 707.

"La Vida Americana, Hispanics in America," Reprints of a series of articles published in *The Dallas Morning News*, December 1981.

National Center for Education Statistics, "The Condition of Education for Hispanic Americans," 1980.

Strategy Research Corporation, National Association of Spanish Broadcasters, "U.S. Hispanics — A Market Profile," 1980.

U.S. Bureau of the Census, "Persons of Spanish Origin in the United States: March 1980 (Advance Report)," *Population Characteristics*, Series P-20, No. 361, May 1981.

Migrants: ENDURING FARM PROBLEM

by

Roger Thompson

June 3
1983

Editor's Note. One week after a court-ordered deadline, the Occupational Safety and Health Administration on March 1, 1984, issued proposed field sanitation rules *(see p. 149)*. The rules require toilet, handwashing and drinking water facilities for workers on farms employing more than 10 persons engaged in hand-labor. The rules would affect an estimated 765,500 farm workers and cost $15.5 million to $22.5 million a year to carry out, according to information in the March 1 *Federal Register*. Final action will be taken after the public comment period closes April 16.

By April 1984, Congress had not agreed on proposed changes in the 1978 Federal Insecticide, Fungicide and Rodenticide Act (FIFRA) *(see p. 149)*, but the previous October the Supreme Court agreed to review a challenge to key provisions of the law. Monsanto Co., a major chemical manufacturer, challenged provisions requiring public disclosure of industry-gathered health and safety data. The data must be submitted to obtain federal registration of a new chemical product. In April 1983, a U.S. district court in Missouri ruled the disclosure requirement unconstitutional because it forced companies to reveal "trade secrets." It is that decision that the Justice Department appealed to the Supreme Court.

MIGRANTS: ENDURING
FARM PROBLEM

"HARVEST of Shame," Edward R. Murrow's television documentary exposing the misery of migrant farm workers, made history 23 years ago. Today, it is hard to imagine a subject that has since been more thoroughly explored by the news media, by scholars and by the government at all levels. But as another harvest season begins, it is clear that the issues raised two decades ago remain — and others have emerged.

Lawmakers responded in the years that followed Murrow's expose with an impressive array of legislation to improve the lives of the nation's farm migrants, who today may number 1.5 million.[1] New laws made them eligible for food stamps, provided rural clinics for medical aid, created special school programs for migrant children and sent federally paid attorneys into the fields and courtrooms to fight migants' legal battles. Yet serious problems persist, causing some advocates of migrant workers to despair that they remain outcasts in a land of plenty. "By and large, all the resources that have gone in have amounted to very little," said Steve Nagler, executive director of the Migrant Legal Action Program, a federally funded program based in Washington, D.C.. "Many of the gains made on paper don't translate into reality. Migrants are still on the bottom."

Even more desperate are the uncounted thousands of illegal aliens, mostly Mexicans, who form a large segment of the farm labor force in some of the Sunbelt states — notably California and Texas. Farmers say they hire illegal aliens because not enough Americans are available and willing to work in the fields. Ironically, farmers are breaking no federal law by hiring illegal aliens. It is the aliens who are breaking the law by accepting the jobs.

Migrant-worker advocates argue that farmers prefer illegal aliens because they work longer hours for less money than Americans and are not safeguarded by minimum wage, workmen's compensation or other laws. Labor unions complain that farmers have no excuse for hiring illegal aliens while unemploy-

---

[1] The figure is based on research conducted by the Migrant Legal Action Program and Rural America. Migrant Legal Action Program, funded by the federally supported Legal Services Corp., is at 806 15th St. N.W., Washington, D.C. 20005. Rural America, a nonprofit organization concerned with low-income people in rural areas, is at 1346 Connecticut Ave. N.W., Washington, D.C. 20036.

ment stays above the 10 percent mark and millions of Americans are looking for work.

Unemployed Americans are not flocking to the fields because they have an alternative in unemployment compensation, said Perry R. Ellsworth, executive vice president of the Washington-based National Council of Agricultural Employers. Unemployment payments vary from state to state, ranging in duration from 34 to 53 weeks. Ellsworth said farmers are willing to hire the unemployed American workers but few of them are willing to relocate for jobs that pay less than they are accustomed. Unemployment compensation recipients must look for work, but they are not required to relocate to find it.

Proposals to end farm employment of illegal aliens have generated intense debate in Congress. President Reagan has urged Congress to enact measures "to regain control of our borders." Like-minded members of Congress advocate penalties for all employers who hire illegal aliens. And they favor a "guest-worker" program, modeled on the discarded "bracero" program *(see p. 152)*, that would admit thousands of Mexicans to the fields on temporary work permits. Critics of the guest-worker idea, including Hispanic groups, point to the difficulty European countries have had in convincing millions of their own guest workers to return home now that Western Europe has more workers than work *(see box, p. 159)*.

Misery in the Fields in Spite of Reforms

Migrants can toil 12 hours a day and still end up owing the crew leader money for cigarettes, beer, and room and board at the end of the week. The median income for a family of six, with children often working, is $3,900 a year, far below the federally defined poverty line of $12,499. Despite federal migrant education programs, only 14 of every 100 children graduate from high school, compared to 75 out of a 100 for the general population. Malnutrition and inadequate medical treatment are as routine as the next day's trip to the fields. Diarrhea and parasites are expected; tuberculosis is common. Pesticide poisoning frequently goes undetected and untreated. Life expectancy is 49 years, roughly two-thirds the national average.[2]

The crew leader system has been blamed for many of the abuses suffered by migrant workers. Most migrants rely on crew leaders to arrange their jobs, transportation, and room and board. Farmers generally deal with crew chiefs, not individual migrants. Sometimes the system works well, especially when the crew leader is a member of an extended family that travels together from state to state. Leaders provide an essential service

---

[2] Statistics based on studies by the Migrant Legal Action Program.

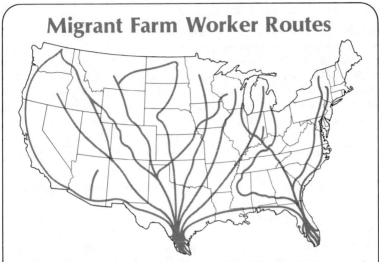

Migrant Farm Worker Routes

Migrant farm workers have developed many discernible routes in their seasonal search for jobs. The main ones are up the East Coast from winter headquarters in Florida, across the Midwest from a home base in the Rio Grande Valley, and up the Pacific Coast from Southern California. Others branch off and fan out into nearly every state. The Sun Belt states, primarily California, Texas and Florida, specialize in winter vegetables and citrus.

The summertime path northward for East Coast migrants leads through peach orchards in Georgia, tobacco fields in the Carolinas and Virginia, and truck farms on the Maryland Eastern Shore and in New Jersey. Appalachian range apple orchards extend the season into the fall and as far northward as New York.

Texas-based migrants are drawn to the grain harvests in the Plains states as far north as Canada, and to Michigan, where they find an abundance of vegetables and cherries. Vineyards in northern California, strawberries in Oregon and apples in Washington await the seasonal flow of farmhands up the West Coast.

Source: Office of Migrant Health, U.S. Public Health Service.

by organizing and delivering a work force when and where it is needed. By its nature, the crew-leader system lends itself to abuses by those who would prey on the helpless.

Three years after Murrow's documentary touched the nation's conscience — it was broadcast Thanksgiving Day 1960 — Congress passed the Farm Labor Contractor Registration Act to correct abuses in the crew leader system. The law required crew leaders to obtain a Labor Department license. Obtaining a license required little: absence of a criminal record and proof of liability insurance on vehicles for transporting workers. In addition, it required crew leaders to inform workers in writing of the conditions of their employment and housing. The law was amended in 1974 after Congress determined it did not deter violators. Stiffer criminal penalties were added and the registration requirement was broadened to include crew leaders who operated solely within one state. The previous law applied only to those who crossed state lines.

Five years passed before new congressional hearings were called. This time the farm lobby complained that the law had "gone wild" because it required corporate agribusinesses, the largest employers of migrants, to register. Spokesmen for farm groups contended Congress never intended for the law to reach into the corporate personnel office. John F. Ebbott, who was then director of the Migrant Legal Action Program, had a different story to tell a House subcommittee: "Many of the abuses which the Farm Labor Contractor Registration Act was enacted to remedy still occur today.... These abuses are perpetrated not only by individual labor contractors, but increasingly by corporate entities." [3]

The hearing also brought out differences over the condition of migrant housing. Perry Ellsworth testified: "Over the past 10 to 15 years, there has been dramatic improvement in housing across the land.... Running hot and cold water and inside plumbing are the rule." That assertion was challenged by migrant spokesmen who contended that camp conditions tended to remain "filthy" and "disgusting."

Even with the registration law, Ebbott testified, "Farmworkers are routinely not told by recruiters what they will be getting into if they accept a job offer.... [They] frequently find they must buy food, cigarettes and other items from the crew leader or the corporate cafeteria. Often the price of these items is hugely inflated. They are soon in debt, and purchases are deducted from their pay, leaving them little or no money. If they try to leave the job, it is not uncommon for the labor contractor, or foreman, to beat them up, threaten to kill them." Ebbott said the Labor Department had failed to enforce the crew leader law.

New Law's Exclusions; OSHA Criticism

Craig Berrington, a deputy assistant secretary of labor, told the subcommittee that the Carter administration had "given high priority" to improving both the living and working conditions of farm workers. He acknowledged the need for stepped-up enforcement but noted that the department's efforts had suffered, "because we have had substantial resistance to even the basics of the act." The resistance he added, came "from the farm owner and the corporate farm community."

It took three more years for a compromise rewrite of the law to clear Congress on Jan. 14, 1983. The new law, entitled the Migrant and Seasonal Agricultural Worker Protection Act, carried over most of the worker protections from the past, with two notable exceptions. Family farms were excluded from coverage, and a damage ceiling of $500,000 was set on class-action law-

---

[3] Transcript of hearing before the House Subcommittee of the Committee on Government Operations, Nov. 13, 1979, p. 80.

Migrant children at Pierson, Fla., quarters also housing 14 adults (1981 photo)

suits brought by farm workers. Farms owned by corporations remained under the act. In addition, record-keeping requirements were extended to growers who in any way supervise field labor. And responsibility for complying with federal housing standards was broadened to include the person who controls the property — that is, the crew leader — as well as the owner.

The change in housing compliance means an end to confusion over who must comply with Occupational Health and Safety Administration (OSHA) standards, said Charles Jeffress, deputy labor commissioner for North Carolina. "In the past, there was a lot of confusion over who to cite and who to bring enforcement action against." Congress created OSHA in 1970 with a mandate to the secretary of labor to prescribe and enforce health and safety standards for the benefit of workers in agriculture and industry. Authorizing legislation stated that OSHA was meant "to assure so far as possible every working man and woman in the nation safe and healthful working conditions." The states were encouraged to develop their own programs; they would be 50 percent federally funded if they equaled or surpassed the federal standards. About half of the states have done so. OSHA quickly issued regulations governing migrant housing.

OSHA's critics took the agency to court as early as 1975 over alleged failure to enforce its migrant housing safety standards. The court ordered the Labor Department — OSHA's parent organization — to improve enforcement, and appointed Washington lawyer Ronald L. Goldfarb to oversee the department's efforts. Goldfarb later recounted: "In 1975 when I called upon

147

OSHA officials to do something about the horrible condition in migrant housing sites around the country, they excused their historic inactivity, blaming overwork and lack of funds. Under pressure, they promised to make a concerted effort to inspect 3,500 migrant housing places in that summer, 10 times the number they had inspected the year before. They actually conducted only 1,825 inspections of migrant labor camps, claiming inadequate enforcement staff and inability to locate migrant camps in some states (as if they could be hidden). And this was with a court order and a court-appointed committee focusing attention on their efforts." [4]

State Minimal Health-Safety Enforcement

Congress in 1977 imposed new restrictions on OSHA's authority to inspect labor camps, barring inspectors from camps with fewer than 11 workers. In New Jersey, for example, eight out of every 10 camps were exempt. Regulations also limited OSHA to pre-season camp checks. Inspectors return only to investigate an alleged violation and only if the complaining worker identified himself. Nagler of the Migrant Legal Action Program said a farm worker who complains can expect to be without a job. The Reagan administration has made matters worse, he added, by cutting back on the number of inspectors. [5]

In states that handle their own OSHA inspections, the situation is reported to be no better. A 1978 housing study of licensed labor camps in eight states that perform their own OSHA inspections — California, Colorado, Florida, Michigan, New York, Ohio, Texas and Washington — found inside running water available in two-thirds of the camps. But two-thirds were without heat, even though most of them were in areas where indoor heat was a common requirement. One-fourth of the kitchens had no working refrigerators, and one-half were without sinks — or even piped-in water, hot or cold. Bedrooms were crowded, though there were not enough beds for all. [6]

Even if OSHA housing regulations were enforced, "the minimum standards still allow you to live in a slum," said Charles Jeffress. "The regulations are meant to prevent people from being electrocuted or falling through holes in the floor, that's all." Aside from minimum housing standards, OSHA in 13 years has issued only two other regulations applying to agriculture. It requires rollover protective structures on tractors, and it sets standards for handling anhydrous ammonia, a liquid fertilizer.

---

[4] Ronald L. Goldfarb, *A Cast of Despair* (1981), p. 45.
[5] Nagler's remarks were made during a telephone interview in April 1983. For background, see John Ripton, "The Surprising Truth About Farm Workers," *The New Jersey Reporter*, May 1982, p. 18.
[6] Study cited by Patricia A. Porter in "The Health Status of Migrant Farmworkers," The Field Foundation, 1980, p. 22. Florida conditions were additionally reported in a series appearing in *The Miami Herald*, March 22-27, 1981.

The absence of standards for field sanitation has been the subject of debate and legal battles for a decade. When OSHA proposed in 1974 to require portable toilets, drinking water and handwashing facilities in the fields, farmers succeeded in killing the idea. They argued that the proposed requirements were unnecessary and too costly. Federal courts subsequently have twice ordered OSHA to write such regulations. The latest ruling came in November 1981 when U.S. District Court Judge June L. Green in Washington, D.C., ordered OSHA to make its "best, good-faith effort" to develop field sanitation regulations within 18 months. She reacted with anger at the agency's claim that it needed another five years to study the matter. "OSHA's actions have been and continue to be irrational and taken in bad faith," she said. "OSHA's timetables belong in Alice in Wonderland's tales: each step forward brings us two steps backward."

Struggle Over Farm Pesticide Poisoning

In August 1980, seven physicians in Kerns County, Calif., were fined $250 each by the state Occupational Safety and Health Administration for failure to report they had treated 54 farm workers for apparent pesticide poisoning. In no other state could there have been made a similar ruling, for no other state requires doctors to report pesticide poisoning. Yet pesticides have become a prime health concern of America's farm workers and the focus of a political battle in Congress. Opposing sides came to a draw at the end of the 1982 session over proposed changes in the law governing pesticides — the 1947 Federal Insecticide, Fungicide and Rodenticide Act (FIFRA). Legislation on the books was extended for the current fiscal year. The battle over substantive changes has been postponed.

The dispute began in 1978 when Congress amended the pesticide law to require chemical manufacturers to make public their previously secret pesticide health and safety studies. The chemical makers responded with a lawsuit that blocked enforcement of disclosure for three years. They argued that divulging the data would amount to giving away trade secrets. When a federal court ruled in favor of disclosure in the summer of 1981, the chemical industry began to lobby Congress for changes in the law. There the industry ran into a coalition of labor and environmental groups that lobbied just as hard for strengthing worker protections.

After the first round of debate last summer, the House Agriculture Committee approved a number of industry-sought changes: to limit public disclosure of health and safety data and to keep states from requiring more information than the federal government does in registering a pesticide for in-state use. The American Farm Bureau Federation backed both changes.

Environmentalist, farm-worker and labor groups argued that eliminating state control over pesticide registration was unwarranted. They viewed the move as an attack on California's tough registration law, which has slowed the introduction of new pesticides in that state. Manufacturers feared other states might follow California's example. Farm-worker advocates also pushed in vain for a proposal to allow farm workers to sue farmers for damages in case of injury from pesticide poisoning. Farm workers are covered now only by workmen's compensation, and only in those states providing such coverage. When the committee-approved bill reached the House floor, it was rewritten by a series of amendments that eliminated the key measures sought by the farm and chemical industry lobbyists. The House bill, however, died at the end of the 97th Congress for lack of Senate action.

No one knows how many farm workers and their children are treated for pesticide exposure each year. Even in California, which has the nation's only mandatory reporting law, many doctors are not aware of the requirement, and some who are do not make the reports. A 1977 study by a California farm-worker group concluded that only 1 percent of the state's pesticide poisonings were reported.[7] Rural America held three regional hearings on pesticide poisoning in 1980. At all three sites — Pharr, Texas; Ocoee, Fla.; and Salinas Calif. — farm workers complained of rashes, vomiting, stomach cramps, burns, skin peeling, blurred and spotted vision and dizziness associated with pesticide exposure.[8]

A majority of the farm workers said they had no idea what chemicals had been used, nor could they obtain any information on the health effects. One worker at the Texas hearing said farmers have used aerial spraying to break up union picketing. Pesticide poisoning is difficult to diagnose, the report stated, because such clinical symptoms as respiratory problems, dizziness and gastro-intestinal disturbances are attributed to flu or other ailments. Few doctors are trained to recognize and treat pesticide poisoning.

The risks associated with pesticide poisoning are even greater for children. Yet the existing federal standards for re-entering fields sprayed with pesticides, set by the Environmental Protection Agency, are based on estimated adult tolerance to pesticide exposure. Of all the chemicals available on the market, EPA has

[7] See "The Committee Report," winter 1981, p. 9, published by the National Farmworker Policy Project, Sacramento, Calif.
[8] The summary report based on the hearings is entitled "Pesticide Use and Misuse: Farm Workers and Small Farmers Speak on the Problem," Rural America, 1980.

developed re-entry times on only 12, according to the Migrant Legal Action Program. There are no separate standards for children for any pesticides.

The absence of such standards triggered a round of lawsuits after Congress amended the Fair Labor Standards Act in 1977. The amendment allowed growers to obtain permission from the secretary of labor to employ 10- and 11-year-olds, provided the growers can prove no harmful effects to the children. Migrant-worker advocates filed suit, charging no studies existed for making such a determination. In March 1981, a federal appeals court ordered the Labor Department to develop safety standards before allowing children to enter pesticide-treated fields. At about the same time, the department and EPA announced a joint, five-year study to determine effects of pesticide exposure on children under 16.

Migrants and Social Policy

THE first migrant farm laborers who trekked into the fields may have been white hobos hired about 120 years ago by a California grower and cattle baron named Henry Miller. They worked for food, not wages, according to a latter-day account which contends that Miller set an enduring tone for the treatment of migrant help. He instructed his cooks to serve the workers last on dirty plates — to discourage any who otherwise might feel at home and wish to settle.[9]

California got a second source of cheap labor after the Union Pacific built its railroad across the nation in 1869. Thousands of Chinese coolies who had been imported to lay the railway suddenly had to find other jobs. By 1880, it is estimated that 100,000 Chinese were at work in California fields holding 90 percent of the farm jobs. Their population increase alarmed trade unionists and small manufacturers who engineered the state's Chinese Exclusion Act of 1882, banning further Chinese immigration.

The next wave of cheap labor came from Japan. By 1910, the state had 72,000 Japanese farm workers. But the federal government slammed the door on virtually all immigrants from Asia in 1924. By this time it was clear that Mexico would supply future farm labor. Thousands of Mexicans fled the country's revolution, which broke out in 1911. The American government wel-

---

[9] The Miller story is told by Richard S. Johnson in "A Denial of Justice," *The Denver Post Empire Magazine*, March 8, 1981, p 34.

Foreign Temporary Workers			
Admitted for Farm Employment			
1958	433,704	1970	47,483
1959	464,128	1971	42,142
1960	447,207	1972	38,752
1961	312,991	1973	37,294
1962	303,638	1974	33,908
1963	243,120	1975	25,434
1964	237,700	1976	22,124
1965	155,671	1977	21,671
1966	64,881	1978	18,679
1967	57,720	1979	18,213
1968	50,782	1980	16,548
1969	43,527	1981	16,190

Source: U.S. Immigration and Naturalization Service

comed their arrival during World War I, at a time when domestic labor was in short supply. The labor shortage became a labor glut during the Depression, and the Mexicans were no longer welcome. America's own economic refugees fled the central plains Dust Bowl for California's verdant fields, as portrayed in John Steinbeck's 1939 novel *Grapes of Wrath* (1939).

Mexicans re-entered the farm labor market in the early 1940s after America's entry into World War II. Farmers again needed a source of cheap labor to replace the farm hands who were drafted or went to work in factories. Legally or illegally, Mexican field hands have remained on the scene ever since. During the war years, upwards of 200,000 Mexican "braceros" — literally strong-armed men — entered the country on temporary work permits to toil in the fields. Congress extended the "wartime" bracero program until 1964 when civil rights groups prevailed in their fight to end what they considered exploitation of foreign workers at the expense of unemployed Americans. But laws prohibiting employment of aliens have been too weak and too poorly enforced to prevent what since has become a flood of Mexican illegal immigrants.

On the East Coast, the history of migrant labor is simpler. Following the Civil War, the sharecropper system replaced slavery. But there wasn't enough work to go around. Desperation set ex-slaves and some poor whites on a seasonal surge northward for work. The East Coast stream took a more definite shape in the 1920s when vast amounts for rich muckland came under the plow in Florida. The state became the winter haven for workers who traveled as far north as New York and Michigan on their cyclical search for jobs. Mexicans joined the stream after cotton harvest mechanization in the early 1950s left thousands without jobs, primarily in Texas. Since 1980, Haitian immigrants have joined the stream and now make up an estimated 10 percent of the migrant work force.[10]

Late-Developing Wage, Welfare Protection

The social history of the past 50 years is replete with examples of government intervention on behalf of the poor, the uneducated, the sick and the young, beginning with the New Deal. But much of it never extended to the fields. While the Social Security Act of 1935 made history, agricultural workers were not covered until 15 years later.[11]

The minimum wage law of 1938, the Fair Labor Standards Act, championed the rights of workers to earn a decent wage without excessive labor. It put a floor under wages at 25 cents an hour, limited the work week to 40 hours, required overtime pay for more than the normal work week and restricted child labor. Agricultural workers were excluded. Twenty-eight years later, in 1966, Congress amended the act to include workers on large farms, thus covering about 30 percent of all farm workers. An additional 10 percent came under the law's coverage with passage of a 1974 amendment. Farm workers still are not eligible for overtime pay.

Enforcing the wage law is difficult. Migrants testified during a legislative commission hearing in North Carolina last fall that crew leaders keep two sets of books, one for the state Labor Department inspector, and one with the real balance sheet. "I've been at this for five years, and I haven't met a farm worker yet who has made the minimum wage for the entire season," said Chuck Eppinette, community education coordinator with North Carolina Farm Worker Legal Services.[12]

Since the 1938 wage law excluded farm workers, their children were not covered by its child-labor provisions. Congress provided some coverage in 1949 by prohibiting children from working in the fields during school hours. But migrant parents usually ignored the law, knowing enforcement was lax or nonexistent. The Senate Labor Committee in 1974 issued a report favoring tougher child labor laws: "Thirty-five years ago, Congress reacted to a national outcry by banning industrial child labor. However, since 1938 the nation has permitted in the fields what it has prohibited in the factories — oppressive and scandalous child labor. The committee once again urges that this shameful double standard no longer be tolerated." [13] Con-

---

[10] For background, see "Refugee Policy," *E.R.R.*, 1980 Vol. I, pp. 385-404.
[11] For background on migrant labor concerns and reform efforts in the 1950s, see "Migratory Farm Workers," *E.R.R.*, 1959 Vol. I, pp. 103-122.
12 Eppinette and Charles Jeffress *(p. 147)* were interviewed by telephone during April 1983.
[13] "Fair Labor Standards Amendments of 1974, S.93-690," Senate Committee on Labor and Public Welfare, Subcommittee on Labor.

gress did not act then, nor has it acted since. The child labor provisions remain unchanged.

Today, all children may work in the fields if they are 14 or older. Children 12 and 13 may do so with parental consent, and those under 12 may do so on a parent's farm or with parental consent on farms not large enough to be covered by minimum-wage provisions. A 1977 report for the Department of Health, Education and Welfare (now Health and Human Services) concluded: "Child labor is an economic necessity for the migrant family due to the low level of income. . . . Many children begin to do some work in the fields by age four, and by age 10 are expected to carry their own weight and usually drop out of school by age 12 to work full time."

Workmen's compensation laws also arose during the New Deal era to assure workers of insurance coverage for job-related injuries regardless of who was at fault. The laws were enacted by the states, which tailored them to meet their individual needs. Today, farm workers remain exempt in nearly half the states. In 13 states and Puerto Rico, migrants are covered on the same basis as other workers; 13 states provide partial coverage with numerous exemptions; the remaining 24 states provide no coverage at all.[14] Farm workers also were excluded from federal unemployment compensation benefits from the time the first bill passed in 1935 until 1976. Since then, migrants and other farm laborers hired by large employers, usually corporate farms, have been eligible for unemployment benefits. Those hired by family farms remain outside the system.

Farm Unions: Success Only in California

Migrant farm workers have not accepted their second-class status without complaint. Chinese laborers organized the first recorded farm strike in 1884 in the hop fields of Kern County, Calif. It failed. So did sporadic strikes by Mexican and Japanese workers in the early 1900s. The Depression brought on a new round of farm work stoppages, 140 by one count.[15] But growers aligned themselves with powerful political and economic forces that broke the resistance.

Farm worker organizers often carried the banner of groups considered to be a threat to the government: the Industrial Workers of the World (Wobblies), the Communist Party or the Socialist Party. For example, the Southern Tenant Farmers Union was set up in the 1930s with funds from the Socialist

---

[14] States providing full coverage are Arizona, California, Colorado, Connecticut, Hawaii, Massachusetts, Montana, New Hampshire, New Jersey, Ohio, Oregon, Pennsylvania and Washington; states providing partial coverage are Alaska, Florida, Illinois, Iowa, Maryland, Michigan, Minnesota, New York, Utah, Vermont, Virginia, West Virginia and Wisconsin.

[15] Goldfarb, *op. cit.,* p. 180.

North Carolina: Slave Question

Some migrants find working conditions so unpleasant they attempt to flee, only to be rounded up by crew leaders or foremen. By definition, that amounts to slavery, a federal crime since 1865. The North Carolina constitution also outlaws slavery, but there are no penalties in state law for enslavement. Thus the U.S. Justice Department's Civil Rights Division must be called on to prosecute all such cases.

In the past five years, 10 such convictions have been obtained in North Carolina, more than any other state. A state study commission in January recommended that the Legislature impose penalties for slavery, making prosecution quicker and surer. The state Farm Bureau Federation opposed an anti-slavery bill introduced this year. It has not been acted on.

Party. It eventualy claimed 25,000 members in five states. But it made no headway. Spontaneous non-union farm strikes took placed in numerous states during the Depression. Labor historians have counted 275 such strikes in 28 states joined by an estimated 178,000 workers.[16] No doubt Congress was aware of agitation on the farm when it excluded farm workers from coverage of the 1935 National Labor Relations Act. The act recognized the right of industrial workers to organize and bargain collectively, but it has never been amended to include farm workers.

"The National Labor Relations Board [created to administer the act] requires employers to bargain in good faith with a union," said Steve Nagler of the Migrant Legal Action Program. "But if that [union organizing] happens in the fields, the crew leader can say, 'I'm sorry, there is no protection for these people. They are fired.'" Arguments for exempting agricultural workers from collective bargaining have remained unchanged. Farm spokesmen contend that agriculture is uniquely vulnerable to work stoppages. The crops cannot wait for a strike to be settled. A farmer facing a strike is at the mercy of the workers, and would be compelled to give in to demands no matter how unreasonable or arbitrary. Collective bargaining would not equalize the bargaining power of farmers and workers; it would make farmers subservient to labor union leaders.

Against this backdrop of resistance, the United Farm Workers union, led by Cesar Chavez, overcame the odds and established its presence in California in the mid-1960s. Chavez, a second-generation Mexican-American, emerged as a national figure during a 1965 strike against Delano, Calif., grape growers. Growers and agribusiness fought unionization while Chavez ap-

[16] *Ibid,* p. 183.

pealed for a nationwide boycott of California grapes and wine. The UFW's major breakthrough came in 1975 when California's newly elected governor, Edmund G. (Jerry) Brown Jr., personally directed negotiations that produced the state's landmark Agricultural Labor Relations Act, patterned after the National Labor Relations Act.

For the first time, California farm workers were given the right to organize and bargain collectively. The act created an Agricultural Labor Relations Board to supervise union elections, hear complaints and develop regulations. Since passage of the act, agricultural employers estimate that in the Monterey-Salinas area 80 to 90 percent of the workers in fresh vegetables are under labor contract. In other vegetable areas, approximately 40 percent are under contract. Fewer than 20 percent of the workers in vineyards, orchards and citrus groves are unionized.[17]

Unionization has brought farm workers higher wages and an array of educational and social service programs funded by union dues. The programs include medical clinics, a pension fund, an economic development fund for workers' centers and language training programs. From the time of the Delano grape strike, Chavez allied his union with the AFL-CIO. Together they fought a bitter jurisdictional battle with the powerful Teamsters Union over the next decade. The two rivals ended the feud in 1975 by signing an agreement giving the United Farm Workers exclusive rights to organize field hands and the Teamsters the right to organize farm workers in transportation jobs.

Chavez has made repeated pledges to lead union drives in other agricultural states, such as Texas and Florida. To date, the UFW's magic has worked only in California. And Chavez's critics say the union is floundering at home because its charismatic leader cannot make the transition from strike organizer to effective manager.

Immigration and the Economy

P ROBLEMS faced by domestic migrants are multiplied for thousands of illegal aliens who live in what has been described as an economic underworld that demands their silence and obedience in return for a job. It operates outside the control and protection of the law. The Census Bureau estimates there

---

[17] Figures from *Seasonal Agricultural Labor Markets in the United States*, Robert D. Emerson, ed., 1981, p. 423.

are three to six million illegal aliens working in the United States, many of them in the fields. Nearly two out of every three come from Mexico.

The number of aliens caught crossing the border illegally has mounted steadily since the bracero program ended in 1964. The Immigration and Naturalization Service deported 1.3 million Mexicans between 1965 and 1970. In 1980 alone more than one million aliens entered the country illegally, most of them Mexican. INS Commissioner Alan Nelson recently told a Senate committee that Border Patrol apprehensions of illegals are at their highest levels in 30 years. In January, 86,811 aliens were caught at the border, a 46 percent increase over the same time a year earlier. But the Border Patrol estimates that only every third person trying to enter is caught. Many keep trying until they cross undetected.

President Carter sent Congress a comprehensive set of immigration law reforms in 1977 to curb the flow of illegal aliens, but the legislation never came to a vote. The Reagan administration has renewed the reform effort and is backing a number of changes, including an amnesty program to allow many illegal aliens already in the country to become permanent residents, and imposing sanctions against employers who knowingly hire them. The administration's proposals were contained in the Immigration Reform and Control Act, popularly known as the Simpson-Mazzoli bill for its sponsors, Rep. Romano L. Mazzoli, D-Ky., and Sen. Alan K. Simpson, R-Wyo. The Senate passed the bill last year, but it died in the House.

The bill was reintroduced in January and again won Senate passage on May 18, after important concessions were made to the agriculture industry. The House Judiciary Committee completed work on the House version of the bill May 13, but it is not expected to reach floor debate until August, following review by the Agriculture, Education and Labor, Energy and Commerce, and Ways and Means committees.

The Senate-approved bill includes a compromise amendment giving agricultural employers three years to phase out their use of illegal aliens. In the fourth year, farmers either would have to employ American workers or obtain foreign laborers through a new "guest worker" program. No cap was put on the number of aliens who could be imported for seasonal work. The House bill currently contains a similar proposal. The phase-out provision was intended to overcome fears that an abrupt change in the labor supply could mean crop losses and higher consumer prices at the checkout counter.

For all other businesses, employment of illegal aliens would become a violation six months after the law took effect. A first offense would draw a $1,000 fine per alien and a second offense

$2,000. Criminal penalties are provided for chronic violators. The Senate bill allows illegal workers who were in the country before Jan. 1, 1977, to qualify for legal resident status, but makes them ineligible for such public benefits as unemployment compensation and food stamps for three years. Workers in the United States before Jan. 1, 1980, would qualify for temporary-resident status but would have no access to public benefits for six years. Hispanic advocacy groups estimate the cutoff date would leave half of the illegal aliens ineligible for citizenship. In contrast, the House bill would grant permanent resident status to aliens who were in the country before Jan. 1, 1982.

Immigration Bill's 'Guest Worker' Concept

The guest-worker program envisioned by both the House and Senate bills is patterned after the 30-year-old "H-2" temporary worker program, named for the section of the 1952 immigration law authorizing importation of foreign laborers. The H-2 program was designed to allow temporary employment for workers performing services for which domestic workers could not be found. The secretary of labor must certify the absence of American labor before H-2 workers may be hired. The program operates under much stricter controls than the old bracero program and therefore has remained far smaller, averaging less than 20,000 workers a year. The program now operates primarily for the benefit of East Coast apple growers, who import about 5,000 Jamaicans each fall, and Florida sugar cane growers, who bring in about 8,500 Jamaican cane cutters during the winter harvest.

Southwestern farmers contend that the H-2 program is too rigid to accommodate their need for thousands of workers on short notice. They acknowledge widespread use of illegal aliens, but blame H-2 red tape for forcing them to hire aliens. Farmers have lobbied for a guest-worker program far more "flexible" than the H-2 program, but the outcome of their efforts remains in doubt. Hispanic groups strongly oppose the guest-worker plan and have called it "a backdoor bracero program" to exploit immigrant workers.

Some economists and politicians suggest that a solution to the illegal immigration problem does not require exclusionary laws. They argue that the only effective approach is economic development in the countries spawning the immigrant stream. This was at least part of President Reagan's rationale — other than security reasons — for proposing a "Caribbean Basin Initiative" to Congress last year. He asked for legislation opening U.S. markets more fully to most Caribbean nations to stimulate their economic growth.[17]

---

[17] The House approved the legislation last year despite organized labor's fear of U.S. job losses, but it died in the Senate when the 97th Congress ended. Reintroduced this year, it was approved May 14 by the Senate Finance Committee.

European 'Guest Workers'

As many as 15 million "guest workers" and their dependents have migrated from of Southern Europe, Turkey and North Africa to Northern and Western Europe since 1960 to find jobs, most of them menial. The host governments encouraged them to come in a time of prosperity and labor shortages — but supposedly on a temporary basis. Though times have changed and far fewer guest workers are needed, only one of every three has returned home.

With the 1973 Arab oil embargo and the ensuing worldwide recession, the labor-importing countries moved to halt or severely restrict further recruitment of aliens. But no country attempted massive expulsions. The belief that guest workers would not settle in the host countries proved false for a number of reasons. The need for foreign labor turned out not to be temporary. Native workers have tended to shun the lowliest jobs, even in times of rising unemployment.

The economic and social consequences of the programs have caused alarm in Europe. It is argued that the social and political costs outweighed the economic benefits. As workers were joined by their families, government expenditures rose for schools, housing, medical care and other social services. In Switzerland, opponents of the guest worker program waged four unsuccessful referendums to restrict their numbers. Racial problems arose in several countries. Tension between aliens and residents occasionally erupted into violence. Backers of the programs contend that Europe's economy would not have prospered and grown as it did without imported labor.

There is another project that seeks a similar objective. It is much more modest in size and does not require new laws or public funding. The small, independent Arizona Farm Workers Union has started a fund to channel money into job-development projects in Mexico. One project is taking shape in La Caja, a small village 185 miles north of Mexico City, where an irrigation project will supply water to 4,000 acres of arid farm land. The villagers' only obligation to the union is to help neighboring villages.

The plan may seem impossible, but so did the union's chances of obtaining its first, and only, contract five years ago when 300 citrus workers went on strike at Arrowhead Ranch in Arizona. Today, the workers have a union contract, live in a $250,000 camp with showers, laundry, a courtyard and communal kitchen. Their wages have doubled and they receive three hot meals a day for only $5. Twenty-three years after "Harvest of Shame," such accommodations remain the exception, not the rule, for the nation's migrant farm workers.

Selected Bibliography

Books

Coles, Robert, *Migrants, Sharecroppers, Mountaineers,* Little, Brown, 1967.
—— *Uprooted Children,* University of Pittsburgh Press, 1970.
Goldfarb, Ronald L., *Migrant Farm Workers: A Caste of Despair,* Iowa State University Press, 1981.
Emerson, Robert D., *Seasonal Agricultural Labor Markets in the United States,* Iowa State University Press, 1983 (forthcoming).
Levy, Jacques. E. *Cesar Chavez,* W. W. Norton & Co., 1975.

Articles

Johnson, Richard S., "Our Historical Abuse of Farm Workers," *The Denver Post Empire Magazine,* March, 1, 1981.
Ripton, John, "The Surprising Truth about Farm Workers," *The New Jersey Reporter,* May 1982.
Selected issues of "FAIR — Immigration Report," The American Federation for Immigration Reform, Box 14131, Washington, D.C. 20044.
Satchell, Michael, "Bent, But Not Broken," *Parade,* Oct. 10, 1982.
Sinclair, Ward, "An Endless Season, Migrants of the East," (series in *The Washington Post*), Aug. 23-27, 1981.
"The New Migrants: Struggles in an Alien Land" (series in *The Miami Herald*), March 22-27, 1981.
"The Border: A World Apart," *Newsweek,* April 11, 1983.

Studies and Reports

Editorial Research Reports: "Migratory Farm Workers," 1959 Vol. I, p. 105; "Europe's Foreign Laborers," 1975 Vol. II, p. 543; "Hispanic America," 1982 Vol. II, p. 549.
Joshua S. Reichert, "The Agricultural Labor System in North Carolina: Recommendations for Change," The Division of Policy Development, N.C. Department of Administration, June 1980.
Legislative Research Commission Report to the 1983 General Assembly of North Carolina, "Migrant Workers," January, 1983.
North, David S. and Houstoun, Marion F., "The Characteristics and Role of Illegal Aliens in the U.S. Labor Market," New TransCentury Foundation, March 1976.
Porter, Patricia A., "Health Status of Migrant Farm Workers," The Field Foundation, March 1980.
Rural America, "Pesticide Use and Misuse: Farm Workers and Small Farmers Speak on the Problem," September, 1980.
Subcommittee on Government Operations, U.S. House of Representatives, "Administration of Laws Affecting Farm Workers" (hearing transcript), November 1979.
The Select Commission on Immigration and Refugee Policy, U.S. Senate, "Temporary Worker Programs: Background and Issues," February 1980.

Graphics: Photos on cover and p. 147 from Migrant Legal Action Program; p. 145 map by Art Director Richard Pottern. Cover photo shows housing for migrant tomato-field workers in Florida.

HOUSING OPTIONS FOR THE ELDERLY

by

Linda Daily

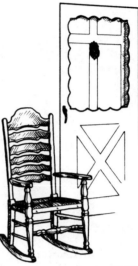

Aug. 6
1982

Editor's Note: Late in 1982, after this report was originally published, Congress authorized $5 million a year during fiscal 1983 and 1984 in grants and loans to private groups to pay start-up costs of establishing home health programs, thus enabling more aged and disabled people to remain in their homes. There is a discussion of similar, proposed services on p. 170.

HOUSING OPTIONS FOR THE ELDERLY

MANY FAMILIES today must face the difficult decision of how to help care for elderly parents or other relatives. But choices are no longer limited to nursing homes or living together under one roof. Older Americans have more housing options than ever before. Contrary to popular belief, only 5 percent of those over 65 live in nursing homes, while 70 percent own their own homes. Others select "continuing care" communities where they live independently with the assurance that all health needs will be taken care of in the future. Those who can afford it often opt for the social/recreational lifestyle found in the retirement havens that have sprung up in the western and southern states.

Choosing where to live is not always a simple matter of preference, however, because of health needs, income limitations and the supply of housing. Innovative living arrangements are emerging as more elderly persons move in with their families or non-relatives to cut down on housing costs and maintain independence. Options include building apartments within existing homes, renting individual rooms or purchasing a separate unit known as an elder cottage or "granny flat." Home and health support services and adult day-care programs help keep more dependent elderly in their own homes or living with family members. Federal projects provide affordable housing for some low-income elderly.

Retirement living is an issue of growing importance. The number of older Americans is rapidly increasing and is expected to grow from 11 percent of the population in 1980 to a projected 20.4 percent by 2030. By comparison, the elderly comprised only 4 percent of the population in 1900. Estimates of the number of elderly living in substandard housing run as high as 30 percent.[1] Budget constraints are forcing a reconsideration of federal housing and other support programs. Elderly homeowners are finding it increasingly difficult to manage the costs of big, older homes. The rental shortage is intensifying.

Health needs and income are closely linked to housing choices. As Dr. Robert Butler, director of the National Institute on Aging (NIA), observed: "The No. 1 cause of distress for most retired Americans is their income. The second is probably their

[1] Robert N. Butler and Myrna I. Lewis, *Aging and Mental Health* (1982), p. 14.

health. The third is their housing." [2] Older Americans generally
have greater health needs than the rest of the population because they are more likely to suffer from one or more chronic
afflictions, such as heart conditions. Despite disabilities, most
elderly are able to live independently. In 1980, more than 30
percent of the older population lived alone. But the need for
help with daily activities — such as dressing and bathing —
increases with age. Families and friends provide most supportive care. But social and population changes may affect the
availability of these informal supports, creating a more dependent elderly population.

The presence of a spouse and the availability of children are
perhaps the two most important factors in keeping elderly
persons out of nursing homes. But more women than ever now
work outside the home, and some families are separated by long
distances. More than 70 percent of nursing home residents are
female, most are widows or single, and nearly half are childless.[3]
Age is another factor. More than 20 percent of those 85 and
older live in nursing homes. This predominantly female, "old,
old" sector of the elderly population is expected to triple in the
next 50 years.

Although only 5 percent of the elderly now live in nursing
homes, utilization of nursing homes is expected to increase more
than 50 percent in the next 20 years. And by 2030, the number
of nursing home residents is expected to be almost 3 million,
compared to 1.3 million today.[4] Total cost of nursing home care
is expected to increase from $24.5 billion in 1981 to more than
$75 billion by 1990, compared to only $2.1 billion in 1965.[5]

Improved Conditions in Nursing Homes

Congressional investigations in the 1970s uncovered widespread deficiencies in nursing homes: unsanitary conditions,
inadequate nutrition, a high percentage of errors in administering drugs, misappropriation of residents' funds and neg-
ligence and abuse of residents causing death and injury. "To the
average older American, nursing homes have become almost
synonymous with death and protracted suffering before death,"
the Senate Special Committee on Aging reported in a 1975
study.[6]

---

[2] Quoted in *U.S. News & World Report*, Feb. 26, 1979, p. 66. Butler is leaving NIA on
Sept. 1, 1982, for New York's Mount Sinai Medical Center, where he will head the geriatric
department.
[3] See "Long Term Care: Background and Future Directions," Health Care Financing
Administration, January 1981, pp. 9-10. Also see "Women and Aging," *E.R.R.*, 1981 Vol. II,
pp. 713-732.
[4] *Ibid.*, p. 12.
[5] Figures from Butler and Lewis, *op. cit.*, p. 283 and U.S. Department of Commerce, "U.S.
Industrial Outlook, 1982," p. 406.
[6] See "Nursing Home Care in the United States: Failure In Public Policy," Supporting
Paper No. 6, U.S. Senate Special Committee on Aging, 1975, pp. xiv-xv.

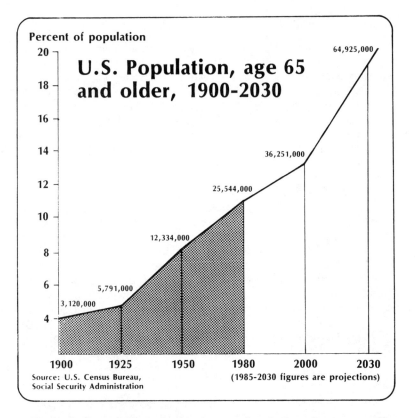

Percent of population

U.S. Population, age 65 and older, 1900-2030

64,925,000

36,251,000

25,544,000

12,334,000

5,791,000

3,120,000

1900   1925   1950   1980   2000   2030

Source: U.S. Census Bureau,
Social Security Administration

(1985-2030 figures are projections)

Today, the quality of care in nursing homes has generally improved for a variety of reasons. Some point to stronger enforcement of state and federal regulations, others to increased public awareness, improvements in geriatric training and recognition of residents' rights. Many homes encourage self-development by offering educational classes and other programs. Others form active ties with the community. Many residents organize resident councils to become more involved in issues affecting their lives.[7]

Challenges remain, however, in upgrading care. One of the most serious problems according to government studies is the lack of training for nurses' aides, who provide 90 percent of the "hands on" care of nursing home residents. Demanding work and low pay are cited as reasons for an annual turnover rate as high as 75 percent.[8] There are other problems, as well, including "a lack of rehabilitative services and specialized mental health services, both of which, if provided, would help people to move on to other housing situations," said Elma Griesel of the National Citizens' Coalition for Nursing Home Reform.

---

[7] See *Long Term Care of the Aging — A Socially Responsible Approach*, American Association of Homes For the Aging (1979), p. 17.
[8] See "Long Term Care: Background and Future Directions," *op. cit.*, p. 28.

Residents often complain about regimented schedules, lack of privacy and other problems associated with the institutional character of nursing homes, 90 percent of which are operated for profit. Horror stories still surface on occasion. An 80-year-old Virginia nursing home resident died late in 1981 after being scalded in a whirlpool bath. In the spring of 1981, a grand jury indicted a Houston, Texas, nursing home corporation and six employees in the deaths of eight patients allegedly caused by neglect and abuse.

New Debate Over Government Regulation

Regulation of nursing homes is a continuing controversy. Last March, Secretary of Health and Human Services Richard S. Schweiker rejected proposed changes in nursing home regulations that had been drafted by his staff. The proposals, which produced an outpouring of congressional and consumer protests, would, among other things, have dropped a requirement that the medical directors of nursing homes be physicians. The department is proceeding, however, with proposals to change the way nursing homes are inspected. The effort is one of the goals of the Vice President's Task Force on Regulatory Relief.

HHS wants to end annual inspections of all nursing homes to concentrate its resources on facilities with poor records of compliance with federal standards. Homes with good records would be inspected every two years. Other changes would eliminate follow-up visits to substantiate correction of problems, and allow a non-governmental commission to inspect nursing homes rather than require state agencies to determine if facilities meet federal standards. Agency officials will review public comments on the proposed regulations before deciding whether to make the changes permanent. The final decision, which could come at any time, rests with Schweiker.

Critics contend the revised inspection rules would cause the quality of care given residents to deteriorate since there would be less oversight at a time when federal funds provided states to enforce standards are being reduced.[9] A new study by the General Accounting Office found that more nursing home residents than ever are infirm and require more intensive care. At the same time, GAO said, the states are seeking ways to reduce nursing home expenditures. Under these conditions, inspection procedures were seen as being particularly important to assure that residents receive quality care.[10]

---

[9] The federal budget allocation for inspecting Medicare facilities dropped to $13.6 million in 1982 from $24.7 million in 1981. Inspection funds for Medicaid facilities fell to $31.8 million in 1982, compared to $42 million in 1980.

[10] General Accounting Office, "Preliminary Findings on Patient Characteristics and State Medicaid Expenditures for Nursing Home Care," July 15, 1982.

The World Assembly on Aging

The global phenomenon of aging populations received close scrutiny during the U.N.-sponsored World Assembly on Aging held in Vienna, Austria, July 26-Aug. 6, 1982. According to U.N. estimates, there were 350 million people aged 60 and over in 1975; this group is expected to reach 590 million by the year 2,000 and 1.1 billion by 2025. The elderly populations in most industrialized countries already have increased significantly, while developing countries are experiencing a more gradual growth.

An international plan of action drafted for the conference proposed basic guidelines and recommendations for countries to consider in deciding how to meet the economic and social challenges of their aging populations. In the area of housing, the plan of action highlighted the importance of a mix of services in helping elderly to remain independent in their communities. Governments also were urged to develop housing policies that keep older people at home as long as possible and support family members in their caretaker role. The international plan of action will be submitted to the U.N. General Assembly later in 1982 for approval. Individual countries will decide what policies to implement.

The skyrocketing expense of nursing home care is hardly good news for federal and state governments struggling to trim already lean budgets. Government funds paid for more than 55 percent of nursing home costs in 1979, with private payments accounting for the rest.[11] Many nursing home residents originally paid for their care, but the high costs — now about $17,000 a year — depleted their savings.[12] Those without adequate personal resources often turn to Medicaid, the federal health care program for the poor, which accounts for 87 percent of government expenditures for nursing home care. Medicaid rules generally make it easier to qualify for care in a nursing home than in a private residence. On the other hand, Medicare, the federal health insurance program for the elderly, pays very little in nursing home benefits because coverage has a 100-day time limit and requires pre-hospitalization.

Congressional studies estimate that 20-40 percent of nursing home residents could live in the community if adequate support services were available.[13] Yet the health care system provides far greater support for institutional and medically oriented care. For every $10 spent on nursing home care, the federal government spends only $1 on home health care.[14]

[11] See "Long Term Care: Background and Future Directions," op. cit., p. 15.
[12] See Butler and Lewis, op. cit., p. 283.
[13] See "Developments in Aging: 1981," U.S. Senate Special Committee on Aging, 1982, p. 359.
[14] See "Working Papers on Long-Term Care," Office of the Assistant Secretary For Planning and Evaluation, Department of Health and Human Services, October 1981, p. 7.

Providing more alternative services, however, is on the agenda of nursing homes across the country, several industry spokesmen told Editorial Research Reports. Because of high construction costs, companies are not planning to build many new nursing homes despite a projected need for 300,000 to 400,000 new beds over the next decade. "We're beginning to see our companies getting into outpatient, home health, day care and retirement communities," said Jack MacDonald, executive vice president of the National Council of Health Centers, which represents chain or investor-owned nursing homes. MacDonald said the number of people coming in and out of nursing homes will increase, but the length of stay will decrease because other services will meet patients' needs.

Non-Institutional Options

MOST OLDER people want to stay in their own homes for as long as possible, despite the burden of high utility and maintenance costs. "If I lose my house, I lose the only important thing in my life," one 88-year-old homeowner recently told the House Select Committee on Aging. New financial arrangements allowing older homeowners to convert home equity into cash are being developed to make that decision easier to afford. Some states also allow elderly homeowners to defer property tax payments until they sell their home or die.

Under one type of equity conversion plan, an investor purchases an elderly homeowner's residence and agrees to lease it back. The monthly payments the buyer makes to the seller exceed the monthly rent, giving the former homeowner a steady income. In reverse annuity mortgages, homeowners take out a bank loan borrowed against the value of their homes, providing a lump sum or monthly payments for a certain period after which the loan must be refinanced or repaid. High interest rates and financial risks associated with such programs have limited their appeal and growth, but several plans are now in existence.[15] Leo Baldwin, housing consultant for the American Association of Retired Persons-National Retired Teachers Association, said in a recent interview that such plans must have strong consumer protections providing legal services, counseling and guaranteeing lifelong occupancy to prevent exploitation of the elderly.

In-home and community-based services also help older

---

[15] See "Developments in Aging: 1981," *op. cit.*, p. 226, and Diana Shaman, "New Hope for the Elderly: Home Equity Conversion," *Real Estate Today*, May 1982, p. 36.

Photo Courtesy of the Department of Housing and Urban Development
Older Americans have more choices in living arrangements than ever before.

Americans live in their own homes or with others. The range and availability of public and private support programs depends on the community, but services often include homemaker assistance, home health aid, personal care, nursing care, medical equipment rental, home-delivered and group-site meals and home maintenance. A variety of federal and state programs — each with its own eligibility criteria — fund community care services, which are managed by government agencies and non-profit and private organizations.

The complexity and fragmentation inherent in the system make it difficult — some say impossible — for elderly persons to get services they need. Information and referral systems are "the only way to serve the public without duplication of services, which we can't afford," Baldwin said. Some cities are taking steps to improve senior citizens' knowledge about programs. Boston, for example, publishes neighborhood service directories. Other cities publish newspapers or newsletters that focus on elderly issues and programs, or operate an "elderly hotline." [16]

Several states, some with the help of federal funds, also are trying to improve coordination of services and upgrade assessments of needs to prevent premature institutionalization. Florida's Community Care for the Elderly Program provides several "core" services to functionally impaired adults 60 and over. Under Connecticut's Promotion of Independent Living Pro-

---

[16] See "Administering Aging Programs, Vol. VI: Serving the Urban Elderly — Issues and Programs," U.S. Conference of Mayors, 1982, p. 39.

gram, staff members assess the needs of elderly clients, develop a plan of care and coordinate and monitor services.[17]

On the federal level, Congress in 1981 approved a provision that allows states to use Medicaid funds for certain home and community-based services if such care is cost-effective for persons who would otherwise be in nursing homes. Legislation has been proposed to establish a coordinated system of non-institutional services (S 861) and to promote development of home health programs and agencies and expand coverage of such services under Medicare and Medicaid (S 234). But neither bill is expected to be acted upon this year. Medicare and Medicaid generally limit coverage of home health services to instances when care is medically necessary, such as after an operation. The Congressional Budget Office estimated in 1977 that 1.7-2.7 million people needed in-home services, but only 300,000 to 500,000 were receiving them.[18]

Adult Day Care: Needed Help for Families

Families seeking support in day-to-day care of elderly relatives sometimes turn to adult day-care centers for help. In 1982, there were more than 800 programs serving 20,000 people[19] compared to 15 in 1974.[20] Some centers, often attached to hospitals and nursing homes, provide medical, rehabilitative and/or therapeutic services, while others combine minimal health monitoring with social activities. One of the most well-known programs is On Lok Senior Health Services in San Francisco, Calif., which was launched in 1972 as a day health center under an Administration on Aging grant. On Lok has since expanded its community care services to include home health services and a specially designed housing center.[21]

Another alternative is respite programs that offer temporary care for elderly persons whose families cannot provide their usual support because of vacation, illness or other problems. The Visiting Resident Program, run by the Metropolitan Jewish Geriatric Center in Brooklyn, N.Y., allows elderly persons living in the community to stay in a nursing home from one to six weeks.

---

[17] See Gail Toff, "Alternatives To Institutional Care For the Elderly: An Analysis of State Initiatives," Intergovernmental Health Policy Project, George Washington University, September 1981, pp. 18-21.
[18] See "Long-Term Care for the Elderly and Disabled," Congressional Budget Office, February 1977, p. x.
[19] Data from interview with Betty Shepherd, coordinator, National Institute on Adult Daycare.
[20] Speech by Edith G. Robins, Special Assistant for Adult Day Health Services, Health Care Financing Administration, Oct. 22, 1980.
[21] See "Adult Day Care Programs," U.S. House Select Committee on Aging, Subcommittee on Health and Long-Term Care, April 23, 1980, p. 88.

As with in-home services, the issue of whether adult day care prevents premature institutionalization is controversial. A 1979 study by the National Center for Health Services Research concluded that day care was not a substitute for nursing home care, but a costly additional service. Critics disputed the study's findings and research methods.[22] Kay Larmer, director of the Annandale (Va.) Elderly Day Care Center, told Editorial Research Reports that when a vacancy does open on her average waiting list of 25-50 people, many people already have gone into nursing homes. "Families are willing to share the burden of care for impaired adults if they get support," she said.

According to Betty Shepherd, coordinator of the National Institute on Adult Daycare established by the National Council on the Aging, centers provide services to an average of 25 people a day for an average daily cost of about $20. Most programs are non-profit and base fees on ability to pay. Funding comes from several sources. In 1980, more than 300 programs relied on Title XX, the Social Services Amendments to the Social Security Act. The program was turned into a social services block grant in 1981 with a 25 percent reduction in funds. A March 1982 study by the Subcommittee on Human Services of the House Select Committee on Aging found that 10 states were reducing adult day-care services. Other funding sources include Title III of the Older Americans Act (also reduced in 1981), state and local governments and private donations. Medicare and private insurance rarely cover adult day-care services and only 14 states and the District of Columbia provide Medicaid reimbursement for the services.[23]

Although the funding situation is serious, "a majority [of programs] will survive — maybe on a shoestring — by turning to their communities for support," Shepherd said. More programs probably will rely on client fees to a greater extent, which could limit their use by the poor. The new Medicaid waiver provision that allows funding for community-based care will help adult day care, Shepherd said, as will a new tax credit enacted in 1981. The credit, which ranges between 20-30 percent of day-care costs, depending upon adjusted gross income, applies only to dependent elderly living with their families.

Innovative Shared-Housing Arrangements

Housing pressures also have led to the development of innovative living arrangements — such as shared housing, acces-

---

[22] *Ibid.*, pp. 18-24.
[23] The 14 states are California, Colorado, Florida, Georgia, Kansas, Maryland, Massachusetts, Minnesota, Nebraska, North Dakota, New Jersey, New York, Texas and Washington. The Older Americans Act was enacted in 1965 to develop new or improved programs for older persons through grants to the states.

sory apartments and elder cottages — that some observers say will revive the concept of the extended family. Shared households range from two unrelated persons sharing an apartment or home to group residences. The Boston chapter of the Volunteers of America opened an elderly group home in 1976. Called McCroham House, it offers residents the help of a house manager and various social services. The Shared Living House, which opened in Boston in 1979, houses 16 men and women, with ages ranging from 24 to 84, although most are over 55. Residents have to be self-sufficient since they share in the upkeep of the home.

The trend toward shared living quarters has spurred the growth of matching programs usually provided without charge by social service agencies. Homesharing for Seniors, which operates in several cities including Seattle and Philadelphia, interviews candidates and coordinates elderly and intergenerational matchups, and "barter" arrangements where services are exchanged for room and board. While home sharing is often not ideal because of inevitable conflicts, the greater economic and personal security it provides usually outweigh the drawbacks.

Senior citizens living in homes they have outgrown, but want to keep, sometimes convert their houses into two-family residences. The Census Bureau estimates there are 2.5 million of these so-called accessory apartments, bringing in average monthly rents of $300-$400. Another innovation is "echo" housing (elder cottage housing opportunity), an idea imported from Australia where it is known as the "granny flat." Energy-efficient, compact, removable homes are designed to be installed in the backyard of the family home for use by aging relatives.

Ed Guion, a housing manufacturer in Lancaster County, Pa., became interested in the concept when a local official tried to launch an elder cottage rental project that never materialized because of funding obstacles. Guion decided to use his own money to build a model unit. With the help of a private investor, he has built three homes and sold two at an average cost of $18,000. According to Guion, echo housing also could be located in clusters, for a village setting, or adjacent to nursing homes.

Although shared housing, accessory apartments and echo housing help the elderly live independently and promote usage of underutilized housing in a tight market, they face significant obstacles in local zoning laws. Most municipal codes restrict the number of unrelated people who can live together. Restrictions in public welfare programs and federal rent subsidies also discourage shared housing arrangements. Single-family zoning regulations usually prohibit echo housing and accessory apartments.

Community opposition to zoning changes legalizing these living arrangements stems from concern that neighborhoods will deteriorate, causing property values to drop. Ignoring illegal conversions of single-family homes, however, could cause even more problems. "We have no way of knowing whether plumbing or electrical work was done properly, whether there are fire exits. We're going to have some fires, people trapped in buildings, see some neighborhoods deteriorating and all hell is going to break loose," said Leo Baldwin. "The answer is to legalize them [accessory apartments] — make it an appropriate way for people to retool existing housing."

There are signs of change. Several communities, including Babylon, N.Y., and Portland, Ore., have legalized accessory apartments. Lancaster County, Pa., has approved zoning waivers for individual elder cottages. Proponents predict other communities will follow. According to Patrick Hare, a housing and planning consultant in Washington, D.C., who has conducted several studies on innovative living arrangements, local planners can change zoning laws without inviting the wrath of property owners by implementing certain restrictions. To legalize accessory apartments, for example, Hare recommends prohibiting any visual changes in the home and allowing only owner-occupiers to install or rent the units.

Attraction of Retirement Communities

More affluent older Americans often choose to live in retirement communities. A new study conducted by the Institute of Gerontology at the University of Michigan estimates there are 970,000 people living in 2,300 retirement communities nationwide.[24] Traditionally located in the Sun Belt, communities such as Sun City, Ariz., are usually age-segregated and emphasize an active, leisure lifestyle. Some experts, like Leo Baldwin, doubt whether large communities like Sun City, with several golf courses, fancy recreation centers and a population of 100,000, will continue to be developed because of economic conditions. Smaller, less elaborate retirement villages may instead become more common.

Leisure World in Silver Spring, Md., for example, has 4,000 residents living in 2,800 single homes, apartments and semi-detached units. Residents have to be at least 50 years old; the median age is 73. Prices of homes start at $60,000 with maintenance fees averaging $150 a month. A variety of educational and recreational programs are offered and a medical center provides routine services.

---

[24] Data from interview with Robert Marans, whose study, "Changing Properties of Retirement Communities," will soon be published by the Institute of Gerontology at the University of Michigan.

In multi-level care centers, meals, social support services and nursing care are provided to elderly persons living in independent housing units. Operated by churches, universities or private companies, these communities vary from a single building to a campus-like setting of individual homes, apartment highrises and nursing facilities. Those concerned about future health needs and medical expenses often seek the security that continuing care communities offer.

Residents of Goodwin House in Alexandria, Va., a single-building facility sponsored by the Virginia diocese of the Episcopal Church, make a down payment ranging from $37,000 for an efficiency apartment to $60,000 for a one-bedroom unit. A monthly fee of about $700 for a single person and about $1,400 for a couple covers meals, personal assistance, maid service, various educational and recreational programs and all nursing care. Contributions from the church support residents who have exhausted personal funds. Administrator James K. Meharg Jr., said in an interview that if inflation remains high, new residents might have to be limited to ensure that the program can pay for the needs of those already in residence. He said a waiting period of three years is common at Goodwin House.

Attempts to Regulate Boarding Home Care

Increasing attention is being focused on the nation's estimated 300,000 boarding homes as safety and financial fraud problems come to light.[25] Also known as rest homes, foster, adult or domiciliary care facilities, boarding homes provide room and board to more than 1 million people. Residents are usually elderly, disabled, or former mental patients who receive Supplemental Security Income (SSI) payments or other public assistance. In the last five years, 143 persons have died in 14 boarding home fires.[26] An investigation of 10 boarding homes conducted by the General Accounting Office in 1980 found operators abusing residents' funds and cheating the government to pad their own pockets. Boarding home residents also have been subjected to poor care and abuse. A 101-year-old woman was locked in a closet and two other elderly residents were told to spend the night in a park by a boarding home operator in Florida who did not want the city inspector to know she had too many boarders.[27]

Public concern about boarding home deficiencies prompted Congress in 1976 to enact an amendment to the Social Security

---

[25] See "Board and Care Homes — A Study of Federal and State Actions To Safeguard the Health and Safety of Board and Care Home Residents," Department of Health and Human Services, Office of the Inspector General, April 1982, p. iv.
[26] See story by Sandra Sugawara in *The Washington Post*, April 23, 1982.
[27] See "Fraud and Abuse in Boarding Homes," U.S. House Select Committee on Aging, June 25, 1981, pp. 2-3.

Act that required states to license and regulate the facilities. The federal law, however, had no enforcement muscle since the only penalty was to withhold SSI payments from boarding home residents to encourage them to move to a licensed facility. The reasoning ignored the physical and mental limitations of many residents and the lack of adequate housing.

The Department of Health and Human Services is implementing a new plan to strengthen protections for residents in "board and care homes," which offer minimal medical and other supervision in addition to room and board. To help carry out its program, the department has established an inter-agency coordination unit, has provided the National Bureau of Standards with $400,000 to complete development of fire safety standards, and is implementing plans to develop a model state statute.

Under the department's new requirements, board and care operators who receive tenants' SSI payments directly will have to prove that their facilities comply with state regulations. States that want to use Medicaid funds for board and care homes also will have to prove they are enforcing standards. The program has been criticized for not including federal aid to states for upgrading enforcement activities, and for proposing to withhold Older American Act funds, which pay for nutrition and other support programs for the elderly, from states that fail to enforce regulations.

Federal Housing Policies Under Reagan

The federal government's involvement in housing efforts for the poor dates back to 1937 when the low-rent public housing program was established. Under the program, construction, financing and some operating costs are paid by the Department of Housing and Urban Development (HUD), although units are managed by state and local agencies. Since then, other housing programs have been launched.

Under Section 8, HUD pays rent subsidies to owners of existing, private rental housing or to developers of new or substantially rehabilitated housing for low-income persons. The subsidies equal the difference between what HUD has determined to be the fair market rent for the dwelling and the tenants' share, which is 25-30 percent of their income.

Under the Section 202 program, HUD provides direct, below-market loans to non-profit sponsors to build rental housing specially designed for independent elderly and handicapped persons with very low incomes. Residents who meet Section 8 requirements pay no more than 30 percent of their income for rent. In 1978, Congress approved the Congregate Housing Services Act making funds available to Section 202 sponsors and

```
┌─────────────────────────────────────────────────────────────┐
                    The "Old-Old"

                    Women                    Men
    75-79          2,945,482              1,847,115
    80-84          1,915,370              1,018,859
    85+            1,558,293                681,428

    Source: U.S. Department of Commerce, Bureau of Census, 1980 figures
└─────────────────────────────────────────────────────────────┘
```

public housing agencies to provide meals in a central dining area and personal and housekeeping services to partially impaired elderly and handicapped residents with the goal of preventing premature institutionalization. (Congregate housing programs, which provide an independent group living environment with the help of non-medical support services, have existed for many years through non-governmental agencies.)

Although Section 202 is the federal government's primary building program for the elderly, 202 units represent only a fraction of federal housing units occupied by the elderly because relatively few have been built. Nearly half of 1.2 million public housing units are occupied by elderly persons. Most new public housing construction in the last 10 years has been for elderly projects, in part because of community resistance to programs for low-income families.[28] Nearly 40 percent of Section 8 units also are occupied by elderly persons.[29]

A redirection in federal housing policy is occurring under the Reagan administration. The private market and local initiative are viewed as the major sources in meeting needs. According to a report by the President's Commission on Housing, affordability — not supply — is the greatest housing problem faced by low-income people.[30] Opposition to federal housing programs stems in part from their long-term financial commitments. For example, the Section 8 existing housing programs involve 15-year contracts for assistance payments.

To carry out its philosophies, the administration has proposed using a voucher system to replace all federally assisted housing programs, with the exception of Section 202. Under this system, qualified recipients would receive cash assistance to help pay for private housing in the community. Critics argue that federal incentives for new construction are crucial because the present housing supply — both public and private — is inadequate and the demand is increasing. The average waiting time to get into public housing programs is several years. One critic also observed that if you increase the amount of money to pay for housing, but do not increase the supply, prices will rise.

[28] See "Working Papers on Long Term Care," *op. cit.*, p. 56.
[29] See "Developments in Aging: 1981," *op. cit.*, p. 214.
[30] President's Commission on Housing, "Interim Report," Oct. 30, 1981, p. 8.

Section 202 is up for renewal this year, but most congressional observers believe the popularity of the program and its good reputation will help ensure its survival. But the congregate housing services program has been put on hold until HUD completes an evaluation due in 1984, despite congressional efforts to continue funding new projects. The 202 budget for fiscal 1983 will fund 10,000 units. Recommendations approved at the 1981 White House Conference on Aging called for the production of 20,000 units annually. Philip Abrams, a HUD deputy assistant secretary, said additional monies will be available from cancellation of 202 projects that have been in the planning stages for more than two years. New design restrictions on 202 projects soon to take effect also will reduce costs. Such policies have met strong criticism from aging and other groups, who stress that 202 programs sometimes incur greater costs in design features and encounter more time delays in construction because of the special needs of the elderly and handicapped people being served.

Economic and Social Issues

WHILE OLDER Americans have more choices in living arrangements than ever before, the need for a broader range of housing and care options is generating increasing attention and support. This is especially true for the frail elderly population. The ideal is to keep people living independently by providing a sequence or continuum of housing arrangements and support services that meet the aging individual's needs for progressively greater care. "For older people, housing and services must be treated as an integral set of concerns. An overriding necessity in meeting the housing-related needs of older people is to promote the development of a continuum of appropriate housing types," concluded a 1980 housing forum held in preparation for the December 1981 White House Conference on Aging.[31]

Delegates to the White House Conference did approve several recommendations urging development of coordinated, community-based services to help impaired elderly live in the least restrictive setting, with nursing homes viewed as the "last resort." Whether a well-developed plan of housing and care options will become a reality is a matter of conjecture. "It's a question of social values," M. Powell Lawton, director of behav-

---

[31] See "Report of the Mini-Conference on Housing for the Elderly," Oct. 22-24, 1980, convened by the National Council of Senior Citizens.

The Issue of Income Adequacy

Older Americans are generally healthier, wealthier, and better housed than in past generations. The number of elderly persons living in poverty dropped from 35.2 percent in 1959 to 15.3 percent in 1981. But inflation has had a significant impact because it is most severe in areas such as housing and medical care where the elderly spend the greatest portion of their income. The result is a decline in purchasing power.

The elderly pay an average of 29 percent of their health-care costs out-of-pocket or about $700-$900 a year. Older homeowners pay more than 25 percent of their income for shelter, while older renters' costs usually exceed 30 percent. Those 75 and over often pay more than 45 percent of their income for housing.

ioral research at the Philadelphia Geriatric Center, told Editorial Research Reports. "In-home health services are a glaring lack, that cost or no cost, need to be funded. If we're going to serve people in need, we've got to pay for it." [32]

Long-Term Public Policy Challenges

Many issues remain to be resolved that will have a significant impact on housing options for older Americans. The growth of the elderly population presents serious challenges for individuals and for government at all levels, especially in a constrained economy. Planning and saving for retirement will become increasingly important. Inflation already is causing some older workers to postpone retirement. Public skepticism about the durability of the Social Security system also remains high. While reform initiatives, such as raising the retirement age or reducing annual cost-of-living adjustments, have met political defeat in recent months, pressure is building for changes because of predicted shortages in trust funds and a reduced work force in future years that will have to support a larger retired population. [33]

Budget pressures are a continuing concern. Even with significant cutbacks in domestic programs such as Medicare and Medicaid and new tax increases, a federal budget deficit of well over $100 billion is expected in 1983. Many states have reduced spending and/or increased taxes to try to reduce multimillion-dollar deficits. More than 25 states are reporting problems in funding Medicaid, with some deciding to limit nursing home payments or freeze new bed construction. [34] Expansion of ser-

[32] The Philadelphia center includes a hospital, nursing home, research institute, two apartment buildings and several small boarding homes on one city block, with a day-care center operating in another part of the city.
[33] See "Retirement Income in Jeopardy," *E.R.R.*, 1981 Vol. I, pp. 169-188.
[34] See "Development in Aging: 1981," *op. cit.*, p. 382.

Health needs and income are closely linked to housing choices for the elderly.

vices and programs under such conditions will become increasingly difficult. And yet, because of the issue's importance, meeting the housing and support needs of the elderly is on the agenda of many local governments. The U.S. Conference of Mayors, at its July 1982 conference, approved a recommendation supporting greater use of alternative living arrangements for the elderly and continued federal support of innovative local programs.

Imaginative, cost-effective approaches to meeting the elderly's housing needs by combining government, business, community and volunteer resources will be much in demand. The National Association of Counties and the U.S. Conference of Mayors help local governments determine needs and develop policies through exchange of information, including innovative programs. Denver, Colo., for example, provides a telephone hotline service through public and private funds to help low-income senior citizens find affordable housing. Jacksonville, Fla., has launched a "Corporate Caring" program where private companies "adopt" elderly congregate living facilities, taking responsibility for both the building and the residents. A new study has found a wide array of successful local strategies that help elderly persons "age in place." [35]

Politics will play the lead role in determining the degree of support for innovative living arrangements and other housing-related needs, according to Leo Baldwin. Local governments will respond with a commitment to older Americans, if they are viewed as an important political constituency.

---

[35] See Phyllis Myers, "Aging In Place: Strategies To Help The Elderly Stay In Revitalizing Neighborhoods," The Conservation Foundation in collaboration with The Urban Institute, 1982.

Selected Bibliography

Books

Butler, Robert, *Why Survive? Being Old in America,* Harper & Row, 1976.
— and Myrna Lewis, *Aging & Mental Health,* The C. V. Mosby Co., 1982.
Percy, Charles H., *Growing Old in the Country of the Young,* McGraw-Hill, 1974.
Powell, M. Lawton and S. L. Hoover, *Community Housing: Choices for Older Americans,* Springer Publishing Co., 1981.

Articles

"Granny Flats: Easing the Housing Crunch for the Elderly," *The Futurist,* February 1982.
Hare, Patrick H., "Carving up the American Dream," *Planning,* July 1981.
"Housing Needs: The Choices Increase," *U.S. News & World Report,* Sept. 1, 1980.
"The Aging of America," *Congressional Quarterly Weekly Report,* Nov. 28, 1981.
Trunzo, Candace E., "Health Costs — Solving The Age-Old Problem," *Money,* January 1982.
Wallis, Claudia, "Day Care Centers for the Old," *Time,* Jan. 18, 1982.

Reports and Studies

Editorial Research Reports: "Retirement Income In Jeopardy," 1981 Vol. I, p. 169; "Plight of the Aged," 1971 Vol. II, p. 863.
Hare, Patrick H., "Accessory Apartments: Surplus Space in Single Family Homes," American Planning Association, Planning Advisory Service Report No. 365, 1981.
Health Care Financing Administration, "Directory of Adult Day Care Centers," September 1980.
House Select Committee on Aging, Subcommittee on Housing and Consumer Interests, "Congregate Housing Services," May 19, 1981; "Housing The Elderly: Present Problems and Future Considerations," July 29, 1981; "Shared Housing," Nov. 17, 1981.
Myers, Phyllis, "Aging In Place: Strategies To Help The Elderly Stay In Revitalizing Neighborhoods," The Conservation Foundation in collaboration with The Urban Institute, 1982.
National Conference on Social Welfare, "Long Term Care — In Search of Solutions: The Need for Long Term Care; Alternative Directions For Change in Long Term Care; Informal Supports in Long Term Care," 1981.
Toff, Gail, "Alternatives To Institutional Care: An Analysis of State Initiatives," Intergovernmental Health Policy Project, George Washington University, September 1981.
U.S. Conference of Mayors, "Administering Aging Programs, Vol. VI: Serving the Urban Elderly — Issues and Programs," 1982.

AMERICAN INDIAN ECONOMIC DEVELOPMENT

by

Tom Arrandale

**Feb. 17
1 9 8 4**

AMERICAN INDIAN
ECONOMIC DEVELOPMENT

A MERICAN Indian tribes may be approaching a crossroad in their struggle for economic independence in Indian country. President Reagan's budget cutbacks are forcing tribal governments to scramble to open industrial parks, trailer courts, tourist stops, bingo halls and other business ventures to bring money and jobs onto impoverished reservations. Shifting world energy markets are presenting some tribes with difficult decisions on managing the coal, oil and gas, uranium and other natural resources that their reservations contain.

In the process, Indian leaders are trying to build self-sufficient reservations — no longer dependent on federal economic assistance — to back up the political self-determination that tribal governments gained in the 1970s. Mescalero Apache Tribal President Wendell Chino declared, "[My] people are still tough and independent, and we are determined to make progress on our own." [1]

The potential for economic self-sufficiency exists. The tribes that control vast energy and timber reserves can exploit those resources, while others can take advantage of scenic reservation lands and fine jewelry- and pottery-making traditions. As self-governing sovereigns, exempt from state and local taxes and regulation, tribes can set the terms for their own growth and offer special incentives to lure investment and industry.

Economic growth is essential to bring some degree of prosperity to remote and desperately poor reservations. Nearly a quarter of the country's Indian families, including Alaskan Eskimos and Aleuts, live on incomes that fall below the poverty level, according to the 1980 federal census. By whatever measure — health, housing, life expectancy, unemployment rates — Native Americans rank near the bottom in U.S. society *(see box, p. 185)*.

Without economic development the plight of the Indians can only worsen. Unemployment among Indians on reservations is staggering. More than half now live off their tribal reservations, seeking decent-paying jobs in Los Angeles, Seattle, Denver, San Francisco, Chicago, New York City and other metropolitan regions. Furthermore, many tribal populations are growing rap-

[1] Quoted in *U.S. News & World Report*, April 5, 1982, p. 64.

idly; the 160,000-member Navajo Nation, already the largest tribe, will have 300,000 people by the turn of the century.

Recognizing the need to develop reservation economies and actually doing it may be two different things. Many of the initial business ventures have failed, the bingo games may be short-term gains and little revenue has been set aside for sustained development. Most tribes have not prepared for their future needs, an oversight many are now trying to remedy by drawing up comprehensive economic development plans.

Tribal leaders and Indian economists agree that tribal governments lack management skills, development capital and effective control over their own natural resources. Tribal leaders blame the federal government for many of these failures, contending the Bureau of Indian Affairs (BIA) in the Interior Department has exercised its power as trustee for Indians and their lands in ways that have crippled tribal governments and perpetuated economic dependence.

Some help may come from the Reagan administration. Stimulation of private enterprise on reservations is the cornerstone of President Reagan's Indian policy, announced Jan. 24, 1983. The president appointed a nine-member presidential commission, including six Indians, to study ways to promote private investment on reservations and "reduce the federal presence in Indian affairs." Co-chaired by Ross O. Swimmer, principle Cherokee Nation chief, and Robert Robertson, a Nevada businessman, the commission in January 1984 began a six-month series of hearings on economic development possibilities in states with large Indian populations.

Although they are eager to spur economic growth, Indian leaders claim that what Reagan has given with one hand, he has taken away with the other. The administration's sharp cutbacks in federal social welfare and economic development programs mean that tribes must use their limited revenues to replace federal funding that helped with day-to-day reservation expenses, leaving little left over to provide the facilities that would attract business investment and making the need to generate new revenues even more urgent. "We really have a pretty big job ahead," 35-year-old Navajo economist Al Henderson, the tribe's former economic development director, acknowledged. [2]

Indian Reservations: Portraits of Poverty

American Indian tribes possess about 30 million acres on 288 reservations in 26 states. Those lands range in size from the huge Navajo reservation, which is as large as West Virginia, to a one-acre "rancheria" in California. Some reservations contain

[2] Aug. 4, 1979, interview.

Indian Reservation Income, 1979
Selected Reservations

Reservation	State	Per Capita Income	Median Family Income	Persons Below Poverty Level
Agua Caliente	Calif.	$6,409	$50,394	34.9%
Osage	Okla.	5,806	15,891	18.5
Onondaga	N.Y.	5,693	17,742	18.9
Penobscot	Maine	4,861	9,208	21.4
Colville	Wash.	4,428	12,394	32.7
Laguna Pueblo	N.M.	4,422	16,675	12.3
Red Lake	Minn.	4,106	12,465	28.9
Potawatomi	Wis.	3,799	3,523	58.9
Lummi	Wash.	3,783	15,893	24.6
Brighton Seminole	Fla.	3,769	7,279	34.4
Turtle Mountain	N.D.	3,339	10,934	40.8
Indian Township	Maine	3,260	15,556	27.8
Eastern Cherokee	N.C.	3,066	9,849	34.0
Crow	Mont.	3,011	9,773	33.1
Mississippi Choctaw	Miss.	2,988	11,054	35.2
Acoma Pueblo	N.M.	2,885	14,225	29.7
Fort Berthold	N.D.	2,730	11,045	37.5
Northern Cheyenne	Mont.	2,512	9,336	41.8
Hopi	Ariz.	2,510	8,145	50.2
Rosebud	S.D.	2,484	8,318	50.2
Navajo	Ariz., N.M., Utah	2,414	9,079	49.7
Fort Apache	Ariz.	2,309	10,129	42.2
Pine Ridge	S.D.	2,209	9,435	48.5
Fort McDermitt	Nev., Ore.	1,982	7,917	61.5
Santa Rosa Rancheria	Calif.	1,322	—	36.4
Muckleshoot	Wash.	1,094	4,452	68.8

Source: U.S. Department of Commerce, Bureau of the Census, 1980 Census

valuable resources, including coal, oil and gas, commercial forests, productive crop lands, extensive rangelands, important rivers and other water sources, major fishing grounds, and attractive recreation sites. The Oklahoma Osage reservation lies on top of one of the country's largest oil pools. California's Agua Caliente tribe has grown wealthy from the Hollywood entertainers and millionaire industrialists who have built homes and golf courses on or near their lands at Palm Springs. Most tribes, however, lack the natural resources, nearby markets, investment capital, technical know-how and cultural traditions needed to compete successfully in the white man's economy. Indian country remains undeveloped, with few paved roads, utilities and the other facilities that support business activity.

Many reservations "might be likened to Appalachia or some of the highly depressed non-Indian areas throughout the United States," Forrest J. Gerard, President Carter's assistant secretary of the interior for Indian affairs, told the House Interior and Insular Affairs Committee in 1979. "For the most part, Indian reservations remain underdeveloped and Indian people lack credit, remain poor, uneducated, and unhealthy," a congressional American Indian Policy Review Commission reported in 1977. "From the standpoint of personal well-being, the Indian of America ranks at the bottom of virtually every social statistical indicator. On the average he has the highest infant mortality rate, the lowest longevity rate, the lowest level of educational attainment, the lowest per capita income and the poorest housing and transportation in the land."[3]

Conditions have not improved much since the commission issued its report. Counting Alaska's Eskimos and Aleuts, Indians fared better than both urban and rural blacks in 1980 census measures of average income levels. But Indians living on and off the reservations lagged far behind white Americans. And Indians, especially those living on chronically depressed reservations, are less likely to benefit from overall U.S. economic recovery. "Even when the nation's economy has been relatively healthy, reservation unemployment has hovered at three to four times the national average, with persistent unemployment on individual reservations in excess of 50 and 60 percent not at all uncommon," Rosebud Sioux Tribal Chairman Carl Waln noted during 1983 Senate testimony.

Short-Term Gains; Long-Term Projects

To advance the Indian campaign for self-determination, many tribes launched ambitious economic development programs in the 1970s. Reagan's budget cutbacks have lent new urgency to these efforts. "Two or three years ago, [economic development] was something they'd like to see happen, but it wasn't at the top of their list of priorities," noted Alan Parker, president of the American Indian National Bank of Washington, D.C. "Today ... developing a viable private sector on the reservation is viewed as an overriding goal by a majority of tribal leaders." [4]

One of the more popular tribal business ventures is gambling. Attempting to cash in on federal court rulings that have de-

---

[3] American Indian Policy Review Commission, *Final Report*, May 17, 1977, p. 7. The commission was headed by Sen. James Abourezk, D-S.D. (Senate 1973-79; House 1971-73), who had proposed its establishment "to determine the nature and scope of necessary revisions" in U.S. Indian policy. Abourezk's sympathies with the Indians dated from his childhood; he was reared on the Rosebud Reservation in South Dakota.
[4] Jan. 24, 1984, telephone interview. Thirteen Indian tribal organizations hold the majority of stock in this commercial bank, which was founded in 1973 to lend money to Indian tribes and business enterprises.

clared reservation lands beyond the reach of state gambling regulations, several tribal governments are running bingo and blackjack games and making plans to build race tracks. At least 50 tribes have opened bingo halls, reaping large profits by using high-stake jackpots to attract non-Indian players from nearby cities. In North Carolina the Cherokee tribe has earned $500,000 since 1982 when they converted a textile mill into a bingo parlor. Florida's Seminole tribe took in $4.2 million from three bingo operations in 1983. New Mexico's Acoma Pueblo paid for a newly opened bingo operation in two months. "Everything they get now is gravy," said Jerry Folsom, BIA economic development adviser in Albuquerque.[5]

**Mississippi Choctaw Band
wire assembly plant**

The quick returns from bingo may not last. Non-Indian churches, lodges, war veteran and charitable groups that raise money by running bingo games subject to state jackpot limits have begun objecting to Indian competition. The U.S. Supreme Court in 1982 refused to review lower court rulings holding that, short of barring all bingo in the state, Florida could not regulate Seminole games. Nonetheless, Arizona, Washington, and Oklahoma officials are trying to control Indian bingo operations.[6] In New Mexico, Acoma leaders are "in it for the short-term," Folsom noted, recognizing that state legislation raising the pot limit on charitable games "would wipe out Indian bingo."

For the long run, tribal governments will have to branch out into more lasting businesses. The Acomas already have drawn up plans to build a restaurant, gas station, motel and resort at an Interstate 40 highway interchange on their lands. New Mexico's Pojoaque Pueblo is opening a 110-unit trailer park just outside housing-short Santa Fe. The Mississippi Choctaw Band operates successful construction, automobile wiring, and greeting card businesses in an 80-acre industrial park in eastern Mississippi. The Navajos operate a forest products business

---

[5] Jan. 5, 1984, interview.
[6] See "Indian War Cry: Bingo!" *Time*, Jan. 2, 1984, p. 58.

employing 624 Navajos and are trying to make an irrigated farming operation profitable. Arizona's Ak-Chin tribe and Washington's Yakima reservation run successful farming operations, while tribes in Maine, Minnesota, and the Pacific Coast states harvest major timber stands.

Before coming to the Reagan administration as assistant secretary of the interior for Indian affairs, Kenneth L. Smith, a Wasco Indian, served as business manager for the Warm Springs reservation, supervising resort, logging and sawmill operations that made the tribe central Oregon's largest employer.[7] Smith now urges individual Indian businessmen to take the lead in building privately owned reservation enterprises. To replace government-funded programs that provide "meaningless makework jobs," the administration wants Indians to "develop instead more real businesses that are competent and competitive and are going to endure to provide jobs and services . . . for years to come," Smith told a 1983 workshop for Indian contractors in Albuquerque. "They will endure because they earn the money they make and they also earn respect."

Federal Indian Politics

BEFORE Europeans colonized North America, Indian tribes practiced a variety of well-developed economic systems. The Pueblo and Hohokam Indians of the Southwest used sophisticated irrigation systems to grow crops. Eastern and Southern tribes also farmed, sharing tobacco and corn with the Pilgrims and other European colonists. Pacific Northwest tribes harvested salmon and other fish from the region's streams. Especially after acquiring horses, the Great Plains tribes based their way of life on hunting the region's vast buffalo herds. But tribal economic systems could not survive after white traders taught Indians a taste for alcohol and trinkets, buffalo hide hunters wiped out the herds, settlers cut down the forests and plowed the plains, and missionaries and government agents tried to turn hunting and gathering tribes into yeoman farmers.

Native American tribes occupy a special place in the U.S. political system. Like the European colonial governments that preceded it, the U.S. government from its inception treated tribes as sovereign nations. Between 1778 and 1868, the U.S. Senate ratified 370 treaties under which Indian tribes ceded nearly a billion acres of land to the national government as

---

[7] See "Business Breakout for America's Indians," *U.S. News & World Report,* May 28, 1979, p. 68.

white settlement spread west into Indian country. The government in return pledged to protect the remaining Indian lands and resources. But throughout its history, the federal government has vacillated between encouraging tribes to govern themselves on self-sufficient reservations and assimilating individual Indians into a predominantly white society.[8]

President Thomas Jefferson in an 1803 message to Congress spoke of leading Indians "to agriculture, to manufactures and civilization." Through most of the 19th century Indians were forced to give up much of their land as white America expanded westward. Most whites thought that Indians were "vanishing Americans" doomed to die off or be absorbed in the country's population. The U.S. cavalry confined defeated and demoralized tribes on large reservations carved from federally owned lands that at the time had little interest for settlers. Eventually — when they were needed for homesteaders or when valuable resources were discovered on them — the government forced tribes to give up even some of those lands.

Congress in 1887 passed the General Allotment Act to speed Indian assimilation. Sponsored by Sen. Henry L. Dawes, a Massachusetts Republican, the law gave the president authority to divide reservations into parcels and give each Indian an individual "allotment" of land formerly owned in common by the tribe. After all living tribal members received allotments, remaining tribal lands were to be opened to non-Indian homesteaders. The Bureau of Indian Affairs after 1887 became the guardians of individuals as well as tribes, assuming power over the most minute decisions in Indian life.

Between 1887 and 1934, tribal lands fell from 138 million acres to 48 million acres. Most individual allotments were too dry for farming, and most Indians could make no productive use of their holdings. With BIA approval, many leased their lands to white ranchers and others who wanted to combine Indian-owned lands with their own holdings. Evidence mounted in the early decades of the 20th century that assimilation policies were failing to improve Indian welfare. In the Indian Reorganization Act of 1934, Congress prohibited future allotment of tribally owned lands, returned remaining surplus lands to the tribes and empowered them to adopt written constitutions and set up governments to manage their internal affairs.

In the 1950s, government policy once again favored assimilation. Congress in 1953 approved a concurrent resolution declaring that the federal government should end supervision of reservations and make Indians subject to the same laws, privi-

---

[8] For background, see "Indian Rights," *E.R.R.*, 1977 Vol. I, p. 267.

leges and responsibilities as other U.S. citizens. Several tribes were "terminated" under this policy in the late 1950s and early 1960s.[9] The policy was eventually abandoned, but Indians continued to fear that the government some day would break up their reservations, consigning Native Americans to a permanent pauper class within white society. Indian frustrations gave rise in the late 1960s and early 1970s to a militant Red Power movement that led to numerous demonstrations. Perhaps the most publicized of these was American Indian Movement (AIM) occupation of BIA offices at Wounded Knee, S.D., in 1973.[10] When it ended after 71 days, two Indians were dead.

Swing Toward Greater Tribal Self-Reliance

The pendulum began to swing back toward tribal autonomy in the late 1960s when the government made tribal governments eligible for a number of federal social welfare and economic development programs. In 1970 President Nixon asked Congress to formally renounce the termination policy.[11] He also reorganized BIA, hired Native Americans for top-level bureau positions and began an expansion of federal funding for Indian programs. Congress endorsed Nixon's policy of encouraging tribal self-determination by passing the Indian Self-Determination and Education Assistance Act of 1974, which permitted Indian tribes to assume control and operation of many federal programs on reservations. In the same year, Congress also passed the Indian Financing Act, which made grants and loans to help Indians utilize and manage their own resources. The government also encouraged federal defense contractors to open electronics assembly plants on Indian lands.

Initiatives taken under these new laws met with mixed success. Many of the development projects were ill-conceived, plagued by inadequate financing and poor management. Several reservation motels and resorts ran consistent losses; tribally built industrial parks stood nearly empty. When the electronics market faltered, some firms closed their reservation plants. Indian militancy also hampered reservation development. In one well-publicized example, Fairchild Camera Corp. in 1975 shut down a Shiprock, N.M., electronics assembly plant that once employed 1,200 Navajos after AIM militants occupied the facility. The stigma of that closing "has stuck for 10 years," said Henderson, the Navajo economist. These failures also made

---

[9] Among these were Wisconsin's Menominees, Oregon's Klamath, the Wyandotte, Peoria and Ottawa tribes in Oklahoma and several small rancherias in California.

[10] Wounded Knee was especially significant because in 1890 it was the site of a massacre of at least 200 Sioux men, women and children by the U.S. cavalry. The incident marked the end of the Indian wars.

[11] Reagan also asked Congress to repeal the termination resolution, but the legislators have not yet acted.

Indians wary of relying solely on federally financed development programs or plants managed by outsiders to bring economic growth to Indian country.

Reagan Policy: More Autonomy; Less Aid

Reagan in his Jan. 24, 1983, Indian policy statement reaffirmed the government's commitment "to pursue the policy of self-government for Indian tribes without threatening termination." [12] Since then the president has followed through on many of his promises. Reagan endorsed and signed new federal laws granting tribes the same tax-exempt status as states and cities and confirming tribal authority to exploit their natural resources through joint ventures and other innovative arrangements with outside industry. BIA launched an economic development fund providing $10 million a year in federal seed money to help tribal governments develop natural resources and attract private investment on reservations.

Administration officials contend that stronger tribal governments and private economic growth on reservations are essential for tribes to achieve full self-reliance. "A tribe cannot really be self-governing if it is economically dependent on the federal government — if its funds are controlled by an outside power," Assistant Secretary Smith told a 1983 symposium at Oklahoma's Northeastern State University.

But at the same time that it is asking Indian tribes to assume more of the costs of governing themselves, the administration is cutting back its federal assistance to Indians. Reagan specifically barred his advisory panel from proposing new federal financial assistance for development projects. Although funding has increased somewhat for direct federal services to reservations, by BIA calculations total federal spending on Indians has fallen by roughly $1 billion during Reagan's term, to $2.5 billion a year. Funding for BIA, which runs reservation schools, provides welfare services, builds roads and manages tribal lands, has risen slightly to $1 billion a year, officials note. The budget for the Indian Health Service (IHS), a U.S. Health and Human Services Department agency that operates 48 Indian hospitals and more than 300 health clinics, also has risen slightly. In addition, Congress in 1982 channeled $100 million a year in federal highway construction funds, financed by a 5-cents-a-gallon gasoline tax increase, to Indian reservations. [13]

[12] In a televised interview five days before Reagan released his policy paper, Secretary of the Interior James G. Watt termed the poverty and social problems in Indian country "an example of the failures of socialism." While Watt quickly backtracked, that comment revived Indians' fears that the national government would terminate its responsibility to act as trustee over Indian lands and its special relationship with sovereign self-governing tribes.

[13] See Iver Peterson, "Bringing Decentralization to the Reservation," *The New York Times*, Oct. 30, 1983.

But budget cuts in a host of additional federal programs that were helping tribes build economic infrastructure, attract outside capital, enlarge tribal ventures and train Indians to run them have been devastating. "They're cutting away all the prerequisites to a well-founded economic development plan," Delfin J. Lovato, chairman of the 19 New Mexico pueblos' All-Indian Pueblo Council, charged at a 1983 economic development seminar.

In testimony before Congress, the National Tribal Chairmen's Association, National Congress of American Indians, and tribal leaders have contested Reagan proposals to curtail specific BIA and IHS programs providing Indians with community health services, free drugs, transportation to hospitals, higher education financial aid and funds for housing and sewer construction. They also protested administration attempts to phase out health, education, and child welfare programs targeted on off-reservation Indians living in urban areas. And they objected to the administration's plans to scrap federally funded legal services, economic development grants, and Comprehensive Employment and Training Act (CETA) job-creating programs available to Indians and non-Indians. Tribal leaders relied heavily on those funds in the 1970s to expand reservation services, increase tribal government employment and attract business to Indian lands. Without such assistance, "the resources and internal ability of tribal governments to meet reservation Indian members' needs, let alone off-reservation members, is for the most part absent," National Congress of American Indians Executive Director Ronald P. Andrade contended in a statement submitted to the Senate Select Committee on Indian Affairs in 1983. "We are being asked to trade the needs of our people now for the hoped-for future benefits of economic development."

Congress saved many of those programs but at sharply reduced funding levels, and the cuts have had a dramatic impact on Indians. Federal aid for the 24,000-square-mile Navajo reservation, which reaches into New Mexico, Arizona, and Utah, fell from $550 million in 1981 to $400 million in 1983, a 27 percent reduction. The cutbacks cost the tribe at least 10,000 jobs; its unemployment rate jumped to 80 percent by mid-1983.[14] Navajo Tribal Chairman Peterson Zah, who took office in 1983 after defeating former Chairman Peter MacDonald in tribal elections, has threatened to return management of police and social service programs to BIA unless the agency demands that the administration and Congress restore funding to previous levels.

---

[14] See James Cook, "America's Oldest Minority, *Forbes,* Aug. 15, 1983, p. 34.

Prospects for Growth

FEW INDIANS underestimate the difficult economic, social, and cultural barriers they must overcome to make reservations self-sufficient. With federal assistance declining, some tribes have to make difficult decisions on expanding economic opportunities that may produce jobs and benefits for their people but also alter Indian ways of life. "Some choices have to be made," Henderson, the Navajo economist, pointed out, "whether Indian tribes are going to isolate themselves from the rest of the world or go ahead with policies . . . that will permit them to survive over the long term."

The most pressing economic problem for many tribes is how to acquire capital. "We have the labor force and land base, but we don't have the capital to create economic activity," Roman Bitsuie, a Princeton University graduate who chairs the Navajo Tribal Council's Economic Development and Planning Committee, said. "We're beginning to address that." [15]

At present, Indian tribes live in what Henderson describes as a "maintenance economy." Money flowing onto reservations from federal agencies, mining leases and other outside sources is spent on day-to-day expenses with nothing left over for investment in developing a more productive economy. Tribal governments, along with BIA offices and IHS clinics, are most tribes' major employers. Tribally owned enterprises have usually been operated to provide jobs rather than to earn consistent profits. Funds for road construction, social services and other programs frequently are distributed on the basis of political patronage. Observers, for example, often compared former Navajo Tribal Chairman MacDonald's government with the big-city political machines that once dominated many major U.S. cities.

There are other barriers to economic growth. Many tribes change leaders frequently, sometimes every year, making the climate for business development unstable. Outdated BIA regulations, some issued 100 years ago, have discouraged individual Indians from opening new businesses. "The Navajo business community has complained that under current procedures it takes up to ten years for a business site lease to be approved," Zah told the Navajo Tribal Council in January. "It is no wonder that every Saturday there is a steady stream of cars and pickups flowing off our reservation so that Navajo

---

[15] Jan. 23, 1984, telephone interview.

people can shop in the thriving 'border towns' surrounding our Nation."

Because so few supplies are available on the reservation, what income Indians earn flows immediately off the reservation to stores, gasoline stations, and automobile dealerships run by non-Indian owners. Most reservations have no Indian-owned banks, savings and loan associations, or other financial institutions where tribal members' savings could provide capital for reservation investments. Indian banks consider reservation businesses risky ventures and are reluctant to lend funds to tribal governments and individual Indians. Because the federal government holds legal title to reservation lands in trust, Indians cannot mortgage their property to acquire development funds. In combination, these limitations make the lack of capital "an overriding problem inhibiting economic development in Indian country," Parker, the American Indian National Bank president, wrote in a 1983 report to the Interior Department.[16]

But even if money were available, many tribes remain divided over how fast to pursue economic development. Some tribes fear rapid growth might bring outsiders onto reservation lands, disrupting religious and cultural traditions. Indian values and work habits often conflict with the acquisitive, competitive methods that the American private enterprise system nurtures, creating tensions with non-Indian managers. Traditional Navajo culture, for example, frowns on the accumulation of individual wealth and discourages risk-taking innovations, anthropologist Charles R. Griffith observed. "Progress, the concept so vital in American thinking to sustain goal-direction, effort, and dedication, is muted in traditional Navajo thought," Griffith wrote in a 1980 Interior Department study. "Saving or accumulating capital (for the proverbial 'rainy day') is still alien to many Navajos," Griffith said. "... There is no question of native Navajo intellectual capacity; rather it is the continuing hold of traditional culture which constrains development more rapidly along lines predicted by classical economic theory of development." [17]

Putting Together Sound Business Strategies

In the past, tribal governments approached economic development in a piecemeal fashion. Now many tribes are trying to put together coherent economic development strategies.

---

[16] Alan R. Parker, *Survey of Indian Economic Development Issues, A Report to the Assistant Secretary of the Interior for Indian Affairs,* February 1983, p. xvi.
[17] Charles R. Griffith, "Fundamentals of Navajo Risk Behavior in Economic Development," Working Paper No. 30, *San Juan Basin Regional Uranium Study,* U.S. Department of the Interior, Albuquerque, N.M., 1980.

Warm Springs Forest Products Industries on Oregon's Warm Springs Reservation

Younger Indians, some with professional training, are working for tribal governments or seeking opportunities to start their own businesses without leaving their tribal homes. And tribal leaders, learning from the failure of federally sponsored economic development programs to produce real growth, are showing renewed interest in attracting industry to Indian country. "Tribes have looked at different things, tried different things, and moved in the direction of private business development," Parker, a Cree from Montana's Rocky Boy Reservation, said.

Navajo Chairman Zah has begun consolidating tribal government agencies and wants to simplify regulations to provide greater opportunities for Navajos to go into business on their own. The tribe's economic planning department has drafted a comprehensive development plan based on creation of four Navajo-controlled financial institutions to finance economic growth. These include a commercial bank and a savings and loan association on the reservation, along with an economic development bank that would use revenues from certain energy leases as collateral to sell bonds and make loans for potential business projects. The fourth would be a Minority Small Business Investment Corp. started with $1 million in tribal funds and $4 million in federal Small Business Administration matching funds. "If we want economic development to happen, we need to own our own financial institutions," Michael Allison, Zah's economic planning director, asserts. "Outside bankers have their own interests at heart, not the tribe's interest." [18]

[18] Jan. 30, 1984, telephone interview.

195

But so far the Navajo council has failed to set aside any tribal energy revenues to finance new economic ventures. Other tribes lack sufficient resources and development potential to create their own financing mechanisms. The National Congress of American Indians has proposed setting up a nationwide Indian development institution to provide long-term venture capital for business development on Indian lands. But that institution would probably require federal funds, and Congress has yet to give it serious consideration.

Indians still are interested in attracting economic ventures to reservations "providing we can run it ourselves," BIA official Folsom, a Choctaw from Oklahoma, declared. "If there's nothing in it for us, we're no longer interested in bringing industry out to the reservation to create jobs that may or may not be there in five years." Some tribes plan to build up a variety of businesses. "We've been putting our emphasis on big corporations, but maybe we'd be better off concentrating on smaller businesses," Zah told *Forbes* in 1983. "A lot of them could generate as much employment as a single large company, but it wouldn't leave us so vulnerable if one should close." [19]

Some reservations, however, simply lack the resources to offer their residents much hope for progress. With or without federal financial assistance, reservations that lie far from major cities or Interstate highways — South Dakota's Pine Ridge Sioux reservation, for example — have few development prospects. "Some tribes just have a hard time because of circumstances, the same circumstances that sat the Osages in Oklahoma on top of one of the largest oil pools in the U.S.," BIA official Folsom noted. "The tribes at the bottom just have to hope for something to fall out of the sky."

Exploitation of Resources on Reservations

More fortunate tribes, on the other hand, may be able to develop their economies by tapping their reservations' natural bounty. Federal studies in the mid-1970s estimated that Indian lands held 5.3 million acres of commercial forests bearing about 38 billion board feet of timber. Another 2.5 million acres is crop land and 44 million acres is rangeland for grazing cattle and sheep. Tribes have been claiming priority rights to harvest Pacific Northwest fish and to use scarce water supplies in the arid West. And about 40 reservations in 17 states contain energy resources.[20] By some estimates Indians own 4 percent of known U.S. oil and gas reserves, 40 percent of the nation's uranium, and roughly 200 billion tons of coal that make up about 30 percent of the West's attractive low-sulfur resources.

[19] Quoted by Cook, *op cit.*
[20] American Indian Policy Commission, *Final Report*, May 17, 1977, p. 7.

Indian Water Rights

American Indian tribes in arid Western states own potentially large shares of the region's scarce and economically valuable water. Tribal governments, recognizing the wealth that water could bring, have been pressing lawsuits and negotiating with federal and state officials to firmly establish Indians' rights to water flowing through their reservations. But those claims, staked out by a 1908 U.S. Supreme Court decision, are putting tribes into conflict with Western farmers, industries, cities and towns that in some areas already use all the water supplies available.

The Supreme Court, in its 1908 *Winters v. United States* decision, declared that Congress when it established Indian reservations also reserved water for tribes living there to use. Western state water laws, however, usually protect the rights of the first person to divert water for beneficial uses. Indians, dependent on federal government assistance to build dams and irrigation canals, have lagged behind non-Indian Westerners in developing water supplies and their claims are clouding the rights of non-Indians who began using water after the dates on which reservations were established.

In recent years, tribal governments and federal agencies acting as Indians' trustees have filed more than 50 lawsuits demanding rights to use Western waters. Western state officials and business interests have called for "quantifying" Indian rights to clarify what future total demands will be for the region's limited supplies. The Supreme Court, in *Arizona v. California* (1963), awarded 1.2 million acre feet of the Colorado River's water to five Indian tribes. The Reagan administration in 1982 negotiated a $15 million settlement to enable Arizona's Papago Indians to develop alternative supplies to groundwater depleted by pumping in nearby Tucson. The Reagan administration favors negotiations to settle Indian water rights, but many tribes are still turning to federal courts to press their claims.

If carefully managed, reservation energy resources could provide "the foundation for overall economic development for a sector of American society which has been overlooked and under-developed for more than 200 years," MacDonald, the former Navajo chairman, told the National Press Club in 1979.[21] Oklahoma Indians have enjoyed handsome oil and gas royalties, and Navajo miners earn $30,000 a year working deposits that the tribe has leased to Utah International Inc., Peabody Coal Co., and Pittsburgh and Midway Coal Co., a Gulf Oil Corp. subsidiary. But over the last decade, tribal leaders have concluded that their people now realize far too little return from extraction of reservation resources that are part of the Indians' heritage.

[21] Quoted by the *Navajo Times*, Aug. 9, 1979.

In the past, they contend, the federal agencies that controlled mineral leasing on Indian lands failed to fully protect tribal interests. On Wyoming's Wind River reservation, Arapahoe and Shoshone tribal leaders were dismayed when investigators found that lax U.S. Geological Survey accounting permitted oil companies to underpay $1 million in royalties and taxes. Navajo officials complain bitterly that BIA negotiated coal leases for the tribe that pay fixed royalty rates of 15 cents to 25 cents per ton and that yield less revenue than the 12.5 percent royalties that the government itself commands by selling nearby federally owned coal deposits. "They're really poor, unconscionable leases," Zah has charged. "We're committed to changing those leases so that we can get a fair market value for our coal, uranium, and oil." [22]

Tribal Divisions on Energy Development

To tighten tribal control over resource development and demand larger revenues from mining operations, tribes holding major energy reserves formed a Council of Energy Resource Tribes (CERT) in 1975. Organized by MacDonald and based in Denver, CERT at first was proclaimed a "Native American OPEC." Officials of CERT, which has 37 member tribes, now play down comparisons with the Organization of Petroleum Exporting Countries. "The mission is to offer the technical assistance the Indian people need to make proper judgments" on developing reservation resources, CERT economist Ahmed Kooros, a former Iranian oil official, explained. [23] The organization has been granted $2 million in federal funds to hire economists, lawyers, energy and environmental experts.

Continuing negotiations that MacDonald began, Zah has been pressing coal mining firms operating on Navajo lands to renegotiate their contracts to pay higher royalties. The Navajo and other tribal governments also have been exploring ways for tribes to participate in developing their minerals instead of simply leasing them. The Jicarilla Apaches, for instance, now drill their own oil and gas wells and are drafting plans to build their own refinery. Tribes have had some success in negotiating joint ventures, service contracts or production sharing arrangements with energy companies that will give them a role in production decisions.

However, the worldwide oil glut has slowed, and in some cases, stopped reservation energy development. Oil and gas revenues have fallen off. Energy companies shut down major uranium mines at Laguna Pueblo and on the Navajo reservation

---

[22] Interviewed on "The MacNeil-Lehrer Report," Public Broadcasting System, Feb. 24, 1983.
[23] 1979 interview with the author.

in the early 1980s as the nuclear industry's troubles mounted. With coal demand weakened, the 7,000-member Crow tribe in southern Montana has gone $41 million in debt and energy companies have shelved plans to build a synthetic fuel plant, a power plant, mines, a coal slurry pipeline and a Pacific Coast coal-loading facility to develop the reservation's 17 billion tons of reserves. "Everyone promised to make us millionaires tomorrow," Dan Old Elk, a Crow tribal member, recalled. "But no one told us how we are going to pay our bills until then." [24]

Other considerations are also affecting development of tribal energy resources. The Northern Cheyenne have imposed strict environmental controls that limit coal mining on their reservations. Some dissident Navajos, influenced by non-Indian environmental and anti-nuclear groups, have protested tribal coal and uranium development plans. Some Navajos also fear that mining will disrupt the traditional tribal life built around sheep and cattle herding on empty rangelands. Navajo ranchers protest that non-Indian miners and oil and gas drilling crews litter their lands with equipment, and medicine men complain that development desecrates burial grounds and tribal holy sites. Such protests have complicated the search for outside investment. One company pulled out of a planned coal gasification plant on the Navajo lands after protests from the local Navajo chapter stalled tribal government approval.

Some tribes remain relatively untroubled by development. On the Laguna Pueblo, where uranium mining began in 1953, "we have not hurt our culture, religion, traditions," former Gov. Floyd Correa maintained. "We've learned to take development in stride." Other tribes, including the Navajo, may have no choice but to develop their energy reserves to pave the way for overall economic expansion. "You can go ahead and use that as a springboard," Henderson, now a private economic consultant in Albuquerque, noted. "There's still a chance, but in the next five years, if leases are not renegotiated, if a tribal accounting process is not in place, then we're stepping back 50 years."

Indian energy reserves eventually will run out. Reagan's budget cutbacks also have made it plain that tribal governments can no longer rely on substantial federal government financing. So tribal leaders recognize that they will have a few decades at best to build alternative economic activity that will sustain their people in the 21st century. "Tribes are aware there are limits to resources," Henderson commented. "Indians know assistance from the federal government is not all the answer either."

---

[24] Quoted by Bill Richards, "Crow Indians Find Huge Coal Reserves Help Them Very Little," *The Wall Street Journal*, Jan. 31, 1984.

Selected Bibliography

Books

Brophy, William A., and Aberle, Sophie D., *The Indian, America's Unfinished Business, Report of the Commission on the Rights, Liberties, and Responsibilities of the American Indian,* University of Oklahoma Press, 1966.

Cohen, Felix, *Handbook of Federal Indian Law,* U.S. Government Printing Office, 1940.

Dippie, Brain W., *The Vanishing American, White Attitudes and U.S. Indian Policy,* Wesleyan University Press, 1982.

Levitan, Sar A., and Johnston, William B., *Indian Giving, Federal Programs for Native Americans,* The Johns Hopkins University Press, 1975.

Sorkin, Alan L., *American Indians and Federal Aid,* The Brookings Institution, 1971.

Native American Studies, University of New Mexico, *Economic Development in American Indian Reservations,* 1979.

Articles

Andersen, Kurt, "Indian War Cry: Bingo!" *Time,* Jan. 2, 1984.

Cook, James, "America's Oldest Minority," *Forbes,* Aug. 15, 1983.

Huntley, Steve, "America's Indians: 'Beggars in Our Own Land,'" *U.S. News & World Report,* May 23, 1983.

Mann, James, "Business Breakout for America's Indians," *U.S. News & World Report,* May 28, 1983.

Peterson, Iver, "Bringing Decentralization to the Reservation," *The New York Times,* Oct. 30, 1983.

Richards, Bill, "Crow Indians Find Huge Coal Reserves Help Them Very Little," *The Wall Street Journal,* Jan. 31, 1984.

Reports and Studies

American Indian Policy Review Commission, "Final Report," May 17, 1977; Task Force Seven, "Report on Reservation and Resource Development and Protection," July 29, 1976.

Editorial Research Reports, "American Indians: Neglected Minority," 1966 Vol. II, p. 623; "Changing Status of American Indians," 1954 Vol. I, p. 381; "Indian Rights," 1977 Vol. I, p. 267; "Preservation of Indian Culture," 1972 Vol. II, p. 847.

Griffith, Charles R., "Fundamentals of Navajo Risk Behavior in Economic Development," Department of the Interior, San Juan Regional Basin Uranium Study, Working Paper No. 30, 1980.

Navajo Tribe, Division of Economic Development, "Navajo Nation Overall Economic Development Plan, 1983-84," September 1983.

Parker, Alan R., "Survey of Indian Economic Development Issues," report to the assistant secretary of the interior for Indian affairs, February 1983.

Graphics: Photos courtesy of the American Indian National Bank

200

INDEX